Probabilistic Knowledge

Sarah Moss is Associate Professor of Philosophy at the University of Michigan, Ann Arbor. She received her A.B. in Mathematics from Harvard University and her B.Phil. in Philosophy from Oxford University, where she studied as a Marshall Scholar. She received her Ph.D. in Philosophy with a minor in Linguistics from MIT in 2009.

Probabilistic Knowledge

Sarah Moss

OXFORD
UNIVERSITY PRESS

Great Clarendon Street, Oxford, OX2 6DP,
United Kingdom

Oxford University Press is a department of the University of Oxford.
It furthers the University's objective of excellence in research, scholarship,
and education by publishing worldwide. Oxford is a registered trade mark of
Oxford University Press in the UK and in certain other countries

Published in the United States of America by Oxford University Press
198 Madison Avenue, New York, NY 10016, United States of America

British Library Cataloguing in Publication Data
Data available

Library of Congress Cataloging in Publication Data
Data available

ISBN 978-0-19-879215-4 (Hbk.)
ISBN 978 0 19 885809-6 (Pbk.)

For my guys—Eric, Liem, and Oliver Swanson

Contents

Preface

This book argues that credences can be knowledge. Say you have .5 credence that a certain coin landed heads, .6 credence that your friend Jones smokes, and .3 credence that your friend Brown smokes. I argue that each of these credences can be knowledge, in just the same way that your full beliefs can be knowledge. Traditional epistemology has focused on the epistemic status of full beliefs in propositions, such as the proposition that you are not dreaming, or that God exists, or that you have hands. But in addition to having knowledge of black and white propositions, we have knowledge that comes in every shade of grey.

This book is about credences, but not just about credences. More generally, it is about probabilistic beliefs. For instance, I argue that you can know that it might be raining outside, where this epistemic modal belief cannot be reduced to full belief in any proposition. Similarly, your conditional beliefs and conditional credences can be probabilistic knowledge. Also, this book is about knowledge, but not just about knowledge—it is also about belief and assertion. There is something common to credences, epistemic modal beliefs, conditional beliefs, conditional credences, and so on. The contents of these attitudes are sets of probability spaces over propositions, or *probabilistic contents*. Just as tradition holds that you believe and assert propositions, I hold that you can believe and assert probabilistic contents. Hence probabilistic contents play a central role not only in epistemology, but in the philosophy of mind and the philosophy of language as well.

Accepting that we can believe, assert, and know probabilistic contents has significant consequences for a wide range of contemporary debates. For instance, my arguments about probabilistic belief support a novel account of the relationship between full belief and credence. As I defend the claim that we can assert probabilistic contents, I develop and defend a formal semantics for epistemic modals and probability operators, as well as a formal semantics for indicative conditionals. Along the way, I give arguments that challenge the celebrated connection between indicative conditionals and conditional probability. In later chapters of the book, I discuss several arguments for the claim that we can perceive probabilistic contents, including arguments informed by Bayesian models of human visual perception. I develop several knowledge norms governing rational belief and action, including norms that have implications for what you should believe when you find out that you disagree with an epistemic peer. I spell out a precise interpretation of the claim that the resources of standard decision theory are inadequate when it comes to decisions about whether to have transformative experiences. I defend perceptual dogmatism from the objection that it is inconsistent with Bayesian principles of rational updating.

Along with many philosophical questions, probabilistic knowledge also helps us answer questions of interest to broader audiences. For instance, accepting probabilistic knowledge should prompt us to rethink common negative evaluations of stereotypically female speech. Probabilistic knowledge plays an important role in legal standards of proof, such as the standard of proof beyond a reasonable doubt. The fact that legal proof requires probabilistic knowledge explains why merely statistical evidence is insufficient to license a legal verdict of guilt or liability. Finally, probabilistic knowledge can be used to explain why acts of racial profiling violate not only moral norms, but also epistemic norms. I hope that in addition to moving many philosophical debates forward, this book will also help move them outward, by identifying practical and political problems to which my central claims may be usefully applied.

Some readers with limited time may be interested in reading selected portions of the book. Epistemologists will hit many important highlights by reading chapter 1, sections 3.5–6, and chapters 5 through 7. Philosophers of language will find it useful to focus on chapters 1–4, chapter 6, and sections 7.4–5. For anyone wishing to read a condensed version of this book, say for one meeting of a graduate seminar or a reading group, I recommend sections 1.1–2, 2.2, 5.6, 5.8, and 6.2–3, with the possible addition of section 2.1 for readers unfamiliar with the literature on epistemic modals, and sections 5.9 and 10.4–5 for readers interested in practical applications of probabilistic knowledge. The main ten chapters of the book are accessible to readers with no background in formal semantics; the appendix is an additional chapter for linguistically-minded readers who would like this book to turn it up to eleven.

Some of the ideas in chapters 3 and 4 of this book appear in "On the Semantics and Pragmatics of Epistemic Vocabulary," *Semantics and Pragmatics* vol. 8, no. 5 (2015). Some of the ideas in chapter 5 appear in "Epistemology Formalized," *Philosophical Review* vol. 122, no. 1 (2013). The other seven chapters are almost entirely new. I am grateful to have gotten feedback on my book manuscript from a variety of audiences, including the philosophy departments at Harvard, MIT, Ohio State, Pittsburgh, Princeton, Purdue, Rutgers University–New Brunswick, University of California at Berkeley, University of North Carolina at Chapel Hill, University of Southern California, University of Texas at Austin, University of Wisconsin at Madison, and Yale. I have also benefited from comments from audiences at the 2015 workshop on Bayesian Theories of Perception and Epistemology at Cornell University, the Lofoten Epistemology Conference, the 2016 Northern

Illinois University Graduate Conference, the 2014 Philosophical Linguistics and Linguistical Philosophy Workshop, the 2014 Rutgers Semantics Workshop, the 24th Semantics and Linguistics Theory Conference, and the 2014 University of Chicago Linguistics and Philosophy Workshop.

In addition to these groups, many individuals provided me with helpful comments on early drafts of material in this book. For helpful discussion and insight, thanks to Maria Aarnio, Liz Anderson, Andrew Bacon, Gordon Belot, Catrin Campbell-Moore, Fabrizio Cariani, Dave Chalmers, Keith DeRose, Josh Dever, Marcello Di Bello, Cian Dorr, Tom Dougherty, Daniel Drucker, Julien Dutant, Kenny Easwaran, Allan Gibbard, Alex Guerrero, Caspar Hare, Scott Hershovitz, Jonathan Jenkins Ichikawa, Jim Joyce, Ezra Keshet, Jason Konek, Ofra Magidor, Ishani Maitra, David Manley, John Morrison, Jessie Munton, Bob Pasnau, Laurie Paul, Richard Pettigrew, Jim Pryor, Peter Railton, Hans Rott, Laura Ruetsche, Jeff Russell, Paolo Santorio, Miriam Schoenfield, Mark Schroeder, Moritz Schulz, Janum Sethi, Ted Sider, Susanna Siegel, Alex Silk, Julia Staffel, Jason Stanley, Zoltán Szabó, Katia Vavova, Brian Weatherson, Roger White, Malte Willer, Robbie Williams, and Seth Yalcin. I am grateful to several undergraduate and graduate research assistants who performed valuable detective work and time-consuming copy-editing tasks: David Boylan, Kevin Craven, Daniel Drucker, Samia Hesni, Zoe Jenkin, Allison Lang, Alexandra Newton, Jonathan Sarnoff, and Joe Shin. The writing of this book was supported by a Charles A. Ryskamp Research Fellowship from the American Council of Learned Societies, and by a Summer Writing Grant from the ADVANCE Program at the University of Michigan.

A number of people were generous enough to read nearly all of this book as it was in preparation. I am grateful to the students in my Fall 2015 graduate seminar, who endured a much less fun version of the manuscript with tremendous enthusiasm and insight. Thanks also to Andy Egan, Branden Fitelson, Dan Greco, Alan Hájek, John Hawthorne, Brian Hedden, Dilip Ninan, Susanna Rinard, Bob Stalnaker, Eric Swanson, and Tim Williamson, each of whom significantly influenced my choices about what to include in this book by contributing insights about my arguments and about how to best present them.

Finally, my family deserves special thanks. I am grateful to my sister, Katie Moss, whose passionate and indefatigable work as a public defender inspired my interest in legal standards of proof. I am grateful to Liem and Oliver for a steady supply of laughter. Above all, I am grateful to Eric Swanson, not only for reading this book but for living with it for the past three years. He is an inspiration, both as a philosopher and as a person, and I know with certainty that I could not have written this book without his support.

1

The case for probabilistic contents

1.1 Probabilistic beliefs

Traditional theories of assertion and knowledge traffic in full beliefs. That grass is green, that you have hands, that you are not dreaming: these are propositions you can believe, assert, and know. In addition to these full beliefs, you have probabilistic beliefs. You may have .5 credence that a certain coin landed heads, for instance. You have high credence that you have hands, and you have low credence that you are dreaming. How should our theories of assertion and knowledge incorporate these probabilistic beliefs? This book defends three central theses. The first is a thesis in the philosophy of mind: we can believe probabilistic contents. The second is a thesis in the philosophy of language: we can assert probabilistic contents. The third is a thesis in epistemology: we can know probabilistic contents.

For example, say you believe your friend Smith smokes, while you have .6 credence that Jones smokes and .3 credence that Brown smokes. Just as your full belief that Smith smokes can be knowledge, your .6 credence that Jones smokes can be knowledge, and so can your .3 credence that Brown smokes. The same goes not just for simple assignments of credence but for more complicated probabilistic beliefs, such as your belief that Jones is more likely to smoke than Brown, your belief that it is between .5 and .7 likely that Jones smokes, and the conditional probability judgment that if Smith smokes then it is fairly likely that Jones does too. These probabilistic beliefs can all be knowledge, namely *probabilistic knowledge*.

The starting assumption of this book is that we have *probabilistic beliefs*, the sort of beliefs that are best represented using probability spaces.[1] Say you ask Smith, "On a scale of one to ten, how likely is it that Jones smokes?" and also "How likely is it that Jones *doesn't* smoke?" Suppose Smith says "Nine!" both times. Then there is something intuitively wrong with Smith. This intuition is naturally explained by

---

[1] As explained in §1.2, my starting assumption that we *have probabilistic beliefs* is distinct from my first central thesis that we *believe probabilistic contents*.

the assumption that Smith has beliefs that ought to reflect the laws of probability, which entail that the negation of a likely proposition is unlikely. The same can be said when Smith bets on long odds that Jones smokes and then also bets that she doesn't. In many ordinary situations, our decisions are informed by certain sorts of opinions, the sorts of opinions that Bayesian epistemologists are in the business of stating norms for. According to Bayesian tradition, these opinions are best represented using probability spaces.[2]

A word of caution: the probabilistic beliefs that I have been talking about are not full beliefs in propositions about probabilities. For instance, they are not merely full beliefs about what is likely given your evidence. They are not full beliefs about objective chance facts. As some might put it, your probabilistic beliefs include your partial beliefs, degrees of belief, degrees of confidence, or subjective probabilities. These sorts of beliefs stand apart from your full beliefs, or outright beliefs. The simplest examples of probabilistic beliefs are credences, which are subjective probabilities measured on a scale from 0 to 1. In addition to credences, though, you also have more complicated probabilistic beliefs that supervene on your credences. When you have .6 credence that Jones smokes and .3 credence that Brown smokes, for instance, your credences thereby have another property, namely assigning higher probability to Jones smoking than Brown. To put it another way, when you believe that it is .6 likely that Jones smokes and that it is .3 likely that Brown smokes, you thereby believe that Jones is more likely to smoke than Brown. This second description of your three beliefs may sound like it is describing full beliefs about probabilities of some sort or other. But on the theory of probability operators defended in this book, it is just another way of describing your credences and your comparative probabilistic beliefs.

Some of my central theses are more radical than others. The thesis that we can assert probabilistic contents is arguably more radical than the thesis that we can believe probabilistic contents, and the thesis that we can know probabilistic contents is more radical still. Accordingly, the majority of this book is dedicated to defending probabilistic assertion and probabilistic knowledge. I defend these two theses using independent arguments for each thesis, as well as conditional arguments for each thesis that presuppose the other thesis. The resulting probabilistic theories of assertion and knowledge are logically independent, but they are strongest when accepted as a package.

---

[2] A *probability space* is an ordered triple consisting of a domain of possibilities, an algebra of propositions, and a probability measure defined on the elements of that algebra. For more detailed discussion, see §2.4.

The central theses of this book not only support each other, but also support my starting assumption that we have probabilistic beliefs. A number of theorists have recently argued that we do not have any probabilistic beliefs such as credences. For some, skepticism about credences might be motivated by the thought that the contents of belief must be potential contents of assertion, together with the thought that only the contents of full beliefs are fit for assertion. For others, skepticism is motivated by the thought that the contents of belief are the sort of contents that can be knowledge, together with the thought that only full beliefs can be knowledge. For instance, HOLTON 2014 encourages skepticism about credences by saying that "a belief is either a piece of knowledge or a failed attempt at knowledge . . . But since knowledge is itself an all-out state, this only adds to the force of what is said here," namely that "we cannot form credences at all" (34). These arguments against credences are undermined by my development of theories of assertion and knowledge in which credences play a central role. Knowledge may be first, as WILLIAMSON 2000 would say. But that does not mean that credences have to be second.

In this chapter, I argue for my first central thesis: we can believe probabilistic contents. In §1.2, I argue that probabilistic contents play certain theoretical roles traditionally assigned to contents of belief. In §1.3, I defend my assumption that the contents of belief are indeed the objects that play these roles. In §1.4, I discuss the relationship between full belief and probabilistic belief. In §1.5, I adapt my arguments for referentialist and relationist theories of belief, and I discuss theories of *de se* belief according to which no one sort of content plays all of the roles mentioned in §1.2. In short, this chapter discusses several foundational debates about content, motivating probabilistic contents of belief for a broad range of positions in these debates.

1.2 An argument for probabilistic contents of belief

The starting assumption of this book is that we have probabilistic beliefs. The first central thesis of this book concerns the nature of these beliefs. What sorts of objects are the contents of probabilistic beliefs, and what sorts of attitudes do we have toward these contents? What I have said so far is consistent with two different accounts. Suppose that you have .6 credence that Jones smokes. This could be a complex attitude with a simple content. The complex attitude is *believing to degree .6*. The simple content is just the proposition that Jones smokes. Alternatively, your probabilistic belief could be a simple attitude with a complex content. The simple attitude is just the attitude of *believing*. The complex content is the content that it is .6 likely that Jones smokes. This content is not a proposition, but a probabilistic content. By definition, a *probabilistic content* is a set of probability spaces. For example, the content that it is .6 likely that Jones smokes is the set containing just those probability spaces with measures that assign .6 to the proposition that Jones smokes. The first central thesis of this book states that the complex content account is correct. The correct analysis of probabilistic beliefs requires enriching the contents of belief, as opposed to enriching the attitudes that we have toward these contents.

The opposing complex attitude account is commonly presupposed in discussions of probabilistic belief. For example, HÁJEK 2013 says that "to the extent that a sentence is appropriate to be the content of a belief-like attitude (such as a degree of belief), it must have truth conditions, and the attitude concerns those conditions being met" (148). Hájek assumes that to have various credences is to have various *belief-like* attitudes, distinct from the simple attitude of belief. In addition to theorists like Hájek who are friendly to credences, the complex attitude account is also presupposed by some skeptics about credences, as they argue that the complex attitude account does not describe any attitudes that ordinary subjects actually have. For example, HOLTON 2014 assumes that according to the credence picture, "our beliefs are essentially probabilistic. This is because probability is ... in the attitude of belief itself" (14). The syntactic structure of credence ascriptions encourages this way of thinking. When we say that you have .6 credence in a certain proposition, we mention a simple content, and we appear to say that you have some complex attitude toward it.[3]

At first, the complex attitude account may appear simpler than the complex content account, since the former can represent your .6 credence without appealing to anything as structured as a set of probability spaces. This appearance of simplicity fades away, though, when we consider more complex probabilistic beliefs. For example, suppose that you have higher credence that Jones smokes than that Brown smokes, conditional on Smith smoking. In colloquial terms, you believe that if Smith smokes, then it is more likely that Jones smokes than that Brown does. On the complex content account, you have a belief with a probabilistic content, namely the set of probability spaces that assign higher probability to Jones smoking than Brown, conditional on Smith smoking. On the complex attitude account, your attitude is much more complicated. Just as your .6 credence is an attitude with one simple content, your conditional belief is an attitude

---

[3] For readers of HOLTON 2014, I should flag an important terminological difference. Holton uses 'probabilistic content' for propositions about probabilities. I have not adopted his terminology. As I see it, propositions about probabilities are not probabilistic contents, any more than propositions about nepotism are nepotistic contents. I reserve the term 'probabilistic contents' for sets of probability spaces.

with three simple contents. Just as you can have the "believing to degree .6" attitude toward one content, you will have the "believing that the first is more likely than the second, given the third" attitude toward the three propositional contents of your conditional belief. There are an unlimited number of belief-like attitudes, many determining different asymmetric relations between their contents. For example, there is an attitude of believing that the first content of your attitude is three times as likely as the second content, given that either the third content is at least .6 likely or the fourth content is less likely than the fifth. And so on. Just like the simple attitude account, the complex attitude account must appeal to structured entities in order to explain what it means to have certain probabilistic beliefs. On the complex attitude account, the relevant structured entities are the "belief-like" attitudes.

If the rival accounts of probabilistic belief are equally complicated, why endorse the complex content account? There are two premises that together entail the thesis that the contents of belief can include probabilistic contents. The first premise is that the contents of belief just are whatever objects play certain theoretical roles. The second premise is that probabilistic contents play those roles. In the rest of this section, I outline four theoretical roles that are traditionally ascribed to contents of belief, and I argue that probabilistic contents play all of them.

The first role played by contents of belief concerns explanations of action. The fact that agents believe the same content often helps explain why those agents act the same way. The fact that Jones and Smith each open up their umbrellas is explained in part by the fact that they believe the same content, namely that it is raining. The fact that Lois Lane looks up and searches the sky on several occasions may be explained in part by the fact that she believes the same content on all those occasions, namely that Superman is flying through the sky above her. For many theorists, explaining action is part of the job description for the notion of content they are interested in. For instance, BLOCK 1991 "simply assumes that the rationale for narrow content is (causal) psychological explanation," and observes that this is "how the notion of narrow content has generally been understood, both by its proponents and opponents" (36).[4]

In addition to theories about relations between belief and action, contents of belief play important roles in theories about relations between beliefs. For instance, at a first pass, subjects *agree* about something just in case they believe

---

[4] For similar assumptions, see FODOR 1987, LOAR 1988, and STALNAKER 1991. A contrasting notion of belief content is discussed by *referentialists* such as Nathan Salmon and Scott Soames. Referentialists say that Superman beliefs and Clark Kent beliefs have the same content, and accordingly deny that belief contents play any of the theoretical roles described in this section. For further discussion of referentialism, see §1.5.

the same content, and *disagree* just in case they believe inconsistent contents. MacFarlane 2014 elaborates: "Asked what disagreement is, I suspect many philosophers' first answer will be what we might call The Simple View of Disagreement. To disagree with someone's belief that *p* is to have beliefs whose contents are jointly incompatible with *p*" (121). Suppose that Jones and Smith are standing together in the middle of Harvard Square. Jones believes that some nearby bar serves coffee, and Smith believes that coffee is not served in any nearby bar. According to the Simple View, the fact that Jones and Smith disagree is explained by the fact that they believe inconsistent contents. Suppose that miles away in Boston, Brown believes that some nearby bar serves coffee. Smith and Brown do not thereby disagree about anything. According to the Simple View, the fact that they do not disagree is explained by the fact that they believe consistent contents.

A third theoretical role for contents of belief concerns relations between beliefs held by one subject at different times. At a first pass, you *change your mind* just in case you believe some content at one time and later believe some content that is inconsistent with it. In other words, you change your mind when you disagree with your earlier self. Smith intuitively changes his mind if Jones convinces him that some nearby bar serves coffee, since then the contents of his earlier and later beliefs are inconsistent. By contrast, Smith does not change his mind if he travels to Boston and then comes to believe that some nearby bar serves coffee, since his Harvard Square belief and his Boston belief have consistent contents. Just like facts about disagreement, intuitive facts about changing your mind are grounded in facts about the contents of beliefs.

Finally, in addition to relations between beliefs held by different subjects and beliefs held at different times, contents of belief play an important role in grounding rational relations between beliefs held by one subject at one time. For instance, ideal rationality demands that your beliefs be consistent. At a first pass, your beliefs are consistent just in case they have consistent contents, and inconsistent just in case they have inconsistent contents. In other words, rationality demands that you do not disagree with yourself. Similarly, ideal rationality may demand that your beliefs be closed under entailment, where this relation between beliefs is grounded in entailment relations between their contents. For instance, if Jones believes that some nearby bar serves coffee, then she may be rationally required to believe that at least one bar serves coffee, since the content of the former belief entails the content of the latter.

I have described four theoretical roles played by the contents of belief. Each of these roles can be played by probabilistic contents. For starters, the fact that agents believe the same probabilistic content can help explain why those agents act the same way. Jones and Smith may each grab an umbrella as they leave the house simply because they each have *some fairly high credence* that it will rain. If they act the same way in virtue of believing the same content, then this content must be a probabilistic content, namely the set of probability spaces that assign some fairly high probability to the proposition that it will rain. Lois Lane may look up and search the sky simply because she has *at least .3 credence* that Superman is flying above her. If she searches the sky in virtue of believing a certain content, then this content must be a probabilistic content, namely the set of probability spaces that assign at least .3 probability to the proposition that Superman is flying above her.[5]

Could it be that ultimately Jones and Smith each grab an umbrella only in virtue of sharing some full belief in a certain proposition? To spell out the intended example more carefully, we may suppose that Jones and Smith are agnostic about whether it will rain, neither believing this content nor its negation. In addition, suppose that Jones and Smith do not have any higher-order beliefs about their evidence, and hence *a fortiori* they do not have any common beliefs about what their evidence supports. Could there nevertheless still be some other proposition that both Jones and Smith believe? Could there be some proposition believed by all and only those subjects who act as if they have a fairly high credence that it is going to rain? Could their common full belief in this proposition explain why these subjects go around grabbing umbrellas, canceling picnics, and more generally doing whatever actions would have highest expected utility for them if they had a fairly high credence that it was going to rain?

Imagine a world with two demi-gods. The demi-gods believe exactly the same propositions. Every proposition that they believe is true, and they believe almost every true proposition. In particular, only two worlds are possible given what the demi-gods believe. In exactly one of these worlds, it will rain later. Although the demi-gods believe the same propositions, they do not have the same probabilistic beliefs. The first assigns .7 credence to the rainy world and .3 credence to the sunny world. The second assigns .3 credence to the rainy world and .7 credence to the sunny world. Accordingly, only the first demi-god grabs an umbrella before leaving the house. There is no proposition believed by only the demi-god with a fairly high credence that it will rain. The fact that the demi-gods act differently is not explained by the fact that they believe different propositions, but by the fact that they believe different probabilistic contents.[6]

---

[5] Some have argued that propositions must be true at centered worlds if they are to play their intended role in action explanations. For a more detailed discussion of *de se* belief contents, see §1.5.

[6] The case of the two demi-gods is intended to resemble the case of the two gods from Lewis 1979a. If my case seems more objectionable, note that one may suppose that the demi-gods themselves are just the gods that Lewis describes, inhabiting centered worlds that differ with respect to whether it will rain later at the location of the center.

The case of the demi-gods is a fanciful illustration of an important moral. Because credences stand apart from full beliefs in propositions, the latter opinions cannot always be substituted for the former in explanations of action. To state a more serious argument in a similar spirit: probabilistic beliefs figure in intuitive explanations of action under conditions of uncertainty. In explaining actions, one may sometimes charitably interpret agents as acting on full beliefs in accordance with principles of instrumental reasoning. But one may sometimes charitably interpret agents as acting on probabilistic beliefs in accordance with principles of standard decision theory. Insofar as your actions are explained by appealing to the contents of your beliefs, decision-theoretic explanations of your actions must appeal to probabilistic contents of belief.

Probabilistic contents also play important roles in theories of agreement and disagreement. The expression 'peer disagreement' is routinely used to describe subjects with different credences in propositions, and this is not some unfortunate misnomer. Suppose that Smith has .6 credence that Jones smokes and Brown only has .3 credence that Jones smokes. Smith and Brown agree that it is at least .3 likely that Jones smokes. But Smith and Brown also intuitively disagree about some questions. For example, they disagree about whether it is at least .5 likely that Jones smokes. If Smith and Brown disagree just in case they believe inconsistent contents, then these contents must be probabilistic. Smith believes the set of probability spaces that assign at least .6 probability to the proposition that Jones smokes, for instance, and Brown does not.

Could it be that ultimately Smith and Brown disagree only in virtue of believing inconsistent propositions? If Smith and Brown have exactly the same evidence, for instance, then they might disagree about some propositions, namely propositions about what their shared evidence supports. In order to isolate the sort of disagreement I am concerned with, we may suppose that Smith and Brown do not have any disagreement of this kind. Suppose that Smith and Brown agree about exactly what credences are supported by any particular body of total evidence. Smith and Brown may nevertheless end up with different credences that Jones smokes, namely in virtue of having different evidence at their disposal. There is an intuitive sense in which Smith and Brown thereby count as disagreeing about the likelihood that Jones smokes. In fact, Smith may disagree with Brown even if he believes that Brown has perfectly rational credences given her total evidence, namely because Smith believes that Brown's total evidence is misleading. The sense in which Smith and Brown disagree simply in virtue of having different credences is the sense that is relevant as you are forming your own credence that Jones smokes. It is the sense in which you must pick sides, the sense in which you cannot agree with them both.

In addition to grounding relations of agreement and disagreement, probabilistic contents ground relations between your beliefs over time. In short, there is an intuitive sense in which changing your credence is changing your mind about something. As BLOCK 1986 puts it, "what corresponds to change of mind in the Bayesian perspective just *is* change of degree of belief" (631). Suppose that you have .6 credence that Jones smokes and then you come to have .3 credence that she smokes. Then intuitively, you have changed your mind about something. As you might put it, first you believe that Jones probably smokes, and then you believe she probably doesn't. If changing your mind just amounts to believing inconsistent contents at different times, then changing your mind by changing your credence amounts to believing inconsistent probabilistic contents at different times.

Finally, probabilistic contents play an important role in grounding rational relations among your beliefs at a given time. Just as ideal rationality demands that your full beliefs be consistent, the same goes for your probabilistic beliefs. For instance, it is inconsistent to have .6 credence that Jones smokes while also having .6 credence that she doesn't. If having inconsistent beliefs just amounts to believing inconsistent contents, then having these inconsistent probabilistic beliefs amounts to believing inconsistent probabilistic contents, namely the set of probability spaces that assign .6 probability to the proposition that Jones smokes and the set of probability spaces that assign .6 probability to its negation. Similarly, suppose that you have .6 credence that Jones smokes and .5 conditional credence that Brown smokes if Jones does. Then ideal rationality may require you to have at least .3 credence that Brown smokes. On the complex content account, this rational requirement has an elegant and familiar explanation, namely that the contents of the first two beliefs entail the content of the third. Even setting aside requirements of ideal rationality, suppose you start with some justified credences and then competently reason your way to others. On the complex content account, your resulting credences are justified for exactly the same reason that full beliefs are justified by inference, namely because you are justified in believing contents that you competently deduce from other contents that you justifiedly believe.

To sum up where we stand: the contents of belief are traditionally assumed to play various theoretical roles, such as explaining rational action, or grounding relations of disagreement or inconsistency between beliefs. These claims about the roles played by contents of belief are usually taken to illuminate theoretical notions, such as what constitutes rational action, disagreement, or inconsistency between beliefs. But insofar as we have some independent grasp of these theoretical notions, the same claims can be understood to illuminate the notion of *content itself*. Having taken this turn, we have repeatedly seen that the theoretical roles for contents of belief can be played not only by propositions, but also by sets of probability spaces over propositions. To put the point another way, there are indeed well-established credence-based theories of rational action, disagreement, and inconsistency between beliefs. We can use these theories to identify the contents of probabilistic beliefs. When we do, we find that the complex content account is correct. Probabilistic beliefs are beliefs with probabilistic contents.

1.3 The roles played by contents of belief

The simplest objection to my §1.2 argument for probabilistic contents of belief comes from the steadfast advocate of the complex attitude account. According to this objection, the theoretical roles described in §1.2 can indeed be played by something other than propositions. However, that does not mean that the contents of belief can be anything other than propositions. Rather, it means that the theoretical roles can be played by something other than the contents of belief. For example, according to the steadfast advocate of the complex attitude account, it is false that subjects agree about something in virtue of believing the same content. Instead, subjects agree in virtue of bearing the *same belief-like attitude* toward some propositional content or contents.

For many theorists, it is analytic that the contents of belief play some or all of the roles described in §1.2. Accordingly, these theorists should dismiss the above objection as misguided. If it is analytic that subjects disagree just in case they believe inconsistent contents, for instance, then in order to argue for the complex content account, it suffices to argue that subjects can disagree in virtue of having different credences in a proposition. But let me grant for sake of argument that it is not analytic that the contents of belief play the theoretical roles mentioned above. Is there a substantive dispute remaining about whether credences are probabilistic attitudes with simple contents, or simple attitudes with probabilistic contents? At first glance, the difference between these accounts may appear to be a mere difference in bookkeeping. However, although the accounts are empirically equivalent, there are theoretical reasons to prefer the complex content account. The complex content account has explanatory virtues that the complex attitude account does not. These virtues are not decisive evidence for the complex content account, but they are significant enough to merit mention here.

For starters, the complex content account can make use of a significant fact about probabilistic contents, namely that they can stand in just the same logical relations as propositions. For instance, sets of probability spaces are consistent just in case there is some probability space in their intersection. They are inconsistent just in case they are disjoint. Some probabilistic contents together entail another probabilistic content just in case the intersection of the former is a subset of the latter. Against this background, the complex content account provides an explanatory theory of rational relations between beliefs. It is rationally inconsistent to have .6 credence that Jones smokes and .6 credence that she doesn't. According to the complex content account, these probabilistic beliefs are inconsistent because their contents are inconsistent, and their contents are inconsistent in virtue of the fact that they are disjoint sets of probability spaces. The same goes for the fact that it is inconsistent to have .6 credence that Jones smokes and .5 conditional credence that Brown smokes if Jones does, and yet have merely .2 credence that Brown smokes. By contrast, according to the complex attitude account, these probabilistic beliefs are inconsistent because they are instances of inconsistent attitudes. Is it a primitive fact that the relevant attitudes are inconsistent? If the inconsistency of various belief-like attitudes is not grounded in similarly simple facts about those attitudes, then the complex content account provides a more satisfying explanation of the inconsistency of these beliefs.

This explanatory challenge for the complex attitude account resembles one interpretation of the Frege-Geach problem for noncognitivist accounts of moral language.[7] Just as it is inconsistent to believe that Jones smoking is both likely and unlikely, it is inconsistent to believe that murder is both permissible and impermissible. According to moral descriptivists, these beliefs are inconsistent because their contents are inconsistent—that is, because there is no world where both of their contents are true. According to noncognitivists, by contrast, the beliefs are inconsistent because they correspond to inconsistent attitudes, such as the attitudes of tolerance and disapproval. SCHROEDER 2008a argues that noncognitivists face an explanatory challenge that moral descriptivists do not face. As Schroeder puts it, "tolerance of murder and disapproval of murder are two *distinct* and apparently *logically unrelated* attitudes toward the *same* content," and therefore the noncognitivist must answer an additional question: "why on earth is it inconsistent to hold them toward the same thing?" (48). The moral descriptivist claims to give a more satisfying account of the inconsistency of certain moral beliefs. Absent any reductive account of the inconsistency of various belief-like attitudes, one might prefer the complex content account of probabilistic belief on similar grounds.

The complex content account not only explains inconsistency relations among probabilistic beliefs, but also allows us to give a unified explanation of inconsistency relations among instances of various belief-like attitudes. Belief itself is

---

[7] SCHROEDER 2008b provides a survey of literature developing this interpretation, including HARE 1970, HALE 1993, UNWIN 1999, and SCHROEDER 2008a.

a belief-like attitude. It is inconsistent to believe that Jones drinks, that Brown drinks, and that it is not the case that both Jones and Brown drink. These full beliefs are inconsistent because they have inconsistent contents. On the complex content account, the inconsistency of probabilistic beliefs can be explained in just the same way. Just like full beliefs, probabilistic beliefs are inconsistent in virtue of having inconsistent contents. On the complex attitude account, by contrast, probabilistic beliefs are inconsistent in virtue of facts about attitudes. For example, consider the three probabilistic beliefs mentioned earlier, namely the belief that it is .6 likely that Jones smokes, .5 likely that Brown smokes if Jones does, and .2 likely that Brown smokes. On the complex attitude account, these probabilistic beliefs are inconsistent in virtue of facts about the belief-like attitudes that they instantiate.

A final argument for the complex content account is that it makes sense of apparent ordinary language quantification over contents. Suppose that Smith and Brown each start with .6 credence that Jones smokes, but then Brown comes to believe that it is merely .3 likely that Jones smokes. Then we could naturally say that Brown comes to believe something that Smith does not believe. We could also naturally say that there is something that Smith and Brown first agree about and then disagree about, namely whether it is .6 likely that Jones smokes. These claims are easy to make sense of on the complex content account, which identifies the objects of their agreement and disagreement as sets of probability spaces. By contrast, the complex attitude account must understand these quantified claims as elliptical for others, such as the claim that there is a certain belief-like attitude toward some contents that Brown comes to have and Smith does not have.

This argument for the complex content account resembles one traditional argument for the existence of propositions.[8] Suppose that Smith believes that Jones is a vegetarian and Brown does not believe that Jones is a vegetarian. Then we could naturally say that there is something that Smith believes and Brown does not. This claim is easy to make sense of on the assumption that there are such things as propositions which are the contents of shared attitudes. In short, ordinary language quantification over propositions gives us some reason to think that we can believe propositions. If this argument is correct, then the same goes for probabilistic contents. The complex content account allows us to take apparent quantification over probabilistic contents at face value.

Advocates of the complex attitude account might try to play the same game, namely finding ordinary language judgments that they are better able to explain. For instance, suppose again that Smith has .6 credence that Jones smokes, while

---

[8] See SPEAKS 2014 for a detailed sympathetic discussion of this argument.

Brown has .3 credence that Jones smokes. Then we might find it intuitive to say that there is something that Smith and Brown have different attitudes about, namely the claim that Jones smokes. The complex attitude account respects this intuition. On the complex attitude account, Smith and Brown have different attitudes about the proposition that Jones smokes, in just the same sense that believing and desiring that Jones smokes are different attitudes about that proposition. Does this constitute a reason for preferring the complex attitude account?

As I see it, the complex attitude account has no big advantage here. The complex content account can explain these same ordinary language intuitions. There is a sense in which beliefs with distinct probabilistic contents may be beliefs *about the same proposition*. It is just the same sense in which on the traditional picture, beliefs with distinct propositional contents may be beliefs *about the same object*. Consider the full belief that Jones smokes and the full belief that Jones drinks. These beliefs are both about Jones. But that does not mean that Jones is a content of the beliefs. In the same sense, Smith and Brown both have probabilistic beliefs about the claim that Jones smokes. But that does not mean that the proposition that Jones smokes is a content of their probabilistic beliefs. The semantics for simple sentences defended in §3.5 further develops this comparison between Jones and the claim that Jones smokes. According to many semantic theories, Jones is the semantic value of her proper name, which is a constituent of sentences such as 'Jones smokes' and 'Jones drinks'. According to my semantics, the proposition that Jones smokes is the semantic value of a constituent of sentences such as 'it is .6 likely that Jones smokes' and 'it is .3 likely that Jones smokes'. These sentences have common constituents with the same semantic value, but they do not therefore express attitudes with the same content.

To sum up, we have to choose some way of talking about probabilistic beliefs. I have stated some theoretical arguments for preferring the complex content account over the complex attitude account, where analogous theoretical arguments are sometimes presented as decisive in the context of other debates. As I see it, the arguments in this section justify my presupposing the complex content account as I defend probabilistic assertion and knowledge. Further reasons to endorse the complex content account will emerge as we go along. That being said, it is also important to note that most of the arguments in this book do not depend on the complex content account of probabilistic belief. Advocates of the complex attitude account can accept much of what I say about probabilistic assertion and probabilistic knowledge, while simply rejecting that these are relations to probabilistic contents. For instance, rather than accepting my third central thesis that probabilistic contents can be knowledge, advocates of the complex attitude account can accept the alternative thesis that degreed belief-like attitudes can be knowledge, in just the same sense as full belief attitudes are knowledge.

1.4 Full beliefs

For each proposition, there is a probabilistic content corresponding to that proposition, namely the set of all and only those probability spaces such that the proposition is true at every world in their domain. These sets of probability spaces are boring. They are *nominally probabilistic* contents: probabilistic since they are sets of probability spaces, but only nominally probabilistic since they represent merely some distinction between possible worlds, namely those that are in their domain and those that are not. All other sets of probability spaces are *thoroughly probabilistic* contents, including the contents of your credences, conditional credences, and many other probabilistic beliefs.

Since propositions correspond to nominally probabilistic contents, there is a sense in which the former contents of belief can be replaced by the latter. Compare LEWIS 1979a on his motivation for representing contents using sets of centered worlds: "when propositional objects of attitudes will do, property objects also will do . . . We have a one-one correspondence between all propositions and some properties. Whenever it would be right to assign a proposition as the object of an attitude, I shall simply assign the corresponding property" (516). In §3.6, I argue that whenever it would be right to assign a proposition as the content of a belief, we may simply assign the corresponding nominally probabilistic content as the strict content of that belief. This argument is part of my argument for a fairly radical conclusion, namely that probabilistic contents should ultimately replace propositions as the fundamental contents of belief. To be more exact, the full beliefs asserted using simple sentences such as 'Jones smokes' have nominally probabilistic strict contents and thoroughly probabilistic loose contents.

Throughout this book, I use 'proposition' for whatever objects are traditionally taken to be the contents of full beliefs. If you already have a favorite view of what sort of objects propositions are, you should understand 'proposition' as I use it to refer to those objects. It is generally agreed that propositions are the sort of objects that are true or false at worlds. But this claim is compatible with any number of detailed theories of propositions. For all I argue, propositions may be sets of worlds, n-tuples of objects and properties, or interpreted logical forms. At a first pass, probabilistic contents are defined to be sets of probability spaces over these same objects. The surprising conclusion of §3.6 is that even full beliefs have probabilistic contents.

We do not merely have probabilistic knowledge on the cheap. It should be understood that when I say that we can know probabilistic contents, I mean that we can know thoroughly probabilistic contents. We do not have probabilistic knowledge merely because we know some propositions and thereby bear a derivative knowledge relation to some corresponding nominally probabilistic contents. In fact, the situation is reversed. When you bear the knowledge relation to the set of probability spaces such that Jones smokes throughout their domain, you thereby bear a derivative knowledge relation to the set of worlds where Jones smokes. Again, compare LEWIS 1979a: when you bear the knowledge relation to the set of centered worlds where Jones smokes, you bear a derivative knowledge relation to the corresponding set of uncentered worlds where Jones smokes. In this carefully limited sense, I accept that propositions can be the contents of belief, assertion, and knowledge. Probabilistic knowledge is fundamental, while propositional knowledge is essentially derivative.

I have argued that the contents of belief are sets of probability spaces, rather than propositions. Why not instead conclude that *propositions are sets of probability spaces*?[9] Strictly speaking, the correct moral of my argument depends on what features propositions have essentially. According to tradition, propositions are the contents of belief, and propositions determine the set of worlds in which a belief is true. I have argued that sets of probability spaces play the former role but not the latter, and I have concluded that not all contents of belief are propositions. But I am not concerned to argue that certain traditional roles of propositions are more essential than others. An alternative conclusion that one might draw from my argument is that it turns out that propositions are not the sort of objects that we thought they were, but rather sets of probability spaces over those objects. According to this conclusion, all sentences have probabilistic contents, and all sentences have propositional contents, because propositions are sets of probability spaces. Readers who prefer this alternative conclusion may translate my arguments accordingly.[10]

1.5 Alternative roles for contents of belief

According to some referentialist and relationist theories, the contents of belief do not play the theoretical roles described in §1.2. These roles are instead played by guises of contents or by relations among contents. At a first pass, debates

---

[9] I am grateful to Zoltán Szabó for encouraging me to address this question.
[10] In the next section, I address questions motivated by specific theories of the contents of belief. Readers may skip ahead to chapter 2 without missing significant positive arguments.

about referentialism and relationism are orthogonal to the main arguments of this chapter. Assume for sake of argument that the referentialist or relationist is right, and that the contents of belief are the objects that have guises that play the theoretical roles described in §1.2, or the objects that stand in the relations that play those roles. Then sets of probability spaces are going to have guises that play these roles, or stand in relations that play these roles, and hence sets of probability spaces are going to be contents of belief.

According to *referentialist* theories of belief, for instance, the content of the belief that Superman flies is the same as the content of the belief that Clark Kent flies. Lois Lane believes this content under one *mode of presentation* or *guise*, namely the Superman guise. She believes the negation of this same content under another guise, namely the Clark Kent guise.[11] Lois has consistent beliefs—she is merely ignorant, not irrational. But according to the referentialist, her consistent beliefs have inconsistent contents. Having inconsistent beliefs does not amount to believing inconsistent contents, then, but believing contents under inconsistent guises. Just like propositions, guises of propositions stand in logical relations to one another, and the referentialist says that these logical relations ground consistency relations among your full beliefs.[12]

At a first pass, the same goes for your probabilistic beliefs. CHALMERS 2011 argues that referentialist theories fail to account for the fact that Superman credences and Clark Kent credences play different roles in the betting behavior of rational agents. On behalf of referentialists, BRAUN 2016 responds by pointing out that referentialist theories can account for this fact in the same way that they account for the fact that Superman beliefs and Clark Kent beliefs play different roles in rational behavior. According to the referentialist, explanations of action must appeal to guises in addition to contents of belief. For example, it is intuitively consistent to have high credence that Superman flies and high credence that Clark Kent doesn't fly. The referentialist can say that these probabilistic beliefs are consistent because you believe the probabilistic content that Superman probably flies under one guise while believing its complement under another. By contrast, if you have high credence that Superman flies and high credence that Superman doesn't fly, then you believe that Superman probably flies under one guise while believing its complement under an inconsistent guise, and so your beliefs are inconsistent. If having inconsistent beliefs just amounts to believing contents under inconsistent guises, then having inconsistent probabilistic beliefs amounts to believing probabilistic contents under inconsistent guises.

---

[11] Classic defenses of referentialism include SCHIFFER 1978, SALMON 1986, SOAMES 1987, RICHARD 1990, and CRIMMINS 1992.

[12] For a recent discussion of this referentialist strategy, see BRAUN 2016.

According to *relationist* theories of belief, neither contents nor guises are adequate to play the theoretical roles described in §1.2. Rather, these roles are played by coordination relations among contents of belief, relations that are not reducible to intrinsic features of those contents. Suppose that Lois believes that Superman flies. According to the relationist view defended in FINE 2009, the reason why Lois can consistently come to believe that Clark Kent doesn't fly is that "the content of the subsequent belief is not appropriately coordinated with the content of the original belief, even though the content of the two beliefs is the same" (78). At a first pass, it seems again that the same goes for probabilistic beliefs. If you have high credence that Superman flies and high credence that Superman doesn't fly, then you believe an appropriately coordinated pair of inconsistent probabilistic contents, and that is why your beliefs are inconsistent. If having inconsistent beliefs just amounts to believing appropriately coordinated inconsistent contents, then having inconsistent probabilistic beliefs amounts to believing appropriately coordinated inconsistent probabilistic contents.

To sum up so far, it seems that both referentialists and relationists should accept that we can believe probabilistic contents. At a second pass, though, some of these theories may have difficulty accepting the complex content account. The difficulty does not arise from referentialist or relationist theories as such, but rather from the fact that many of these theories appeal to structured propositions. And the difficulty does not arise from the complex content account as such, but from the fact that it is not trivial to extend theories of full belief in structured propositions to any sort of theory of probabilistic belief.

To spell this out: suppose that propositions are unstructured sets of possible worlds.[13] Then propositions are the right sort of object to form an *algebra*, a collection of sets that is closed under finite operations of complement and union. As a result, functions assigning credences to propositions can be the right sort of object to satisfy the probability axioms. By contrast, suppose that propositions are interpreted logical forms, cognitive event types, or structured Fregean propositions. According to many such theories, propositions are not sets of anything. They are not the right sort of object to form an algebra on which probability measures can be defined. Probabilistic beliefs must be constrained by the axioms of probability. But for many advocates of structured propositions, it is not trivial to say what object is meant to satisfy these axioms.

Advocates of structured propositions might pursue several strategies here. For instance, as long as guises of propositions stand in logical relations, they may form an algebra-like structure, and thereby ground logical relations among guises

---

[13] For a classic defense of this view, see STALNAKER 1984. For alternative theories of unstructured propositions, see LEWIS 1979a, STALNAKER 2008, CHALMERS 2011, and NINAN 2012.

of probabilistic contents. Similarly, coordination relations among propositions may ground coordination relations among probabilistic contents. Absent the development of more detailed proposals, though, it is difficult to tailor the complex content account to suit particular referentialist or relationist theories. For present purposes, the important point is that the arguments of this chapter are independent of particular strategies for extending theories of propositions to theories of probabilistic belief.

A final challenge for the central argument of §1.2 does not come from any special theory of belief contents, but rather from observations about a special sort of belief. Some of your beliefs are about what the world is like, while others are about your location within it. Self-locating beliefs, or *de se* beliefs, appear to present a problem for the theoretical roles for belief contents discussed in §1.2. As NINAN 2016 neatly summarizes, "Contents have standardly been thought to play a role in the explanation of action and a role in the characterization of interpersonal cognitive relations like agreement. *De se* attitudes reveal that no single object can play both roles" (88). The theoretical roles proposed for contents of belief appear to come apart in both directions. For example, Jones and Brown might each open their umbrellas because each believes that she herself is about to get rained on. But they may not thereby agree about anything, if they are opening their umbrellas in different places or at different times. Conversely, you and I might agree that I am in danger of drowning, but believing this content may cause me to thrash around while it causes you to run for help. Agents can be motivated to do the same action without being in agreement, and they can be in agreement without being motivated to do the same action. Hence being motivated to do the same action and being in agreement cannot each just amount to believing the same content.

There are several strategies for responding to this final challenge for my inventory of roles played by contents of belief. LEWIS 1979a privileges the role of belief contents in action explanations, denying the assumption that subjects agree just in case they believe the same content. Alternatively, one might maintain that contents of belief can indeed explain action and also ground agreement facts, arguing that one can reconcile the apparent tension between these roles. For instance, some theorists argue that contrary to appearances, the content that I am in danger of drowning does in fact motivate us to do just the same actions. MAGIDOR 2015 suggests that incidental constraints could account for the difference between our actions as I thrash and you run for help. Just as an agent may believe that it is raining but fail to open his umbrella because of some temporary paralysis of the arms, some bystander may fail to thrash my arms around in order to save me from drowning merely because she is physiologically unable to do so. As DEVER AND CAPPELEN 2013 would put it, thrashing my arms around is not an *actionable content* for her. Finally, STALNAKER 2008 and Moss 2012c defend another strategy for reconciling the multiple theoretical roles played by contents of belief—namely, associating multiple contents with a single belief state. For instance, my state of believing that I am drowning may have one *de se* content that explains my thrashing, as well as a second *de dicto* content such that our both believing it explains our agreeing about my predicament.[14]

Any answer to the challenge leaves my §1.2 argument intact. Given any answer, the contents of belief can be identified as the objects that play at least one of the theoretical roles described in §1.2. Since probabilistic contents play all of these roles, it follows that probabilistic contents play the theoretical roles that are played by the contents of belief. For instance, according to Lewis, certain actions are explained only by your believing certain sets of probability spaces over *de se* propositions. According to other theorists, the same actions can be equally well explained by your believing certain sets of probability spaces over *de dicto* propositions. In any event, sets of probability spaces over propositions play a valuable theoretical role in explaining action. Just like many theories of propositions, many theories of *de se* beliefs are consistent with the thesis that probabilistic beliefs are beliefs with probabilistic contents.

---

[14] I am indebted to NINAN 2016 for clarifying the nature of this strategy, as well as its potential shortcomings.

2

The case for probabilistic assertion

2.1 Familiar arguments against propositional contents of assertion

According to many traditional theories of mind and language, beliefs and assertions essentially serve to distinguish between possibilities. The content of a belief determines a set of possible worlds, namely those where things are just as they are believed to be. The content of an assertion also determines a set of possible worlds, namely those where things are just as they are asserted to be. In the first chapter of this book, I argued for the central thesis that we can believe probabilistic contents. The content of a belief can be a set of probability spaces that does not correspond to any set of possible worlds. In this chapter, I argue that the same goes for contents of assertion. This is the second central thesis of this book: we can assert probabilistic contents.

The rejection of traditional contents of assertion has recently gained momentum in the literature on epistemic possibility modals, expressions such as 'might' and 'possibly' as used by speakers who are not entirely sure about some subject matter. I begin this chapter by recounting some familiar arguments against the claim that we always assert propositional contents, applying these arguments to sentences containing probability operators. Then in §2.2, I develop three novel arguments for the thesis that we can assert probabilistic contents. The arguments that I develop are different from familiar arguments against traditional theories of assertion, in part because my arguments are more foundational in character. In §2.3, I elaborate on the thesis that we can assert probabilistic contents, namely by describing a model on which probabilistic contents are part of the common ground of a conversation. On this model, probabilistic contents can not only be contents of assertion, but also contents of presuppositions shared by conversational participants.

For simplicity, my arguments in the first three sections of this chapter concern a narrow range of probabilistic beliefs, namely your credences and their consequences. The same can be said for the first chapter of this book. But your thoroughly probabilistic beliefs include more than just these beliefs. Almost everything I say about credences goes equally for probabilistic beliefs expressed using epistemic modals and indicative conditionals, which I briefly discuss in §2.4. Finally, I conclude this chapter in §2.5 by spelling out the relationship between my arguments and contemporary debates about epistemic modals, which I introduce in the remainder of this section.

The starting point for standard truth-conditional theories of epistemic modals is the contextualist semantics defended in KRATZER 1977. According to this semantics, speakers use epistemic modals to assert propositions about contextually determined bodies of evidence, such as the total evidence possessed by certain contextually relevant subjects. For instance, 'Jones *might* smoke' is true at a context just in case it is *consistent* with the contextually relevant evidence that Jones smokes. At a first pass, epistemic probability operators could be interpreted relative to the same body of evidence, with the result that 'Jones *probably* smokes' is true just in case the evidence makes it *probable* that Jones smokes. The same goes for other epistemic vocabulary, including epistemic adjectives, epistemic comparatives, and other quantitative measures of epistemic probability. At a second pass, contextualists may prefer to interpret probability operators relative to some contextual feature richer than a body of evidence. KRATZER 1991 interprets 'probably' relative to an ordering source intended to represent normality relations between worlds, for instance. Another natural contextualist proposal is that probability operators are interpreted relative to a contextually relevant probability space.[1]

However these details are spelled out, truth-conditional theories of epistemic vocabulary have recently come under fire for failing to explain four sorts of intuitive judgments about sentences containing epistemic vocabulary. For starters, some opponents argue that contextualist theories fail to explain how assertions made using epistemic vocabulary are assessed by eavesdroppers and other third parties observing conversations from the outside. To modify an example from EGAN 2007, imagine that some spies in London are eavesdropping on some criminals in Paris. The criminals are trying to figure out where James Bond is located. The eavesdropping spies are confident that Bond is in London. They overhear that the criminals have collected a lot of misleading evidence suggesting that Bond is in Paris. In addition, the eavesdroppers overhear the following:

(1)   *Criminal in Paris*: It is unlikely that James Bond is in London.

---

[1] SWANSON 2008 and YALCIN 2010 present problems for the semantics for probability operators defended in KRATZER 1991. For discussion of alternative contextualist proposals, see LASSITER 2015.

EGAN 2007 suggests that among themselves, the eavesdroppers may then say:

(2)   *Eavesdropper in London*: No it's not—Bond is almost certainly in London.

According to one version of the eavesdropping argument, contextualist theories fail to explain why the criminal and eavesdropper are justified in asserting (1) and (2), respectively. On the one hand, suppose the criminal uses 'unlikely' in (1) to talk about what is unlikely given some restricted body of evidence, such as her current evidence about Bond's location. Then the eavesdropper should agree with her assertion, rather than contradicting it. On the other hand, suppose the criminal uses 'unlikely' to talk about some greatly expanded body of evidence that includes the knowledge of the eavesdropper. Then it is not clear that she is justified in asserting (1) to begin with, since she can't rule out the possibility that this expanded body of evidence supports Bond being in London.[2]

A second concern is that contextualist theories fail to explain retractions of assertions made using epistemic vocabulary. Suppose the criminals eventually find out that Bond is probably in London. Then the criminal who said (1) may retract her assertion, saying that she has discovered that what she said was wrong, that she has changed her mind about it, and that she no longer agrees with what she said. These informed judgments pose the same challenge for the contextualist as the judgments of informed eavesdroppers. If the criminal initially uses (1) merely to talk about some restricted body of evidence, then she should still agree with that assertion after getting more evidence. But if her initial assertion concerns some expanded body of evidence, then again it is not clear why that assertion is licensed. Hence it seems difficult for the contextualist to account for the fact that the initial assertion and the later retraction both sound perfectly fine.[3]

A third concern for contextualist theories concerns the embedding behavior of epistemic vocabulary. For example, YALCIN 2007 observes that it sounds fine to suppose that it is not raining but that it is probable given some specific body of evidence that it is raining. For instance, (3) sounds fine when embedded in sentences such as (4) and (5):

(3)   Given our evidence, it is probably raining.

(4)   Suppose it is not raining and that given our evidence, it is probably raining.

(5)   If it is not raining and it is probably raining given our evidence . . .

---

[2] For further discussion of eavesdropping arguments, see EGAN ET AL. 2005, HAWTHORNE 2007, and VON FINTEL AND GILLIES 2008.

[3] For further discussion of retractions of assertions made using epistemic vocabulary, see MACFARLANE 2011 and YALCIN AND KNOBE 2014.

According to Yalcin, contextualist theories therefore predict that (6) should sound fine in (7) and (8):

(6)   It is probably raining.

(7)   #Suppose it is not raining and it is probably raining.

(8)   #If it is not raining and it is probably raining . . .

After all, contextualist theories say that we use (7) to assert roughly the same sort of content as (4), namely some proposition about whether it is raining and about what is probable given some body of evidence. The same goes for (8) and (5). Hence Yalcin concludes that the contextualist fails to explain why sentences such as (7) and (8) sound much worse than any sentences that the contextualist might identify as their explicit counterparts.

A fourth and final concern for contextualist theories is that they fail to identify the intuitive subject matter of sentences containing epistemic vocabulary. For instance, YALCIN 2011 argues that sentences like (9) are not adequately paraphrased by sentences like (10)–(12):

(9)   It is likely that Jones smokes.

(10)   Given my evidence, it is likely that Jones smokes.

(11)   Given our current evidence, it is likely that Jones smokes.

(12)   Given everything we know or could easily find out, it is likely that Jones smokes.

When you say (9) and then give reasons for what you say, your reasons do not concern your evidence, but rather the first-order proposition that Jones smokes. According to Yalcin, your beliefs in (10)–(12) partly concern facts about your mental states, whereas your belief in (9) is intuitively not a second-order state of mind. To give another example, your dog Fido can believe that you are probably about to take him outside without being capable of entertaining any second-order belief about what is consistent with his evidence.

These four concerns for contextualist theories motivate alternative theories of assertion, namely theories according to which we do not use sentences containing epistemic vocabulary to assert propositions. In particular, these concerns are addressed by theories on which we use these sentences to assert probabilistic contents. Suppose that the content of 'it is unlikely that Bond is in London' is the set of probability spaces that assign less than .5 probability to Bond being in London. The eavesdropping spies will reject that content because they believe an inconsistent probabilistic content, since they have high credence that Bond is in London. The criminal will later retract her assertion of that content for just the same reason. The content of 'it is probably raining' and the content of 'it is not raining' could easily be disjoint sets of probability spaces, which would explain why it sounds bad to suppose their conjunction. Finally, your dog Fido could believe that you are probably about to take him outside in virtue of having high credence in this claim, without believing any proposition about what is probable given his evidence. In each case, the distinctive behavior of epistemic vocabulary is explained by a theory on which we use it to assert probabilistic as opposed to propositional contents.

The four concerns outlined in this section are the most familiar arguments against contextualist theories of epistemic vocabulary. As I see it, these arguments are intimately connected with the four arguments for probabilistic contents developed in the first chapter of this book. In §1.2, I argued that sets of probability spaces play four theoretical roles that are played by the contents of belief. Facts about probabilistic contents ground facts about when subjects agree or disagree about something, facts about when you count as having changed your mind about something, and rational relations between your beliefs. In addition, probabilistic contents play an important role in rational explanations of action. These four theoretical roles for contents correspond to our four concerns for contextualist theories. The assessments of eavesdroppers reflect the fact that subjects can disagree in virtue of believing inconsistent probabilistic contents. The retraction of assertions made using epistemic vocabulary reflects the fact that mind changing can involve believing inconsistent probabilistic contents at different times. The embedding behavior of epistemic vocabulary reflects the fact that relations between probabilistic contents ground relations of entailment and consistency between beliefs. And very roughly, our intuitions about the subject matter of sentences containing epistemic vocabulary reflect the role of probabilistic contents in rational explanations of action. The fact that Fido has high credence that you are about to take him outside may help explain why he is fetching his leash, for instance, given that fetching his leash is rational for him under those circumstances. Sometimes agents can be intuitively described as acting on probabilistic beliefs, even when they cannot be intuitively described as acting on second-order mental states. The familiar arguments against contextualist theories recounted in this section are natural consequences of my first central thesis that the contents of belief can be probabilistic. The contextualist fails to identify the contents that play various theoretical roles, namely in virtue of casting these roles with propositional rather than probabilistic contents.

Arguments against contextualist theories of epistemic vocabulary support probabilistic theories of assertion. In addition, they support the starting assumption of this book, namely that we have probabilistic beliefs. According to many skeptics about credences, your belief that Jones probably smokes is just another full belief, such as the belief that your evidence supports the claim that Jones smokes. LANCE 1995 proposes that "the very subjective probability assignments of Bayesianism themselves should be understood as accepted propositions" (166), namely propositions concerning "the evidence presently available to us" (174). WEISBERG 2013 proposes that credences constitute full beliefs about epistemic probabilities, where your epistemic probability for a proposition is the extent to which your knowledge provides evidence for it. According to the anti-contextualist, there are several reasons to deny that probabilistic assertions are in fact just assertions of propositions about your evidence. Analogously, there are several reasons to deny that probabilistic beliefs are in fact just full beliefs in propositions about your evidence. Assessments, retractions, embeddings, and paraphrases of your belief that Jones probably smokes provide evidence that that it is not a full belief in any proposition, but a thoroughly probabilistic belief.

2.2 Foundational arguments for probabilistic contents of assertion

The anti-contextualist arguments I have recounted are controversial. A number of theorists have defended contextualism against these arguments, including BARNETT 2009, SORENSEN 2009, DOWELL 2011, VON FINTEL AND GILLIES 2011, and DORR AND HAWTHORNE 2012. In particular, many have challenged the ordinary language judgments on which most of these arguments depend. In light of these challenges, I want to provide alternative arguments for the claim that we can assert probabilistic contents. To be precise, our aim will be to compare the following views: the *propositional content view* according to which all assertions have propositional contents, and the *probabilistic content view* that at least some assertions have probabilistic contents. In addition to arguments concerning ordinary language judgments about particular sentences, we have theoretical reasons to prefer the probabilistic content view. These sorts of reasons do not play a significant role in the existing literature on epistemic modals, although they are occasionally hinted at by several authors. For instance, FORREST 1981 argues that we use 'probably' to express a high degree of belief, on the grounds that "to be able to express a high degree of belief rather than merely express a belief is so useful an ability that we should be most surprised if we had no way of expressing a high degree of belief" (44). SWANSON 2011 makes a similar argument, and the final paragraph of YALCIN 2012a contains a rhetorical question in the same spirit: "If we are indeed creatures with probabilistically structured and plan-laden states of mind, why should we have adopted a linguistic practice compelling us to squeeze these highly structured states always into a simplistic propositional medium for conversational transmission?" (156–7). In the rest of this section, I develop detailed arguments in the spirit of these abstract claims. Compared with the propositional content view, the probabilistic content view provides us with accounts of belief and assertion that are more unified in three significant respects.

First, the probabilistic content view provides a more unified account of the communication of full beliefs and probabilistic beliefs. According to the opposing propositional content view, full beliefs are communicated directly, while probabilistic beliefs are not. When I believe that Jones smokes, I can assert the very content that I believe. But the contents of probabilistic beliefs are communicated only as a result of the assertion of some propositional content. When I have high credence that Jones smokes, for instance, the propositional content view says that you can only come to share my probabilistic belief in virtue of coming to fully believe some proposition that I assert, such as the content that it is objectively likely given my evidence that Jones smokes. By contrast, the probabilistic content view allows that communicating subjects come to share probabilistic beliefs in just the same way that they come to share full beliefs. When I have high credence that Jones smokes, the probabilistic content view allows that I can assert the very content that I believe.

Second, the probabilistic content view provides a more unified account of the relation between belief and assertion. If we start with the assumption that you believe probabilistic contents, what may we conclude about the contents of occurrent judgments, thoughts that figure in ordinary reasoning? STAFFEL 2013 gives a thorough and convincing defense of the claim that we can reason with probabilistic beliefs in just the same way that we reason with full beliefs. To modify an example from Staffel, suppose you are having a party and you want it to be attended by as many of your friends as possible. Say that you have one hundred friends, each of whom is such that you have .5 credence that they would come to the party if you held it on Friday. And say you are certain that exactly five friends would come if you held the party on Saturday. Then you may decide to have the party on Friday on the basis of your credences about your friends, rather than on the basis of your full beliefs about which friends would come on each day. Staffel concludes that "any plausible theory of reasoning needs to include degrees of belief among the attitudes that can be involved in reasoning processes" (3550).

Along with this claim, one may reasonably accept the further premise that if your occurrent judgments can have probabilistic contents, then so can your assertions. Just as you can reason to yourself about whether to hold your party on Friday or Saturday, for instance, you can reason with the same probabilistic contents as you think out loud. This idea has deep roots in the analytic tradition. For example, WITTGENSTEIN 1916 remarks, "it is becoming clear why I thought that thinking and language were the same. For thinking is a kind of language" (82). SELLARS 1962 states that "thoughts not only are the sort of things that find overt expression in language, we conceive of them as analogous to overt discourse . . . It is no accident that one learns to think in the very process of learning to speak" (32). DUMMETT 1973 adds that "judgment . . . is the interiorization of the external act of assertion" (362). In short, there is no restriction on what can be said in outer as opposed to inner speech. If the latter contents can be probabilistic, so can the former.

A number of theorists defend additional reasons for identifying the contents of belief and assertion. FINE 2009 argues that the "simplest and most natural view is that there is no more to the content of my belief than there is to the content of my words; I say what I believe" (76). Other theorists take the contents of belief to be potential contents of assertion because they define belief in terms of assertion. According to the Assertion View of Belief defended in KAPLAN 1996, for instance, you believe that p just in case you would prefer to assert that p under certain conditions. Similar connections between believing that p and having a disposition or commitment to assert that p are defended by DE SOUSA 1971, VAN FRAASSEN 1980b, and MAHER 1993, among others. For each of these authors, the first central thesis of this book gives us reason to accept the second. If we can believe probabilistic contents, then we can assert them.

Along with these arguments, it is important to take account of potential motivations for distinguishing the contents of belief and assertion. For example, RAMSEY 1927 points out that intuitively there is some sense in which chickens may believe that certain caterpillars are inedible, even though they could not express this belief in thought or language.[4] In light of this fact, we should charitably interpret the theorists mentioned in the previous paragraph as talking about a more demanding sense of belief. As many have noted, there are multiple natural states corresponding to our rough folk notion of belief. After observing that chickens may have certain sorts of beliefs about caterpillars, Ramsey adds that it is often valuable to focus on another sort of belief, namely the sort of belief that must be expressed in "words, spoken aloud or to oneself or merely imagined" (40). In a similar spirit, MALCOLM 1973 distinguishes *thinking* from *having thoughts*, where only the latter act closely corresponds to assertion. Malcolm argues that neither of these acts deserves to be regarded as more fundamental than the other,

---

[4] I am grateful to Andy Egan for encouraging me to discuss examples of this sort. See MARCUS 1990 for further discussion of similar examples.

since "there is no reason to believe that the concept of thinking has that kind of unity" (15). In the context of my second argument for probabilistic assertion, the sort of belief at issue is the mental state corresponding to the active probabilistic reasoning described in STAFFEL 2013. The point of the argument, as BROOME 2009 puts it, is that "active reasoning itself might require you to express your attitudes to yourself" (223). To sum up, some beliefs involved in active reasoning have probabilistic contents. The probabilistic content view of assertion allows that these contents are contents that you can assert, while the propositional content view does not.

A third argument in favor of the probabilistic content view of assertion is that it provides a more unified account of the belief states of communicating subjects. The default view is that beliefs can be shared; the privacy of mental states is at best an exception that demands explanation. The private language argument in WITTGENSTEIN 1953 famously challenges the notion that we have private thoughts that we cannot share with others, thereby confirming theories of communication according to which we think and reason together. KORSGAARD 1996 draws out a useful application of the private language argument as she argues against an egoist theory of reasons. According to the egoist, when we are discussing some joint decision, you can only ever state some consideration that is a reason for you, and after consulting my reasons for taking your reasons into account, I may decide that it is also a reason for me. Korsgaard points out that the more plausible account of joint reasoning is that we can reason together, each stating collective reasons whose normative force is not mediated by private reasons. Joint reasoning provides a structurally similar and equally compelling case for probabilistic assertion. In just the same way that probabilistic beliefs can figure in your personal reasoning and guide your individual actions, they can figure in our joint reasoning and guide our collective actions. Consider an exchange of reasons.[5] A friend comes to your office door and says: 'We need to buy Jones a birthday gift. Do you have ideas?' and you say 'She is probably going away for the summer, so she might appreciate something that would fit in her suitcase.' And your friend says 'But if she is bringing her cats along, she is almost certainly going to be driving instead of flying.' What is happening here? On my view, you and your friend are engaged in the sort of practical reasoning governed by standard decision theory, figuring out which gift is best in light of your collective probabilistic beliefs. The probabilistic content view of assertion allows that probabilistic beliefs are beliefs with which we can reason together.

---

[5] For comparison, see §4.2.9 of KORSGAARD 1996.

To sum up the big picture: so far in this chapter, I have recounted four familiar arguments *against* the claim that all assertions have *propositional* contents. According to these arguments, we do not always use sentences containing epistemic vocabulary to assert propositions. I have also developed three positive arguments *for* the claim that assertions can have *probabilistic* contents. According to these arguments, we can use sentences containing epistemic vocabulary to assert sets of probability spaces. The rest of this chapter and the next two chapters of this book defend more detailed claims about how to model the assertion of probabilistic contents, and about exactly what probabilistic contents we use particular epistemic expressions to assert.

2.3 Modeling communication

The assertion of probabilistic contents requires some revision of traditional theories of assertion. How much revision is required? For present purposes, assume that your probabilistic beliefs are represented by a single probability space, and that this space is contained in all and only those probabilistic contents that you believe. How exactly should we model the communication of these probabilistic beliefs?

According to theories in the tradition of GRICE 1967, the contents that we assert are added to the *common ground* of our conversation. According to this model of conversation as developed by STALNAKER 1978, the contents of assertion are sets of worlds, and the state of our conversation is represented by the *context set*, which is the intersection of all the contents in the common ground. On this traditional model, sets of possible worlds play four roles. First, they are the contents of individual beliefs. Second, they also represent your total belief state, since the intersection of all the contents that you believe is itself another set of worlds. Third, sets of worlds are the contents of individual assertions. And fourth, they also represent the total state of a conversation, since the intersection of all the contents that have been asserted is itself another set of worlds.

Because sets of worlds play all four of these roles, the traditional model of communication has two elegant features. The first elegant feature is that the same sort of object plays the second and fourth roles mentioned above, representing your total belief state and the total state of a conversation. As a result, there is a sense in which our conversational context resembles a third subject, an imaginary audience member whose beliefs are only just as informed as everything we have said so far. In sharing information with this third subject, we share information with each other. The second elegant feature of the traditional model of communication is that there is a simple interaction between objects in the third and fourth roles, namely the contents that we assert and the context set. As we make assertions, the context set of our conversation is updated by intersection with the contents that we assert.[6]

The communication of probabilistic beliefs calls for adding probabilistic structure to the conversational common ground. This is the thesis of *context probabilism* defended in YALCIN 2012b. Yalcin distinguishes two versions of context probabilism, each with different consequences for our discussion here. According to *sharp context probabilism*, the state of a conversation is represented by a single probability space. According to *blunt context probabilism*, the state of a conversation is represented by a set of probability spaces. On either probabilistic model of communication, sets of probability spaces replace sets of worlds in the first and third roles mentioned above. Sets of probability spaces are the contents of individual probabilistic beliefs, and they are the contents of individual probabilistic assertions. However, sets of probability spaces do not play the second role mentioned above, since your total belief state is represented by a single probability space. As a result, the elegant features of the traditional model of communication cannot both be preserved. Sharp context probabilism preserves the first elegant feature, using the same object to represent your total belief state and the state of the conversation. Blunt context probabilism preserves the second feature, saying that the context set is a set of probability spaces updated by intersection with asserted probabilistic contents.

To make a long story short, blunt context probabilism is better. As Yalcin points out, single probability spaces are far too opinionated to represent conversational states. For example, the common ground may fail to contain the content that Jones probably smokes and also fail to contain its complement. If no one has said anything about the likelihood of Jones smoking, then it is neither presupposed that she probably smokes nor presupposed that she probably doesn't. As long as your total belief state is represented by a single probability space, the first elegant feature of the traditional model must be abandoned. As I develop and defend my probabilistic semantics for epistemic vocabulary, I will assume that the state of a conversation can be represented by a set of probability spaces, and that this probabilistic context set contains only probability spaces contained in all the probabilistic contents that we assert and come to presuppose.

However, blunt context probabilism is not the end of the story. According to more refined models of probabilistic belief, single probability spaces are also far too opinionated to represent rational belief states. Just as our conversational context may be agnostic about the exact likelihood that Jones smokes,

---

[6] This feature is sometimes identified as definitive of static as opposed to dynamic conversation systems. See ROTHSCHILD AND YALCIN 2016 for further discussion.

conversational participants may also be agnostic about this probabilistic content. According to one recent tradition in formal epistemology, the rational assignment of likelihood to a proposition may be an *imprecise* credence, rather than a single real number value. In this tradition, authors such as LEVI 1974, JEFFREY 1983, and VAN FRAASSEN 1990 have argued that the total belief state of a rational agent may be represented by a set of probability spaces, rather than a single probability space. If we adopt this imprecise credence model of belief states, then we must revisit our earlier questions about how to model the communication of probabilistic beliefs. Are total belief states and conversational states ultimately best represented by the same sort of object, namely a set of probability spaces?[7] Alternatively, are certain roles in our best theories of belief and assertion ultimately played by sets of *sets of* probability spaces? For present purposes, we may set aside these questions. The possibility of agnosticism about probabilistic contents plays a central role in my discussion of knowledge norms of belief in §8.2, since a single precise probability space is far too opinionated to represent a belief state that could be reasonably expected to satisfy the knowledge norm of belief. But for the first seven chapters of this book, we may adopt the tradition of using a single probability space to represent your total belief state.

2.4 Epistemic modals and indicative conditionals

The examples of probabilistic beliefs discussed so far in this chapter have been limited to certain sorts of beliefs, namely those that supervene on your credences. For example, your credences determine whether you believe that it is unlikely that James Bond is in London, whether you believe that it is probably raining, and whether you believe that Jones is almost certainly going to be driving if she is bringing her cats along with her on vacation. But the arguments of this chapter apply equally well to any probabilistic beliefs, i.e. to any beliefs represented using probability spaces.[8] Formally, a *probability space* is an ordered triple consisting of a domain of possibilities, an algebra of propositions containing those possibilities, and a probability measure defined on the elements of that algebra. Your total belief state is represented by a probability space, and your credences are the probabilities assigned by the third element of that space. In addition to

---

[7] WILLER 2013 develops a dynamic variant of blunt context probabilism for subjects with more refined belief states, although his model is restricted to beliefs expressed using possibility and necessity modals.

[8] The use of probability spaces to represent subjective degrees of confidence is a traditional but unforced choice. Alternative models of confidence include plausibility measures and Popper functions. The central arguments of this book do not essentially depend on representing confidence using probability spaces as opposed to these other models.

your credences, you have probabilistic beliefs represented by the first and second element of that same space. These probabilistic beliefs include beliefs that you express using epistemic modals and indicative conditionals.

For example, suppose that you are throwing darts, and suppose that your next dart is equally likely to hit each of the uncountably many points on the dartboard, including its point-sized bullseye. You believe that you might hit the bullseye with your dart, and you do not believe that you might hit the Eiffel Tower, though you assign 0 credence to both of these events. Someone else could have exactly your same credences but different beliefs about which events might happen, simply by ruling out the possibility of your hitting the bullseye. The content of your belief that you might hit the bullseye is a set of probability spaces that are distinguished not by the probabilities that they assign to propositions, but rather by the fact that their domains contain some possible world where the dart hits the bullseye.[9]

In addition to believing that something might be the case, you can assert that something might be the case. All of the familiar arguments against contextualism recounted at the start of this chapter apply to epistemic possibility modals, and indeed many familiar versions of these arguments are directed at contextualist theories of 'might' sentences. For instance, it has been argued that contextualist theories fail to explain how we assess utterances of (13) and (14), when we retract an assertion of (15), and why we are reluctant to utter (16):

(13)   She might be in Prague. (EGAN ET AL. 2005, 132)

(14)   Bond might be in Zurich. (EGAN 2007, 2)

(15)   Joe might be in Boston. (MACFARLANE 2011, 150)

(16)   #Suppose it is raining and it might not be raining. (YALCIN 2007, 985)

In short, these 'might' sentences do not behave as if they state propositions to the effect that something is compatible with a certain relevant body of evidence. YALCIN 2011 adds that contextualist theories fail to identify the intuitive subject matter of 'might' sentences, since these sentences are not adequately paraphrased by sentences about any contextually determined body of evidence. BENNETT 2003 states a similar argument for indicative conditionals. For instance, when someone utters a conditional, "common sense and the Ramsey test both clamour that [she] is not assuring me that her value for a certain conditional probability is high, but is assuring me of that high value . . . She aims to convince me of that probability, not the proposition *that* it is her probability" (90).

---

[9] LEWIS 1980b and SKYRMS 1980 propose an alternative content for your belief that the dart might hit the bullseye, namely the set of probability spaces that assign at least some *infinitesimal* probability to that event. For decisive objections to this proposal, see WILLIAMSON 2007 and EASWARAN 2014.

In the case of indicative conditionals, it is often argued that triviality results in the spirit of LEWIS 1976 provide additional motivation for the claim that we can assert non-propositional contents. If the content of an indicative conditional is a proposition, it cannot be that your rational credence in that proposition always matches your conditional credence in the consequent of the conditional given its antecedent. In light of this result, many have concluded that we do not use indicative conditionals to assert propositions (cf. ADAMS 1975, GIBBARD 1981, EDGINGTON 1986, BENNETT 2003, YALCIN 2012c, SWANSON 2016b). The fourth chapter of this book discusses this line of thought in much greater detail. Finally, variations of familiar triviality results can be used to challenge truth-conditional theories of other epistemic expressions as well. SWANSON 2011 extends triviality results for conditionals to argue against truth-conditional theories of epistemic comparatives, for instance. RUSSELL AND HAWTHORNE 2015 prove analogs of triviality results for epistemic possibility modals and probability operators, adding fuel to the fire for probabilistic semantic theories of these expressions.

2.5 A test battery for probabilistic content

This chapter began by describing some distinctive behavior exhibited by epistemic vocabulary, including facts about assessments and retractions of assertions made using epistemic vocabulary, as well as embeddings and paraphrases of sentences containing epistemic vocabulary. In the literature on epistemic modals, many have argued that standard contextualist theories cannot account for uses of epistemic vocabulary that exhibit this distinctive behavior. However, in the debate between contextualists and their opponents, there is one fact that both sides should agree about. It should be uncontroversial that some uses of epistemic vocabulary do not exhibit this behavior.

For starters, consider uses of epistemic expressions accompanied by explicit restrictors, as in the following sentences:

(17)   It is unlikely given our evidence that Bond is in London.

(18)   As far as those soldiers in the jungle know, there might be snipers nearby.

In contrast to the sentences discussed in §2.1, eavesdroppers will not reject (17) on the basis of their high credence that Bond is in London:

(19)   a. *Criminal in Paris*: It is unlikely given our evidence that Bond is in London.
       b. *Eavesdropper in London*: ?No it's not—Bond is almost certainly in London.

Along similar lines, (18) sounds perfectly fine in constructions such as the following:

(20) Suppose that there might be snipers nearby as far as those soldiers in the jungle know, and there aren't snipers nearby . . .

(21) If there might be snipers nearby as far as those soldiers in the jungle know, and there aren't snipers nearby . . .

These examples do not pose any challenge for theories according to which we use sentences containing epistemic vocabulary to assert propositions about specific bodies of evidence.

Furthermore, even in the absence of explicit restrictors, some uses of epistemic vocabulary do not pose any challenge for contextualist semantic theories. A number of theorists have observed that there are *exocentric* uses of epistemic modals that behave just like explicitly restricted modals.[10] For instance, in the presence of substantial contextual cues, 'there might be snipers nearby' can behave just as if 'might' was explicitly restricted. To modify an example from EGAN ET AL. 2005, imagine that you are in the military, and your commanding officer gives you the following advice on jungle warfare:

> There are a lot of deadly snipers in the jungle. Before you walk into an area where there are lots of high trees, if there might be snipers hiding in the branches, clear away the foliage with flamethrowers. Do not worry about wasting equipment. Burn the foliage *whenever* there might be snipers. If there might be snipers and there aren't snipers, you will have wasted a flamethrower. But if there are snipers and you do not use that flamethrower, you will have wasted human lives.

In the context of this monologue, (22) sounds fine, and simply equivalent to (23):

(22) If there might be snipers, and there aren't snipers . . .

(23) If there might—for all you know—be snipers, and there aren't snipers . . .

Hence as uttered in some contexts, sentences can sound fine even if they have the same form as the infelicitous sentences discussed in YALCIN 2007.

The same qualification holds for the other anti-contextualist arguments recounted in §2.1. Suppose that several soldiers are deliberating about various battle strategies. As they deliberate, one of the soldiers calls a commanding officer to ask for advice:

---

[10] LASERSOHN 2005 introduces 'exocentric' for uses of predicates of personal taste. STEPHENSON 2007 adopts the expression for uses of epistemic modals. For further discussion of exocentric uses of epistemic modals, see chapter 4 of CAPPELEN AND HAWTHORNE 2009, WEATHERSON 2011b, DORR AND HAWTHORNE 2012, and §7.2.6 of MACFARLANE 2014.

(24) a. *Soldier*: Should we use flamethrowers to clear the foliage?
   b. *Commander*: Well, could some snipers be hiding in the foliage?
   c. *Soldier*: There might well be snipers hiding in the very tops of the tree branches.
   d. *Commander*: Then obviously you should be using your flamethrowers.

Suppose that some military students are engaged in a training exercise in which they must eavesdrop on the soldiers in the jungle and evaluate their decisions. The eavesdropping students may say (25), even if they know that there are no snipers in the branches:

(25) They should use their flamethrowers, since there might be snipers.

It is easy to identify the truth conditions of 'there might be snipers' in (25). This sentence is paraphrased by the explicitly restricted modal sentence introduced at the start of this section, namely 'As far as those soldiers in the jungle know, there might be snipers nearby'. By all accounts, 'there might be snipers' in the context of (25) should be interpreted to express full beliefs about the evidence of the jungle soldiers, rather than probabilistic beliefs about whether there might be snipers in the branches.

At first glance, exocentric uses of epistemic vocabulary might appear to be at odds with the probabilistic content view of assertion. But in fact, they merely demonstrate that *at least some* uses of sentences containing epistemic vocabulary have just the same sort of contents as simple sentences. Any probabilistic semantics for 'might' must contain the resources to predict its behavior when it is accompanied by explicit restrictors. Advocates of probabilistic semantic theories should use just the same resources to explain the behavior of exocentric uses of 'might' and other epistemic vocabulary.[11] This conclusion is consistent with the thesis that some other uses of epistemic vocabulary demand the revision of standard truth-conditional theories. The familiar revisionary arguments recounted in §2.1 demonstrate that some uses of epistemic vocabulary exhibit distinctive behavior when it comes to the assessments of eavesdroppers, the retraction of assertions, indicative suppositions, and so on. These arguments support the view that at least some sentences containing epistemic vocabulary have thoroughly probabilistic contents.

As explained in §2.2, I do not rest my case for the probabilistic content view on the distinctive behavior of epistemic vocabulary. However, we can make useful

---

[11] For one promising account of exocentric uses of epistemic modals, see the "shifty proposal" described in §3.2.

sense of this behavior in light of my more foundational arguments for probabilistic assertion. I propose that facts about assessments, retractions, embeddings, and paraphrases are best understood as providing us with *diagnostic tests*. These facts should play a role in the literature on epistemic vocabulary like the role played by facts about projection behavior in the literature on presupposition.[12] In both cases, some distinctive behavior calls out for the modification of a standard theory of content. And in both cases, the behavior itself is so distinctive that it may adequately function as partly definitive of the sort of language that is best modeled by the modified theory. Just as GEURTS 1999 introduces the Projection Test Battery as a defeasible diagnostic test for identifying presuppositional content, we can introduce a similar test battery for thoroughly probabilistic content.

For example, suppose we must decide whether some assertion of 'there might be snipers in the nearby branches' has a thoroughly probabilistic content. Then we should test: could an eavesdropper reject the assertion simply in virtue of having certain probabilistic beliefs? Could the speaker herself later retract it on that basis? Can we accept the assertion under the supposition that there are no snipers in the branches? Can we identify some specific interpretation of probability that the assertion is describing? These sorts of questions can be used to isolate thoroughly probabilistic readings of sentences containing epistemic vocabulary, separating these readings from propositions about epistemic probabilities, objective chances, statistical frequencies, and so on.

Throughout the rest of this book, it will be important to keep in mind that sentences containing epistemic vocabulary are sometimes used to assert thoroughly probabilistic contents, and sometimes used to assert contents about contextually determined bodies of evidence. This book is concerned with the readings of sentences that present challenges for the propositional content view of assertion. The aforementioned test battery is intended to identify these readings of sentences. By understanding the behavior of epistemic vocabulary as being revealed by diagnostic tests, we avoid resting our case against contextualism on interpretations of any specific sentence as uttered in any specific context. The arguments against contextualism recounted in §2.1 are best understood as supporting a more general claim, namely that some uses of epistemic vocabulary form a natural kind in virtue of exhibiting a family of distinctive behaviors, where taken together, these behaviors motivate non-standard theories of assertion.

For simplicity, so far I have assumed that there is a fact of the matter about the correct reading of a modal sentence as uttered in a context. For example,

---

[12] For an introductory discussion of the distinctive projection behavior of presuppositions, see KARTTUNEN 1973.

one might assume that speaker intentions determine whether an utterance of 'there might be snipers in the branches' is used to assert a thoroughly probabilistic content or a proposition about some contextually determined body of evidence, just as speaker intentions might determine the correct resolution of lexical or syntactic ambiguities in a sentence. If this assumption is correct, then my probabilistic theory of assertion is motivated by certain utterances of modal sentences, namely those determined to have thoroughly probabilistic contents. However, for all I argue here, the interpretation of modal sentences may turn out to be more complicated. For example, suppose that one eavesdropper judges that your assertion of 'there might be snipers in the branches' is false because there are no snipers in the branches, while another eavesdropper judges that it is true because it is compatible with your evidence that there are snipers in the branches. There may be no fact of the matter that determines which eavesdropper is correct.[13] Ultimately, the assignment of a certain content to an utterance of a sentence may be correct for certain theoretical purposes and incorrect for others. If this more radical conclusion is correct, then the upshot of this section is that the assignment of probabilistic contents to utterances is itself motivated by certain theoretical purposes. For instance, it is motivated by the desire to account for the distinctive behavior of epistemic vocabulary, and the desire to explain the direct communication of the sort of beliefs that govern rational action according to standard decision theory. Throughout the rest of this book, these theoretical purposes should be in the foreground, and sentences containing epistemic vocabulary should be interpreted accordingly. To sum up: for some purposes, we should assign probabilistic contents to uses of sentences containing epistemic vocabulary. The next two chapters of this book are devoted to this task, developing and defending a probabilistic semantics for epistemic modals, probability operators, and indicative conditionals.

---

[13] I am grateful to Andy Egan for raising this point in conversation.

3

Epistemic modals and probability operators

3.1 Motivations for my semantics

The first two chapters of this book argue that we can believe and assert thoroughly probabilistic contents, sets of probability spaces that do not correspond to any set of possible worlds. In particular, we believe and assert these contents using epistemic modals, probability operators, and indicative conditionals. These central theses about belief and assertion form the skeleton of a probabilistic theory of content. The third and fourth chapters of this book put meat on the bones. This chapter defends a probabilistic semantics for epistemic modals and probability operators:

(1)   It might / must / has to / couldn't / can't be raining.

(2)   It is unlikely to be / .3 likely to be / probably / very likely raining.

This semantics naturally extends to epistemic comparatives and epistemic adjectives:

(3)   It is just as / half as / twice as likely to be raining as it is to be snowing.

(4)   That job candidate is a possible / probable / likely / definite hire.

According to the semantics defended in this chapter, the semantic value of each of these sentences relative to a context is a set of probability spaces. According to the semantics defended in chapter 4, the same goes for indicative conditionals.

The central project of this book is to argue that we can believe, assert, and know probabilistic contents. The semantics defended in chapters 3 and 4 helps this project in several ways. First, my semantics provides proof of concept, implementing the abstract notion that we should associate sentences with sets of probability spaces as opposed to propositions. There are many existing non-truth-conditional semantic theories of epistemic modals, including dynamic and expressivist theories that are in the same spirit as my preferred theory. But existing non-truth-conditional theories face serious challenges. For instance, existing theories have trouble interpreting nested occurrences of epistemic vocabulary, constructions such as 'it must be likely that Jones smokes'. In §3.2, I call attention to several significant features of nested epistemic vocabulary. In §3.3, I argue that existing non-truth-conditional theories fail to account for these features. In §3.4, I develop a semantics that succeeds in accounting for them.

Having a successful account of nested epistemic vocabulary is important not only for the development of an adequate semantics for epistemic vocabulary, but also for the development of arguments in later chapters of this book. For example, there is a philosophical tradition of rejecting fallibilism in favor of the claim that knowledge requires certainty. According to this tradition, if you know something, you can't also believe that it might not be the case. As applied to probabilistic knowledge, rejecting fallibilism means saying that if you know that it is likely that Jones smokes, then you can't also believe that it might be unlikely that she smokes. In order to understand this rejection of fallibilism, one must understand what it means to believe that it *might* be *unlikely* that Jones smokes. My semantics for epistemic modals and probability operators provides an account of the content of this belief.

This chapter explains how epistemic modals and probability operators inter-act with each other. Chapter 4 explains how epistemic modals and probability operators interact with indicative conditionals and other logical operators. I argue that the behavior of epistemic modals under disjunction resembles their behavior under epistemic vocabulary, and I defend a compositional semantics that provides a unified account of that behavior. This account represents significant progress for non-truth-conditional theories of epistemic modals, as many existing theories are conspicuously silent about the semantics of epistemic modals under disjunction. Furthermore, just like my account of nested epistemic vocabulary, having an account of the interaction of epistemic vocabulary and logical vocabulary is important not only for its own sake, but also for the sake of my arguments in later chapters. For example, I argue in §7.4 that my semantics helps answer an argument for the claim that we do not have any significant probabilistic knowledge at all. At first glance, this skeptical argument appears to be perfectly sound. Fortunately, my semantics for logical operators helps explain why it is in fact invalid.

Finally, the semantics developed in this chapter helps my overall project by casting light on the relationship between credence and full belief. In §3.5, I give a semantics for *simple sentences*, namely sentences such as 'Jones smokes' that do not contain any epistemic vocabulary. In §3.6, I defend a probabilistic account of the full beliefs that we use these simple sentences to express. According to my account, simple sentences are themselves associated with thoroughly probabilistic contents, in addition to the nominally probabilistic contents corresponding to the propositions they are traditionally taken to express. Hence probabilistic belief and knowledge are not merely an appendage to the full belief and knowledge studied by traditional epistemologists. They are in fact vital to our understanding of these basic mental states.

A quick clarification of the dialectic is in order. The probabilistic semantics that I defend is opposed by two sorts of theories, namely truth-conditional theories of epistemic vocabulary, and non-truth-conditional alternatives to my semantics. Truth-conditional theories are the target of the familiar arguments against propositional contents of assertion in §2.1, as well as the foundational arguments for probabilistic contents of assertion in §2.2. By contrast, this chapter and the next mainly present problems for other non-truth-conditional theories that one might adopt instead of my own—that is, problems that motivate my particular revisionary semantics for epistemic vocabulary. Readers with little interest in formal semantics should read sections §3.5–3.6 and then skip ahead to chapter 5, and refer back to chapters 3 and 4 to fill in the details of my later arguments as needed.

Another note of clarification concerns the relationship between my central thesis about assertion and my probabilistic semantics. In chapter 2, I argued that the contents of assertion are sets of probability spaces. In chapters 3 and 4, I argue that the semantic value of a sentence relative to a context is a set of probability spaces. The conjunction of these arguments raises the customary question of how to define the relationship between assertoric content and semantic value. It is often noted that the content that you assert when you utter a sentence in a context may not be identical with the semantic value of that sentence relative to that context. Traditional concerns about identifying assertoric content and semantic value are largely independent of my arguments. For instance, I agree with DUMMETT 1973 and LEWIS 1980a that sentences used to assert the same content may embed differently under intensional operators, and I discuss intensional operators embedding epistemic vocabulary in §7.5. But in the meantime, I give a semantics for a fragment of natural language without any tense or modal operators, in which merely intensional distinctions do not make a difference to our judgments. On a related note, I agree with YALCIN 2014b that one cannot simply assume or stipulate that the assertoric content of a sentence is the same sort of object as the semantic value of a sentence at a context. It is a substantive consequence of my preferred theories that sets of probability spaces play both of these roles—or more precisely, that there is a useful level of abstraction at which formal semantic theories can assign probabilistic contents to sentences at contexts.

3.2 Embedded epistemic vocabulary

Once we go in for a probabilistic semantics, a lot of epistemic modals and probability operators seem to wear their semantic values on their sleeve. For instance, it may appear easy to associate sets of probability spaces with sentences such as:

(5)   It is .3 likely that Jones smokes.

(6)   Jones probably smokes.

(7)   Jones might smoke.

According to one line of thought, the content of (5) should be the set of probability spaces that assign exactly .3 probability to the proposition that Jones smokes. The content of (6) should be the set of probability spaces that assign that proposition at least .5 probability, and the content of (7) should be the set of probability spaces that assign it at least some minimal threshold probability. In short, the contents of sentences containing an epistemic expression should contain just those probability spaces that assign some range of probability values to a certain proposition, namely the content of the sentence embedded under that epistemic expression.

This line of thought is tempting. In fact, it is not far wrong about the contents of sentences as uttered in many contexts. But it cannot be the correct semantics for epistemic modals and probability operators. The central mistake in this line of thought is hidden in the final assumption, namely that the sentence embedded under an epistemic expression has a *proposition* as its content. We cannot always associate propositions with sentences embedded under epistemic modals or probability operators. And that is because those embedded sentences may themselves contain epistemic vocabulary, which means that their contents are not propositions, but *sets of probability spaces*. For instance, epistemic modals can embed epistemic adjectives:

(8)   Smith is a likely smoker, and Jones might be a likely smoker.

(9)   Smith is a possible smoker, and Jones might be a possible smoker.

(10) A large terrorist organization might be a more likely user of reactor-grade plutonium.[1]

---

[1] BODANSKY 2005, p.496.

Epistemic modals can embed other epistemic modals, as well as probability operators:

(11)   I have no idea what she's talking about. She definitely might be a crazy person.[2]

(12)   It might be at least somewhat likely that Jones smokes.

(13)   The time is now near at hand which must probably determine, whether Americans are to be, Freemen, or Slaves.[3]

And probability operators can embed just the same range of epistemic vocabulary:

(14)   Jones is probably not a likely smoker.

(15)   Jones is probably not all that likely to be smoking.

(16)   It was a little fever of admiration; but it might, probably must, end in love with some.[4]

The above constructions highlight several facts that our semantics for epistemic vocabulary should explain. For starters, nested epistemic expressions make sense. Our semantics should provide well-defined interpretations for these expressions. There should be no semantic type restriction preventing epistemic vocabulary from taking scope over other epistemic vocabulary, for instance.

Furthermore, nested epistemic expressions have an interesting range of interpretations. In some sentences, nested epistemic modals are redundant. For example, GEURTS AND HUITINK 2006 observe that the following sentence has a "modal concord" reading on which the nested epistemic modals are equivalent with a single possibility modal:

(17)   You may possibly have read my little monograph upon the subject.

However, nested epistemic modals are not always redundant. Geurts and Huitink point out that in addition to modal concord readings, nested epistemic modals have *cumulative* readings. For example, (9) says something different about Jones than it does about Smith:

(9)   Smith is a possible smoker, and Jones might be a possible smoker.

---

[2] BARNHOLDT 2014, p.18.
[3] George Washington's address to the Continental Army before the Battle of Long Island, August 27, 1776.
[4] AUSTEN 1818, p.55.

More generally, a string of nested epistemic possibility operators is not always equivalent to a single possibility operator.[5] This brings us to a second fact that our semantics should explain, namely that we can use nested epistemic modals to say something different from what we would use single epistemic modals to say.

The same fact holds for combinations of epistemic modals and probability operators. For example, (18) says something different about Jones than (19) or (20) does:

(18) It is probably the case that Jones is a possible hire.

(19) It is probably the case that Jones is a hire.

(20) Jones is a possible hire.

Comparing (18) and (19), only the latter provides sufficient reason to bet at even odds that Jones is a hire. Comparing (18) and (20), the latter is intuitively more decisive than the former. If you assert that Jones is a possible hire, it sounds as if you have a certain settled opinion about Jones. By contrast, if you merely say that it is *probably* the case that Jones is a possible hire, it sounds as if you have not yet settled on an opinion about Jones. Either Jones is a possible hire, or she is not a possible hire, and you are more inclined to side with the former opinion. A string of epistemic modals and probability operators is not always equivalent to a single modal or probability operator.

Another fact to be explained by our semantics for epistemic vocabulary is that it is often easiest to make sense of nested epistemic vocabulary by imagining situations in which you are torn between different probabilistic opinions. Suppose you are a detective on a murder investigation. If you say that it *might* be probable that Jones is the murderer, it sounds as if you are unsure about exactly what credence to have in the proposition that Jones is the murderer. Your uncertainty might come from either of two sources. You might be unsure about what credence to have because you are unsure about some first-order facts. For example, you might have high credence that the murderer was the person last seen with the victim, but you might be unsure whether that person was Jones or Smith. Alternatively, you might be sure about all of the relevant first-order facts, but unsure what credences they support. For example, you might be torn between various theories about the murder, and perhaps even believe that rational people could disagree about which theory is best supported by your evidence. In either case, you have different conditional credences that Jones is the murderer, given different hypotheses about the first-order facts or different hypotheses about

---

[5] SORENSEN 2009 observes this point in his critical discussion of YALCIN 2007.

what your evidence supports. These conditional credences correspond to different probabilistic opinions that you are torn between.

Suppose you are torn between believing that the murderer is at least .6 likely to be Smith and believing that the murderer is at least .6 likely to be Jones. If you say that it is *fairly probable* that the murderer is at least .6 likely to be Jones, then it sounds as if you have a fair amount of evidence supporting the latter opinion. In addition to reflecting the weight of your evidence—that is, how much evidence you have for an opinion—the strength of an epistemic expression can also reflect the resilience of your opinion.[6] For example, consider the following case:

> *Birdwatching*: Jones and Smith are avid birdwatchers. They are each visiting a remote island in order to collect information about its canary population. Jones has seen 8,000 canaries, and 5,000 of them have been yellow. Smith has seen eight canaries, and five of them have been yellow. Jones and Smith go out birdwatching together without sharing any evidence they have collected about the canaries. They hear a canary in the forest. Jones and Smith cannot see the canary yet. But they both believe that the canary is likely to be yellow.

Based on their respective evidence, Jones and Smith may have just the same credence that the canary in the forest is yellow. But they cannot use just the same nested epistemic vocabulary to talk about the canary. Smith can only assert (21), whereas Jones is intuitively licensed in asserting (22):

(21)   The canary is probably likely to be yellow.

(22)   The canary is definitely likely to be yellow.

The assertability of (22) tracks two differences between Jones and Smith. Jones bases her credences about the canary on more evidence. In addition, her high credence that the canary is yellow is more resilient. In other words, the weight of her evidence and the resilience of her credences are reflected in the strength of the epistemic operator under which she can embed (23):

(23)   The canary is likely to be yellow.

As Smith acquires more and more evidence, his high credence that the canary is yellow will become more and more resilient, and he will be able to embed (23) under stronger and stronger epistemic operators.

To sum up, our semantics for epistemic modals and probability operators should account for several facts. Nested epistemic expressions have well-defined interpretations. Their interpretations do not always coincide with those of single

---

[6] For precise definitions of the notions of *weight* and *resilience* at issue here, see JOYCE 2005.

epistemic expressions. Nested epistemic expressions are often used when multiple probabilistic opinions about some subject are in play. Finally, the strength of an epistemic operator that embeds an epistemic sentence often reflects the weight of your evidence for the content of that sentence, as well as the resilience of your belief in that content.

3.3 Challenges for other theories

How do existing semantic theories of epistemic modals and probability operators fare with respect to our observations about nested epistemic vocabulary? Standard truth-conditional theories have no trouble assigning cumulative interpretations to nested epistemic expressions. But having argued against truth-conditional theories in chapter 2, I shall focus here on evaluating non-truth-conditional alternatives to my semantics. Here the verdict is grim: the observations in §3.2 present serious challenges for existing non-truth-conditional theories of epistemic modals and probability operators.

For example, ROTHSCHILD 2012 defends a variation of the tempting line of thought mentioned at the start of §3.2. Rothschild argues that 'it is likely that' denotes a function that takes a proposition and yields the set of probability measures according to which that proposition is at least .5 likely. On this semantics, probability operators shift the semantic type of their arguments. As a result, Rothschild predicts that nested occurrences of probability operators are not even well defined. For example, consider the following:

(24) It is probably the case that Jones is a likely hire.

For sake of argument, suppose that Rothschild correctly identifies the content of 'Jones is a likely hire' as the set of probability measures according to which it is at least .5 likely that Jones is a hire. This content is not equivalent to any proposition. The argument of 'it is probably the case that' in (24) has a thoroughly probabilistic content. But according to Rothschild, the denotation of this probability operator is only defined on propositions, not on probabilistic contents. Absent further bells and whistles, this semantics incorrectly predicts that (24) is not interpretable at all.

By contrast, nested epistemic expressions are interpretable according to most non-truth-conditional theories of epistemic vocabulary, including theories defended by STALNAKER 1970a, VELTMAN 1996, BEAVER 2001, YALCIN 2007, VON FINTEL AND GILLIES 2007, and WILLER 2013. But nested epistemic modals still pose a serious challenge for each of these theories—namely, because the theories incorrectly predict that nested epistemic modals do not have any cumulative readings. On each of these theories, the semantic entries given for possibility and necessity modals entail the characteristic axioms of the modal logic S5, with the consequence that any string of epistemic modals is equivalent to the innermost modal in the string. To give an especially painful example, these theories predict that the following sentences are equivalent:

(25)   a.   Jones might have to be the murderer.
       b.   Jones has to be the murderer.

Some advocates of non-truth-conditional theories explicitly embrace this result, claiming that "embedding an epistemic modal under another epistemic modal does not in general have any interesting semantic effects" (WILLER 2013, 12). YALCIN 2007 adds that "iterating epistemic possibility operators adds no value on this semantics . . . This may explain why iterating epistemic possibility modals generally does not sound right, and why, when it does, the truth-conditions of the result typically seem equivalent to $\Diamond\phi$. I will generally ignore iterated epistemic modalities" (994).

Similarly, the semantics for epistemic modals and probability operators in YALCIN 2012b predicts that many strings of epistemic modals and probability operators are equivalent to the innermost operator in the string. For example, (26-a) and (26-b) are predicted to be equivalent:

(26)   a.   It is probably the case that we might hire Jones.
       b.   We might hire Jones.

The same goes for (27-a) and (27-b):

(27)   a.   It might be the case that we probably hired Jones.
       b.   We probably hired Jones.

These predictions fail to capture the intuitive meanings of (26-a) and (27-a). More generally, it is hard to see how semantic proposals in this spirit could explain our extensive use of nested epistemic vocabulary, or the many observations about nested epistemic expressions discussed in §3.2.

Among advocates of non-truth-conditional theories, there has been one substantive recent attempt to account for cumulative readings of nested epistemic modals. In YALCIN 2012c, Yalcin admits that sometimes nested modals do "allow for coherent interpretations not equivalent to corresponding expression with the most narrow modal. The latter case is not provided for by the above semantics. In such cases I would be inclined to appeal to tacit shifting of the information state parameter" (1019). For further explanation, we are directed to the following passage in YALCIN 2007: "interpretation may involve a tacit shift in the information parameter . . . to the target state of information for the context. Aside from

Gricean considerations of charitable interpretation, it is not obvious whether general principles are involved in the interpretation of such tacit shifts" (1013). MACFARLANE 2014 provides some helpful context for interpreting these brief passages, namely by pointing out that shifting the information state parameter is the semantic function of explicit restrictors of epistemic modals. For instance, according to MacFarlane, 'for all α knows' is used "to shift the information state to what was known by the person or group denoted by α at the time of evaluation, and to quantify over worlds in the shifted information state" (265), thereby changing a sentence that may be information-sensitive into one that is not. Just like explicitly restricted modals, and like the exocentric uses of epistemic modals discussed in §2.5, the relevant shifted uses of epistemic modals are used to talk about some contextually determined body of evidence.

To return to the passages quoted above, Yalcin is proposing that an embedded modal sentence is interpreted as if it had the same sort of boring content as a sentence without epistemic vocabulary. The same strategy could be applied to any embedded sentence containing epistemic vocabulary. According to this proposal, (22) says something about a specific probability measure, just like (28) and (29):

(22)   The canary is definitely likely to be yellow.

(28)   It is definitely the case that my evidential probability that the canary is yellow is high.

(29)   It is definitely the case that our evidential probability that the canary is yellow is high.

The sentence (22) may say just the same thing as (28) in some contexts, for instance, and just the same thing as (29) in other contexts. This is the most promising proposal that I will consider on behalf of the theories that I am currently arguing against, namely existing non-truth-conditional theories that seem unable to account for cumulative interpretations of nested epistemic vocabulary. Call it the *shifty proposal*, in light of the suggestion that we use embedded epistemic vocabulary to talk about the value of some shifted information state parameter. According to this proposal, every epistemic expression embedded under epistemic vocabulary is interpreted relative to some contextually determined body of evidence.

The shifty proposal accounts for the fact that nested epistemic expressions have well-defined interpretations. In addition, the shifty proposal correctly predicts that nested epistemic expressions are not always redundant. For instance, on the shifty proposal, (22) does not merely say that the canary is definitely yellow, or likely to be yellow. Unfortunately, however, the shifty proposal has many of the same shortcomings as traditional contextualist theories of epistemic vocabulary. Recall from §2.1 that we have several reasons to doubt that the unembedded (23) concerns some particular contextually determined probability space, in the way that (30) and (31) concern some particular probability space:

(23)   The canary is likely to be yellow.

(30)   My evidential probability that the canary is yellow is high.

(31)   Our evidential probability that the canary is yellow is high.

Analogous concerns tell against the assimilation of these sentences when they are embedded under epistemic vocabulary. Just like many unembedded sentences containing epistemic vocabulary, many embedded sentences containing epistemic vocabulary pass the test battery for thoroughly probabilistic content described in §2.5. For example, eavesdroppers may target the embedded modal sentence in (32) and correctly evaluate it relative to their own epistemic situation:

(32)   *Criminal in Paris*: It's certain that James Bond might be in Brussels.

(33)   *Eavesdropper in London*: That's not certain at all! In fact, it is highly improbable that James Bond might be in Brussels.

If the criminal uses 'might' in (32) merely to talk about what is compatible with her evidence, then the eavesdropper should not correct her assertion, since the eavesdropper is also certain that it is compatible with the criminal's limited evidence that Bond is in Brussels. On the other hand, if the criminal uses 'might' to talk about what is compatible with an expanded body of evidence that includes the eavesdropper's evidence, then it is not clear that she is licensed in uttering (32) to begin with. In a similar spirit, the shifty proposal fails to explain why it sounds fine for the criminal to assert (32) but also sounds fine for her to later retract her assertion after learning that James Bond couldn't be in Brussels.

Another concern for the shifty proposal concerns embedded epistemic contradictions. For instance, it sounds fine to express some confidence that our limited evidence is consistent with the false proposition that it is not raining:

(34)   Here's something probable—that it's raining and our evidence leaves open the possibility that it is not raining.

Adapting the central argument of YALCIN 2007, the concern is that the shifty proposal incorrectly predicts that it should sound just as good to say:

(35)   ?Here's something probable—that it's raining and it might not be raining.

After all, the shifty proposal says that (35) has the same general sort of content as (34), namely some content concerning the likelihood of some proposition about whether it is raining and what is probable given some body of evidence. According to the line of argument that Yalcin defends, we should reject the shifty proposal on the grounds that it fails to explain why certain sentences containing nested epistemic vocabulary sound worse than any sentences that might be identified as their explicit counterparts.

Another concern for the shifty proposal is that it fails to identify the intuitive subject matter of sentences containing embedded epistemic vocabulary. For instance, (22) is not adequately paraphrased by (28) or (29):

(22)   The canary is definitely likely to be yellow.

(28)   It is definitely the case that my evidential probability that the canary is yellow is high.

(29)   It is definitely the case that our evidential probability that the canary is yellow is high.

Smith cannot utter (22) after seeing eight canaries in *Birdwatching*. But he can utter (28), because he knows with certainty that according to his limited inductive evidence, it is likely that the canary that he hears in the forest is yellow. Also, just as your dog Fido could believe that you are definitely likely to take him outside without entertaining second-order beliefs about his evidence, subjects could believe (22) without entertaining second-order beliefs about their shared evidential probabilities. Hence (22) is not accurately paraphrased by either (28) or (29).

A final objection to the shifty proposal concerns the interpretation of elided epistemic vocabulary. For example, if we associate the embedded sentence in 'The canary is definitely likely to be yellow' with some proposition about contextually determined evidence, we are still left with the problem of interpreting the following dialogue:

(36)   a. *Smith:* Is that canary likely to be yellow?
       b. *Jones:* Definitely.

It is difficult to motivate the claim that we pre-emptively interpret (36-a) as containing a tacitly shifted information parameter. There must be some way of making sense of (36-b) without associating (36-a) with any propositional content. This interpretation of (36-b) should guide our interpretation of (22). The relevant interpretation will be a thoroughly probabilistic interpretation on which neither epistemic expression is interpreted relative to contextually determined evidence.

To sum up: familiar arguments against contextualist theories of epistemic vocabulary yield analogous arguments against "shifty" dynamic or expressivist theories—that is, theories that resort to interpreting embedded epistemic vocabulary relative to contextually determined bodies of evidence. Insofar as these arguments motivate revisionary theories of epistemic vocabulary, they motivate a theory of embedded epistemic vocabulary that is more thoroughly revisionary than the shifty proposal considered here.

3.4 A semantics for epistemic modals and probability operators

The behavior of nested epistemic expressions provides useful clues about what individual epistemic expressions mean. As explained in §3.2, we often use nested epistemic expressions when we are torn between various opinions about the likelihood of some proposition. For example, consider the following sentence:

(18)   It is probably the case that Jones is a possible hire.

Suppose that you are torn between various ways of evaluating job candidates. It is not clear how to weigh research quality against teaching experience and professional service, and you are open to information that would decide this question in different ways. If research is important, then Jones is a possible hire. But if research is unimportant, she is not. Furthermore, you are fairly confident that research is important. In this context, a certain partition of logical space is salient, namely a partition of propositions that say whether research is important. As a result, two sorts of opinions are salient when you utter (18). First, you have opinions conditional on the partition propositions. For instance, you believe that Jones is a possible hire, conditional on research being important. Second, you have unconditional opinions about the partition propositions. For instance, you have high credence that research is important. At a first pass, my semantics says that opinions of the first sort are associated with embedded epistemic expressions, while the latter are associated with the vocabulary under which those expressions are embedded.

More precisely, my semantics says that sentences containing epistemic vocabulary are context sensitive. Just as context might provide a domain for the interpretation of a quantifier, or a standard for the interpretation of a gradable adjective, context provides a partition of logical space for the interpretation of an epistemic modal or probability operator. This partition is a set of propositions. Whether you believe the content of a sentence containing nested epistemic expressions depends on the credences that you assign to the propositions in the partition, and it also depends on your credences updated on those propositions. The credences that result from your updating on the different partition propositions correspond to different opinions that you are torn between.

As a useful shorthand, let us say that a proposition *p accepts a probabilistic content S relative to your credences* just in case *S* contains the result of updating your credences on *p*.[7] Returning to our example, we may then describe your beliefs about Jones as follows: relative to your credences, the proposition that research is important accepts that Jones is a possible hire, and the proposition that research is unimportant accepts that she isn't. These propositions are the elements of the partition that context provides for the interpretation of 'probably' in (18). With this partition in mind, we can describe your credences by saying that some proposition accepts that Jones is a possible hire, and some proposition accepts that she isn't. That is the sense in which you are torn between two opinions about whether Jones is a possible hire. The opinions are your conditional credences, given the contextually relevant claims about the importance of research for hiring.

Just as context may provide distinct domains for the interpretation of distinct quantifiers in a sentence, and distinct standards for the interpretation of distinct gradable adjectives, context may provide distinct partitions for the interpretation of distinct epistemic expressions. An epistemic modal quantifies over propositions in the partition that context provides for its interpretation. In the shorthand introduced above, 'it might be that *S*' means that some possible proposition accepts that *S*. In more precise terms, the content of 'it might be that *S*' contains your credences just in case some possible proposition in the partition that context provides for the interpretation of 'might' is such that your credences updated on that proposition are contained in the content of '*S*'. Analogously, 'it *must* be that *S*' contains your credences just in case *every* possible proposition in the partition that context provides for the interpretation of 'must' is such that your credences conditional on that proposition are contained in the content of '*S*'. Finally, just like epistemic modals, probability operators are also interpreted relative to contextually determined partitions. The content of 'probably, *S*' contains your credences just in case when it comes to the possible propositions in the partition that context provides for the interpretation of 'probably', you give more than .5 credence to the union of propositions that accept that *S* relative to your credences.

---

[7] For ease of exposition, we may also say that a proposition *accepts a content*, leaving the relevant probability space implicit. I adopt this shorthand where it will not cause confusion. Also, sometimes I use 'credences' for the probability space representing your total belief state, trusting that careful readers will distinguish as necessary between probability spaces and the probability measures given by their third coordinates. Appendix A.1 formally defines the result of updating an entire probability space on a proposition.

Returning again to our example, the content of 'Jones *might* be a possible hire' contains your credences because *some* proposition accepts that Jones is a possible hire, namely the proposition that research is important. The content of 'Jones is *probably* a possible hire' contains your credences, because you give *more than .5 credence* to that same proposition. But the content of 'Jones *must* be a possible hire' does not contain your credences, because it is not the case that *every* proposition accepts that Jones is a possible hire. If you update on the proposition that research is unimportant, your resulting credences are not contained in the content that Jones is a possible hire.[8]

This semantics for epistemic modals and probability operators explains the facts about nested epistemic vocabulary described in §3.2. For starters, nested epistemic expressions are well defined. The definitions of epistemic expressions do not presuppose that they embed simple sentences. The argument of an epistemic modal or probability operator can denote a set of probability spaces, rather than just a proposition. Moreover, strings of nested epistemic expressions are not automatically equivalent with the innermost expression in the string. For example, my semantics successfully distinguishes the contents of the following sentences:

(18)   It is probably the case that Jones is a possible hire.

(20)   Jones is a possible hire.

To put it roughly, your credences are contained in the content of (18) just in case a weighted majority of contextually relevant propositions accept the content that Jones is a possible hire, whereas they are contained in the content of (20) just in case some contextually relevant proposition accepts that Jones is a hire.

In addition, my semantics explains why it is often easiest to make sense of nested epistemic expressions by imagining situations in which you are torn between different probabilistic opinions. The relevant opinions are your conditional credences, conditional on different propositions in the partition that context provides for the interpretation of the embedding epistemic expression. These conditional opinions are thoroughly probabilistic beliefs, rather than full beliefs about what some body of evidence supports. But each conditional opinion may be accompanied by full beliefs about what some body of evidence supports, just as your unconditional credences are often accompanied by full beliefs about what some body of evidence supports—namely, your total evidence.

---

[8] The informal theory presented here is precise enough for readers without any formal semantics background to understand the main arguments of this chapter. Appendix A.2 contains a detailed formal semantics for epistemic modals and probability operators, as well as discussion of several interesting side issues.

Finally, my semantics explains why the strength of an embedding epistemic modal or probability operator often reflects facts about evidential weight and credal resilience. JOYCE 2005 points out that evidential weight often manifests itself in credal resilience when your credences are mediated by chance hypotheses. As Joyce puts it, "the weight of evidence tends to stabilize [your] credence in a particular way: it stabilizes credences of chance hypotheses, while concentrating most of the credence on a small set of these hypotheses" (166). The same goes not just for chance hypotheses, but for any partition of hypotheses that rationally support particular opinions. As you get more and more evidence, you often assign more and more credence to propositions that support one conditional opinion in particular. For example, recall that Jones can say not only (21), but also (22), when her high credence that the canary is yellow is resilient and based on a lot of evidence:

(21)   The canary is probably likely to be yellow.

(22)   The canary is definitely likely to be yellow.

Just as some credences are mediated by chance hypotheses, the credences of Jones and Smith in *Birdwatching* are mediated by hypotheses about what proportion of canaries on the island are yellow. Having seen 5,000 yellow canaries and 8,000 total canaries, Jones concentrates almost all of her credence on a small set of hypotheses about the proportion of yellow canaries on the island. That is why she has such a resilient high credence that the canary that she hears in the forest is yellow. According to my semantics, that is also why Jones can say (22). Intuitively, the modal 'definitely' in (22) is interpreted using just these same hypotheses about the canaries, and Jones believes only hypotheses that accept that the canary in the forest is likely to be yellow. By contrast, Smith gives considerable credence to hypotheses that reject that the canary is likely to be yellow. For instance, there is a significant chance by Smith's lights that there are many more red canaries on the island than yellow canaries, although he has just happened to see more yellow canaries so far. Hence Smith's credences are not contained in the content of (22). When your credences are mediated by certain hypotheses, getting more evidence for your probabilistic beliefs simultaneously makes those beliefs more resilient, and also licenses your embedding corresponding sentences under stronger epistemic expressions.

3.5 A semantics for simple sentences

What about sentences that do not contain any epistemic vocabulary? Is the content of 'Jones smokes' just an ordinary proposition, or is it a set of probability spaces? At first glance, one might be tempted to say that the content of 'Jones smokes' is just the proposition that Jones smokes. For example, one might say that 'Jones smokes' denotes the set of worlds where Jones smokes, whereas 'it is likely that Jones smokes' denotes a set of probability spaces. More generally, one might be tempted to adopt a disjunctive semantics, according to which sentences can have either propositional or probabilistic contents.

However tempting it might be, this disjunctive theory is ultimately unacceptable. Simple sentences and sentences containing epistemic vocabulary stand in logical relations to each other, which means their effects on the common ground cannot be modeled independently. For example, (37) is consistent with (38) but inconsistent with (39), in just the same sense in which the latter sentences are inconsistent with each other:

(37)   Jones smokes.

(38)   It is likely that Jones smokes.

(39)   It is unlikely that Jones smokes.

According to one natural definition of consistency for sentences with unstructured contents, sentences are inconsistent just in case their contents are disjoint. But given this definition, the disjunctive theory incorrectly predicts that (37) and (38) have inconsistent contents. Relatedly, many ordinary inferences involve both simple sentences and sentences containing epistemic vocabulary. For instance, we can use sentences containing epistemic vocabulary in valid arguments for conclusions stated using simple sentences:

(40)   a. Jones probably smokes.
     b. If Jones probably smokes, then Smith smokes.
     c. Therefore, Smith smokes.

According to one natural definition of validity for sentences with unstructured contents, an inference is valid just in case the intersection of the contents of its premises is a subset of the content of its conclusion. If the disjunctive theory were correct, (40) would have sets of probability spaces as premises and a set of worlds as its conclusion, and would therefore be invalid. And intuitively invalid inferences such as (41) would be trivially valid:

(41)   a. Jones smokes.
     b. Smith probably smokes.
     c. Therefore, Brown smokes.

To sum up, disjunctive theories fail to give a straightforward explanation of consistency and entailment relations between simple sentences and sentences containing epistemic vocabulary.

The logical relations between simple sentences and sentences containing epistemic vocabulary are best explained by a semantics that assigns probabilistic contents to simple sentences. Simple sentences have *nominally probabilistic* contents. Recall from §1.4 that a set of probability spaces is nominally probabilistic just in case it contains all and only the probability spaces such that some particular proposition is true throughout their domain. To put it another way: a proposition is *certain* according to a probability space just in case it is true at every world in the domain of that space, and a nominally probabilistic content contains the probability spaces according to which some particular proposition is certain. The content of a simple sentence is the set of probability spaces according to which its traditional propositional content is certain. The simple sentence 'Jones smokes' has a constituent denoting the proposition that Jones smokes, along with a covert operator that shifts the semantic type of that constituent, producing a sentence that denotes the set of probability spaces according to which it is certain that Jones smokes.[9]

By contrast with disjunctive theories, my probabilistic semantics is compatible with natural definitions of logical relations between simple sentences and sentences containing epistemic vocabulary. Whether or not they contain epistemic vocabulary, sentences are consistent just in case their contents are not disjoint. The content of one sentence entails the content of another just in case the former content is a subset of the latter. In addition, the more specific fact that simple sentences have *nominally probabilistic* contents explains more specific facts about their logical relations to other sentences. For example, as discussed in the previous chapter, (42) sounds like a contradiction:

(42)   #Jones smokes, and Jones might not smoke.

This fact is explained by my semantics for simple sentences and epistemic possibility modals. The content of 'Jones smokes' contains a probability space just in case Jones smokes in every world in its domain. The content of 'Jones might not smoke' contains a probability space just in case there is some relevant collection of worlds in its domain where Jones does not smoke. These contents are disjoint, and that is why their conjunction sounds contradictory.

It is instructive to compare my semantics with an alternative "threshold" semantics for simple sentences and epistemic possibility modals. Suppose that the content of 'Jones smokes' contained just those probability spaces that assign *at least some high threshold probability* to the proposition that Jones smokes, and suppose that the content of 'Jones might not smoke' contained just those

---

[9] For further discussion of the logical form of simple sentences, see Appendix A.3.

probability spaces that assign at least some minimal threshold probability to the proposition that Jones doesn't smoke. For certain judiciously chosen thresholds, these probabilistic contents would indeed be disjoint, and so our semantics would successfully predict the fact that (42) sounds contradictory. However, the simple sentence contents assigned by this threshold semantics are not strong enough. Suppose you are throwing a point-sized dart at a dartboard, as in the example introduced in §2.4. The dart is equally likely to hit each of the uncountably many points on the dartboard. For any point on the dartboard, including the point-sized bullseye, you believe that the dart might hit that point. In light of this fact, it is rationally permissible for you to refrain from believing the content of (43):

(43)   The dart won't hit the bullseye.

But unfortunately, you have *credence 1* in the traditional propositional content of (43), and so you will automatically count as believing the content of (43) according to any threshold semantics. This example illustrates that there is no threshold high enough such that your having that threshold credence in some proposition guarantees that you believe the content of the corresponding simple sentence. Hence the content of a simple sentence cannot be the set of probability spaces according to which its traditional propositional content has some high threshold probability. Rather, the content of a simple sentence must be the set of probability spaces according to which its traditional propositional content is certain.

By this point, our discussion may be starting to sound familiar. In particular, the threshold semantics considered above resembles the familiar proposal that rational subjects believe a proposition just in case their credence in that proposition exceeds some high threshold probability.[10] The similarity of these proposals is not a coincidence. The nominally probabilistic contents under discussion are not just the contents that we use simple sentences to assert. They are also the contents of the beliefs that we use simple sentences to express. In other words, the contents of simple sentences are the contents of our full beliefs. In determining whether simple sentences have probabilistic contents, we are determining whether full beliefs have probabilistic contents. To use the vocabulary of more familiar debates, we are investigating the relationship between full belief and certainty, and we are determining whether the attitude of full belief can be understood in terms of credence.

In response to these familiar questions, many theorists have defended disjunctive theories according to which full beliefs and credences figure in fundamentally

---

[10] This claim and close variants of it are known as *the Lockean thesis*, following the introduction of this term in FOLEY 1992.

distinct modes of reasoning. According to some of these theorists, we reason with full beliefs because we must cope with cognitive limitations that prevent us from reasoning with credences.[11] However, in light of our present discussion, we can see that acts of reasoning with full beliefs and acts of reasoning with credences are not so easily separated. In ordinary reasoning, full beliefs justify credences, and credences justify full beliefs. These beliefs stand in logical relations and appear together in valid inferences. Put a bunch of formal epistemologists and traditional epistemologists together in a room, and the members of each group may stick to interacting with each other—but the attitudes that they are studying do not. A disjunctive theory of mind that fundamentally distinguishes reasoning with full beliefs from reasoning with credences faces the challenge of explaining how we can just as easily reason with both at once.

Against the disjunctive theory, I have proposed a unified probabilistic theory of full belief and probabilistic belief. At a first pass, the content of your belief that Jones smokes is just the same as the content of your belief that it is certain that Jones smokes. This proposal has recently been defended by Greco 2015.[12] More precisely, Greco argues that "binary belief is maximal degree of belief—it is the endpoint of the scale of degreed belief" (179). As I see it, this statement of the proposal is in need of only a couple of minor revisions. First, as Greco later acknowledges, full belief should be identified with certainty rather than with credence 1. As the dartboard example illustrates, credence 1 is actually not sufficient for full belief. And second, there is no scale of attitudes such that maximal degree of belief is at one end of the scale. There is just one attitude of belief, and subjects can bear this attitude toward probabilistic contents. Hence we should not say that binary belief can be reduced to some degreed belief attitude, but rather that full beliefs can be reduced to beliefs with probabilistic contents.

Having spelled out this theory of the relation between full belief and probabilistic belief, I can finally discuss an obvious worry for it. At first glance, identifying full belief and certainty yields terrible predictions about what actions are rationally licensed by full beliefs. In order to believe the nominally probabilistic content that Jones smokes, you must have credence 1 in the proposition that Jones smokes. However, as Weatherson 2016 neatly summarizes, "If we identify beliefs with credence 1, and take credences to support betting dispositions, then a rational agent will have very few beliefs. There are lots of things that an agent,

---

[11] For sympathetic discussion of disjunctive theories of full belief and credence, see chapter 6 of Maher 1993. For critical discussion of several recent accounts according to which we form full beliefs in response to cognitive limitations, see Tang 2015.

[12] For another proposal in a similar spirit, see Clarke 2013.

we would normally say, believes even though she wouldn't bet on them at absurd odds" (1). CLARKE 2013 calls this the "betting worry," noting that it is often cited as an argument against identifying belief with credence 1.[13] Along similar lines, probabilistic contents are just the sort of contents that others may come to believe when you make an assertion (cf. §2.2). At first glance, the probabilistic content of a simple sentence appears much too strong to play this role. A theory of simple sentences must explain why you can believe and assert that Jones smokes without being willing to bet your life on it.

To sum up where we stand: any theory of full belief faces a formidable challenge. The dartboard example suggests that full belief requires nothing less than certainty. The betting worry suggests that full belief does not require anything as strong as certainty. WEDGWOOD 2012 discusses the betting worry and arrives at a similar conclusion, arguing that there is a fundamental tension in our intuitions about what full belief requires. An adequate theory of full belief must resolve this tension, simultaneously accounting for our intuition that the content of your belief that Jones smokes is just the same as the content of your belief that it is certain that Jones smokes, while also accounting for our intuition that the latter content is strictly stronger than the former.

3.6 The relationship between credence and full belief

This final section answers the formidable challenge posed in §3.5. There is a sense in which full beliefs have nominally probabilistic contents, and there is also a sense in which full beliefs have significantly weaker contents. To fully explain these different notions of full belief contents, we must understand the distinction between them as an instance of a more general distinction, namely the distinction between strict and loose contents of belief.

If you say that Jones smokes, then perhaps strictly speaking, you have said that Jones certainly smokes. And strictly speaking, you do not believe anything nearly as strong as that content. But by asserting that Jones smokes, you communicate something that you do strictly speaking believe. This phenomenon is familiar. If you say that it is 3:00, then perhaps strictly speaking, you have said that it is 3:00 *on the dot*. And strictly speaking, you do not believe anything as strong as that content. But by asserting that it is 3:00, you communicate another content altogether, something that you do strictly speaking believe. Following LAUER 2012 and DORR AND HAWTHORNE 2014, let us identify the content that you

---

[13] Versions of the betting worry are defended by MAHER 1993, KAPLAN 1996, CHRISTENSEN 2004, and FRANKISH 2009, among others.

communicate as the *loose content* of your assertion. The assertion that it is 3:00 and the assertion that it is exactly 3:00 have the same strict content, but distinct loose contents. The same goes for the assertion that Jones smokes and the assertion that it is certain that Jones smokes. Furthermore, the same distinction between strict and loose contents intuitively holds for contents of belief. The belief that it is 3:00 and the belief that it is exactly 3:00 have distinct loose contents, and as a result, they may play different roles in your practical reasoning. In exactly this same sense, the belief that Jones smokes and the belief that it is certain that Jones smokes have distinct loose contents.

The classification of simple sentences as loose speech is supported by several remarkable analogies between simple sentences and paradigmatic instances of loose speech. Probabilistic contents can be more or less precise. Just as you may say that it is 2:58, for instance, you may say that it is .98 likely that Jones smokes. The precision of the probabilistic contents of simple sentences can be explicitly modulated by *slack regulators* in the sense of LASERSOHN 1999. Just as you may say that it is *exactly* or *precisely* 3:00, for instance, you may say that Jones *certainly* or *definitely* smokes. Another distinctive feature of loose speech is that although many slack regulators strengthen the loose content of an assertion, there do not seem to be slack regulators that merely weaken that content, as opposed to weakening the strict content of the assertion itself. The same goes for probabilistic speech. Just as you may assert that it is *around* 3:00, you may assert that Jones *almost certainly* smokes. But in both cases, your hedging intuitively weakens the strict content of your assertion, as opposed to merely affecting its loose content. Finally, as pointed out by LASERSOHN 1999, LAUER 2012, and others, intuitive judgments about logical relations generally reflect the strict contents of sentences, as opposed to their loose contents. For instance, (44) sounds just as bad as (45), whereas (46) sounds perfectly fine:

(44)   #Jones arrived at 3:00, namely at 3:02.

(45)   #Jones arrived at exactly 3:00, namely at 3:02.

(46)   Jones arrived at around 3:00, namely at 3:02.

In these sentences, 'Jones arrived at 3:00' patterns with 'Jones arrived at exactly 3:00', which expresses its strict content, as opposed to 'Jones arrived at around 3:00', which expresses its loose content. According to the hypothesis that simple sentences are instances of loose speech, one should expect to find the same patterns in our judgments about simple sentences. And indeed, these are just the patterns we find:

(47)   #Jones smokes, although she might not smoke.

(48)   #Jones certainly smokes, although she might not smoke.

(49)   Jones is likely enough to smoke, although she might not smoke.

As these sentences illustrate, our intuitive judgments about logical relations generally reflect the strict contents of simple sentences, as opposed to their loose contents.

The general practice of using loose speech has significant benefits. Loose speech is a convenient way to communicate complicated contents, namely tempered counterparts of the contents that you strictly speaking assert. For instance, you may say 'Jones arrived at 3:00' to communicate that Jones almost certainly arrived within five minutes of 3:00, and probably within three minutes of 3:00, and additional information that perhaps could not even be paraphrased in natural language. It is often practically useful to communicate this sort of content in conversation. In the same way, simple sentences are a convenient way to communicate complicated probabilistic contents. You may say 'Jones smokes' to communicate that it is almost certainly at least .9 likely that Jones smokes, and probably at least .99 likely that she smokes, and so on. It is not only useful to communicate these contents, but also useful to think and reason with them. Your faculties of memory and reasoning would soon be overwhelmed if all of your beliefs about time had to be precise to the nearest tenth of a second, and the same goes for keeping track of practically useless probabilistic information.

The complexity of credences is sometimes used to motivate skepticism about whether ordinary subjects have any credences at all. As HOLTON 2014 puts it, "Unless their powers of memory and reasoning are very great, those who employ credences risk being overwhelmed . . . rather than just discarding the propositions that aren't believed and focussing on those that are, they will have to keep track of all of them and their associated credences" (14). According to Holton, creatures with our limited cognitive powers do not have the ability to store or reason with the amount of information needed to assign credences to propositions.[14] However, it is not clear that concerns about memory and reasoning lend support to the claim that we only ever have full beliefs. After all, the analogous argument concerning beliefs about time does not support the claim that we only ever keep track of time to the nearest hour. The relevant insight is rather that it is often useful to round to the nearest certainty in belief and speech, just as it is often useful to round to the nearest hour. Just as with other forms of loose speech, the use of loose probabilistic speech has significant benefits.

---

[14] HARMAN 1986 defends arguments in a similar spirit. For critical discussion of these arguments, see STAFFEL 2013.

Almost by definition, the use of loose probabilistic speech has no significant costs. LAUER 2013 says that a speaker might assert that Mary arrived by 3:00 without strictly believing that she arrived by 3:00, "if he believes that the exact time of Mary's arrival is irrelevant to his future (linguistic and non-linguistic) action choices," meaning that "acting as though one believes that 'Mary was here by three' is true is just the same as acting as though one believes that 'Mary was here shortly after three' is true" (101). The strict content that Mary arrived by 3:00 is close enough to the truth. Close enough for what? As Lasersohn puts it, "close enough not to obscure pragmatically relevant details or distinctions" (525). This account of loose speech bears a striking resemblance to contemporary theories according to which full belief is something akin to certainty for practical purposes. For example, WEDGWOOD 2012 defines outright belief in p as "the state of being stably disposed to assign a practical credence of 1 to p, for all normal practical purposes" (321). WEATHERSON 2016 argues that to believe a proposition is roughly to be disposed to not change any attitude toward salient questions upon updating on that proposition, where salient questions include what bets you should accept. And SCHROEDER AND ROSS 2014 argue that to believe a proposition is to have a default disposition to use the proposition in reasoning, such as practical reasoning about what bets to accept.[15] These authors all favor something like the view that you believe that Jones smokes just in case practically speaking, it is just as if you are certain that Jones smokes—just as Lasersohn might say that you believe it is 3:00 just in case practically speaking, it is just as if you believe it is exactly 3:00.[16]

If we are having a conversation, then our practical purposes include our conversational purposes. Asserting that Mary arrived at 3:00 leads to our accepting for purposes of conversation that she arrived at exactly 3:00, which is why it can sound bad to elaborate by saying that she arrived at 3:02. STALNAKER 2002 points out that the same goes for the strict probabilistic contents of simple sentences. As Stalnaker puts it, asserted propositions are accepted for purposes of conversation, where this acceptance is incompatible with doubt: "to accept a proposition is to treat it as true for some reason. One ignores, at least temporarily, and perhaps in a limited context, the possibility that it is false" (716). This fact explains the infelicity of sentences such as (42):

(42)   #Jones smokes, and Jones might not smoke.

---

[15] For additional theories in this spirit, see GANSON 2008 and LOCKE 2013.

[16] According to some theories of loose speech, this claim is strictly speaking false. But it is close enough to true for many philosophical purposes.

Asserting that Jones smokes leads to our accepting for purposes of conversation that it is certain that Jones smokes, which is why it sounds bad to follow up by saying that Jones might not smoke after all.

To sum up our discussion so far, the strict content of a simple sentence is nominally probabilistic. The same goes for the strict contents of assertions made using simple sentences, and also for the strict contents of full beliefs. This is the sense in which subjects can bear a derivative belief relation to a proposition, as mentioned in §1.4—namely, by having a belief whose strict content is the nominally probabilistic content according to which that proposition is certain. The same goes not just for derivative belief relations between subjects and propositions, but also for derivative relations of assertion and knowledge. In addition to strict contents, simple sentences and full beliefs also have loose contents— namely, thoroughly probabilistic contents that are equivalent with their strict contents for practical purposes. The previous section of this chapter posed a difficult challenge, namely spelling out the relationship between full belief and certainty. This challenge is answered by explaining that relationship in terms of the relationship between loose and strict contents of belief.

What exactly is the relationship between loose and strict contents of belief? The jury is out. A wide range of philosophers of language would agree that as uttered in context, the sentence 'it is 3:00' can be associated with a stronger content and a weaker content, where the former is independent of context and the latter varies depending on pragmatic concerns. And many would agree that the following sentences are also instances of loose speech:

(50) Odessa has a population of one million. (WACHTEL 1980, 204)

(51) I now weigh 80 kilos. (TRAVIS 1985, 199)

(52) Amherst is 90 miles from Boston. (ELGIN 2002, 304)

(53) I wrote this article in twenty-four hours. (KRIFKA 2009, 117)

These observations leave open some important questions. For instance, are ordinary utterances of 'it is 3:00' literally false? Should the literal content of this sentence be identified with its strict content, or with its loose content? LASERSOHN 1999 assumes that utterances of 'it is 3:00' are often false: "It is a truism that people speak 'loosely'—that is, that they often say things that we can recognize not to be true, but which come close enough to the truth for practical purposes" (522). At the same time, other theorists assume that such utterances are often true. For instance, HAWTHORNE 2004 says that 'it is 3:00' is false as uttered at 3:01 in the context of a rocket launch, but that "there are plenty of ordinary, less demanding contexts, where intuitively [it] expresses a truth" (99).[17] In short, it is a controversial question whether sentences like 'it is 3:00' are often literally false, and we should look to our best semantic and pragmatic theories to answer that question.[18] Similarly, it is controversial whether you believe the literal content that you use the simple sentence 'Jones smokes' to assert, merely in virtue of having some very high credence that Jones smokes.[19]

The close connection between full belief and loose speech constitutes another consideration in favor of the first central thesis of this book. It is this thesis that enables us to use theories of loose and strict speech to explain the relationship between your full beliefs and your thoroughly probabilistic beliefs. Theories of loose speech distinguish different contents of belief, such as the loose and strict content of your belief that it is 3:00. Once we accept that probabilistic beliefs have probabilistic contents, we can similarly distinguish the loose and strict probabilistic contents of simple sentences. We can see the relationship between believing that Jones smokes and believing that Jones certainly smokes as being just the same as the relationship between believing that it is 3:00 and believing that it is exactly 3:00.

In the first chapter of this book, I argued that the claim that *belief comes in degrees* is actually best understood as a claim about the content of your probabilistic beliefs, rather than as a claim about the attitude of belief itself. In a similar spirit, I have argued in this chapter that the controversial claim that *full belief is certainty* is actually best understood as a claim about the content of your full beliefs, rather than as a claim about the attitude of full belief itself. This gestalt shift enables us to understand the latter controversial claim as targeting the strict contents of your full beliefs, without targeting their loose contents. We have thereby answered the difficult challenge from the previous section of this chapter, namely explaining the intuitive similarities and differences between full belief and certainty. In addition, we have explained remarkable analogies between our use of simple sentences and other uses of loose speech. The strength of these explanations lends further support to the central thesis that they presuppose: we can believe probabilistic contents.

---

[17] I am grateful to Keith DeRose for calling my attention to these conflicting assumptions about loose speech.

[18] For an overview of relevant literature, see PREYER AND PETER 2007.

[19] As hinted in fn. 16, it is also controversial whether the following is literally true: that you believe that Jones smokes just in case practically speaking, it is just as if you are certain that Jones smokes.

4

Indicative conditionals

4.1 Probabilities of conditionals as conditional probabilities

The first and second chapters of this book argue that we can believe and assert probabilistic contents. The third chapter develops these central theses by assigning probabilistic contents to sentences containing epistemic modals and probability operators. This fourth chapter extends my probabilistic semantics to indicative conditionals. According to the semantics defended in this chapter, the semantic value of an indicative conditional relative to a context is not a set of worlds, but a set of probability spaces.

There is a long tradition of drawing connections between indicative conditionals and probabilistic beliefs. To cite one especially influential example, RAMSEY 1931 introduces the following proposal concerning conditionals and degrees of belief:

> If two people are arguing 'If p will q?' and are both in doubt as to p, they are adding p hypothetically to their stock of knowledge and arguing on that basis about q . . . We can say that they are fixing their degrees of belief in q given p. (247)

This proposal has inspired many theories of conditionals, with each theory providing a precise interpretation of the passage quoted above.[1] A common first step of interpretation is to identify the relevant "degrees of belief in q given p" as conditional credences. For instance, suppose that a baseball game was scheduled to happen yesterday, and that we are arguing about the following conditional:

(1)   If it rained, the game was cancelled.

Ramsey could be interpreted as saying that you believe that it is *probable* that the game was cancelled if it rained just in case you have *high conditional credence*

---

[1] For some classic examples, see STALNAKER 1970b, ADAMS 1975, VAN FRAASSEN 1976, GIBBARD 1981, EDGINGTON 1986, and BENNETT 2003.

that the game was cancelled given that it rained. The same goes for more precise probability assignments: you believe that it is .8 *likely* that the game was cancelled if it rained just in case you have .8 *conditional credence* that the game was cancelled given that it rained, and so on. In general, you believe a conditional is as probable as your conditional credence in its consequent given its antecedent.

In order to further interpret the passage from Ramsey quoted above, we must explain what it means to believe that some conditional is probable, or .8 likely, and so on. If the content of a conditional is a proposition, then believing a conditional is .8 likely is simply having .8 credence in its content. A tempting second step of interpretation carries this idea through for every degree of belief. The resulting claim is the notorious hypothesis defended by STALNAKER 1970b, namely that one can interpret the indicative conditional as an operator producing propositions such that according to the credences of any rational agent, the probability of an indicative conditional proposition equals the conditional probability of its consequent given its antecedent.[2] Unfortunately, LEWIS 1976 famously argues that Stalnaker's Hypothesis fails. According to the triviality results proved by Lewis and extended by many others, conditionals do not express propositions such that their rational probabilities are simply conditional probabilities. In light of these triviality results, fans of Ramsey do not need to resign, but they do need to regroup. How can one retreat from Stalnaker's Hypothesis while still preserving the central insight of the passage from Ramsey quoted above?

Adopting a probabilistic semantics gives us valuable resources for answering this question. Assume that the content of a conditional is not a proposition. Then a probability function will not be defined on the content of a conditional. But the result of applying a probability operator to a conditional may still have a well-defined content. Hence we can take the first step of interpretation described above without taking the second. According to this probabilistic interpretation of Ramsey, believing that a conditional is probable *does not* amount to having high credence in any proposition. However, believing a conditional is probable *does* amount to believing a certain probabilistic content. For instance, believing that (1) is probable just amounts to believing the content of the following sentence:

(2)   It is probable that if it rained, the game was cancelled.

In order to preserve Ramsey's insight, we could say that the content of (2) is the set of probability spaces that assign high conditional probability to the proposition

[2] Stalnaker's Hypothesis is often discussed in tandem with Adams' Thesis. The latter thesis is usually taken to concern degrees of assertability of conditionals, following ADAMS 1965, though Adams ultimately trades in the notion of assertability for something like probability in ADAMS 1975.

that the game was cancelled, given that it rained. Similarly, we could say that the content of (3) is the set of probability spaces that assign .8 conditional probability to the proposition that the game was cancelled, given that it rained:

(3)   It is .8 likely that if it rained, the game was cancelled.

The same goes for every embedded conditional and every degree of belief. At a first pass, advocates of a probabilistic semantics could say that the content of a conditional under a probability operator is the set of probability spaces assigning that conditional probability to the consequent of the conditional, given its antecedent.

Given this semantics for sentences like (2) and (3), is there a natural accompanying semantics for simple conditionals that are not embedded under any probability operators? Recall that according to my arguments in §3.5, the simple sentence 'Jones smokes' has the same strict content as 'it is certain that Jones smokes'. At a first pass, the simple conditional 'if it rained, the game was cancelled' could have the same strict content as 'it is certain that if it rained, the game was cancelled'. Recall that even though 'Jones smokes' has a strong strict content, it may be used to express probabilistic beliefs that are close enough to certainty that Jones smokes. In the same sense, an indicative conditional could in principle be used to express conditional probabilistic beliefs that are close enough to certainty of its consequent, conditional on its antecedent.

This first pass semantics has some valuable features. There appear to be robust connections between conditionals and conditional probability, and probabilistic semantic theories appear perfectly suited to account for these connections. However, on reflection, the connection between conditionals and conditional probability is more complicated than it first appears. In the next section of this chapter, I spell out a semantics for conditionals that significantly improves on the semantics described above. Then in the rest of the chapter, I argue that my improved semantics accounts for a variety of observations about conditionals, including observations that challenge their celebrated connection with conditional probability.

4.2 A semantics for conditionals

In addition to arguments discussed later in this chapter, there is an easy argument that our first pass semantics for conditionals is inadequate. This semantics suffers from the same problem as the first pass semantics for epistemic modals and probability operators in §3.2. According to that semantics, an epistemic operator such as 'probably' is used to assert a probabilistic content, namely the set of probability spaces that assign some probability to the propositional content of the sentence embedded under that operator. Recall that the problem with this semantics is that the sentence embedded under an epistemic operator cannot necessarily be identified with any propositional content, since that embedded sentence may itself contain epistemic vocabulary. In just the same way, epistemic vocabulary may occur in the scope of indicative conditionals. For instance, indicative conditionals may embed epistemic adjectives:

(4)   If they hired Jones, then Smith is a possible hire.

(5)   If Smith is a possible hire, then they hired Jones.[3]

The antecedents and consequents of indicative conditionals may also embed epistemic modals:

(6)   If they hired Jones, then they might be hiring Smith.

(7)   If they might be hiring Smith, then they definitely hired Jones.

(8)   If you drive a small compact car that has never been washed, you might be a liberal.[4]

The same goes for epistemic comparatives:

(9)   It is more likely than not that the vase broke if it was dropped on concrete.

(10)   If massive neutron stars exist, they are more likely to have formed in systems of high initial mass.[5]

And finally, the same goes for other conditionals. There are well-known examples of right-nested and left-nested indicatives:

(11)   If a Republican wins the election, then if it's not Reagan who wins it will be Anderson.[6]

(12)   If this cup will break if you drop it, then it's fragile.[7]

According to our first pass semantics, you use a conditional to express your high conditional credence in its consequent, given its antecedent. Hence the content of the antecedent and the content of the consequent must be objects on which

---

[3] HACQUARD AND WELLWOOD 2012 give attested cases of epistemic vocabulary in indicative antecedents, while arguing that pragmatic considerations may limit the distribution of epistemic vocabulary in indicative antecedents and similar linguistic contexts.

[4] CURTIS 1997, ch.5.   [5] VANBEVEREN 2001, p.132.   [6] McGEE 1985, p.462.

[7] This example is a variant of an example from GIBBARD 1981. As Gibbard observes, some left-nested conditionals are harder to interpret than others. For compelling arguments that this observation deserves a pragmatic explanation, see SENNET AND WEISBERG 2012.

probability functions are defined. In other words, they must be propositions. But the antecedents and consequents of conditionals cannot always be identified with propositions. At least sometimes, as in examples (4)–(12), the antecedents and consequents of conditionals have thoroughly probabilistic contents.

Any complete semantics for conditionals must provide well-defined semantic values for conditionals embedding epistemic vocabulary. Such conditionals demonstrate that the traditional connection between conditionals and conditional probability is limited at best. A conditional probability function is not always defined on the content of the consequent of a conditional. And a conditional probability function cannot always be constructed by conditionalizing on the content of the antecedent. The first pass semantics for conditionals proposed in §4.1 is revisionary in virtue of saying that conditionals have probabilistic contents. But in fact, the embedding of epistemic vocabulary in conditionals motivates an even more revisionary semantics. In spelling out a precise understanding of RAMSEY 1931, one cannot even take the first step of interpretation described at the start of this chapter. Your degree of belief in a conditional cannot always be your conditional credence in its consequent given its antecedent.

An improved semantics for conditionals should provide semantic values for conditionals embedding epistemic vocabulary, just as my semantics for epistemic modals and probability operators provides semantic values for nested occurrences of these expressions. In fact, the latter semantics serves as a useful guide for the former. Just like epistemic modals and probability operators, we use conditionals when we are torn between various opinions. Imagine that you are a cancer specialist. Jones and Smith have come to you to determine whether they have a rare form of cancer. The diagnostic tests are not conclusive. The best interpretation of the results is controversial. According to one leading theory, blood tests are more probative than ultrasound screenings. According to another leading theory, ultrasound screenings are more probative. In this context, whether you believe that Smith might have cancer depends on your conditional opinions, opinions corresponding to the different ways in which you might evaluate what your evidence supports. You believe the content of 'Smith might have cancer' just in case you have some conditional opinion according to which Smith has cancer. The same conditional opinions determine whether you believe the contents of indicative conditionals. You believe the content of 'if Jones has cancer, then Smith has cancer' just in case every relevant opinion according to which Jones has cancer is an opinion according to which Smith has cancer.

In chapter 3, I argued that sentences containing epistemic modals and probability operators are context sensitive. Conditionals exhibit just the same sort of context sensitivity. In particular, context provides a partition of logical space for the interpretation of a conditional. The propositions in this partition could reflect different sources of evidence, for instance, or different ways of evaluating what your evidence supports. An indicative conditional is a strict conditional over these propositions, in the following sense: the content of a conditional contains your credences just in case the consequent is accepted by every possible proposition that accepts the antecedent relative to your credences. In other words, among the various possible opinions that you find yourself torn between, every opinion in the content of the antecedent of the conditional is also in the content of the consequent.[8]

According to our improved semantics for conditionals, whether you believe a conditional does not depend on your opinions *conditional on the propositional content* of the antecedent. Rather, whether you believe a conditional depends on your conditional opinions that *accept the probabilistic content* of the antecedent. As desired, the contents of antecedents and consequents of conditionals may be sets of probability spaces that do not correspond to any proposition. Arbitrary combinations of conditionals, epistemic modals, and probability operators have well-defined semantic values, which are straightforwardly determined by the semantic values of the individual epistemic expressions they contain, according to standard semantic rules of composition.

4.3 Why probabilities of conditionals are not conditional probabilities

Even for conditionals with simple antecedents and consequents, the connection between conditionals and conditional probability is not as robust as it may appear at first. In addition to conditionals embedding epistemic vocabulary, there is a second problem for the claim that probabilities of conditionals are just conditional probabilities. Consider the following example:

> Jones is standing on the roof of your office building. The local fire department occasionally hangs a net along the roof to protect workers doing construction. The net is strong enough to safely catch anyone who falls off the building. Just a few minutes ago, you happened to notice that there was no net along the roof. As a result, you do not believe that Jones is going to jump off the roof. Jones is a thrill-seeker who might jump into a net for fun, but she definitely does not have a death wish. And without a net, anyone who jumped off the roof would surely fall to the ground and die.[9]

---

[8] In this context, I use 'credences' for the probability space representing your total belief state. A proposition is *possible* according to your credences just in case it is true in some world in the domain of your credences. For a more precise statement of my semantics for conditionals, see Appendix A.4.

[9] This example is inspired by example (15) in chapter 8 of LYCAN 2001, which builds on the discussion of subjunctive conditionals in SLOTE 1978 and LEWIS 1979b.

On the one hand, since you believe there is no net along the roof, you are intuitively justified in asserting:

(13)   It is highly probable that if Jones jumps off the roof, she will die.

On the other hand, you are confident that Jones does not have a death wish. If you were informed that Jones jumped off the roof of your office building, you would conclude that the fire department must have put up a net in the past few minutes. As you consider this information, you are intuitively justified in asserting:

(14)   It is highly improbable that if Jones jumps off the roof, she will die.

To make these observations more vivid, suppose someone asks you whether there is a net along the roof of the building. They know that you promised the fire department that you wouldn't go around telling people whether or not there was a net along the roof, but they persist in pestering you for information. It is intuitively fine for you to respond:

(15)   Look, I can't answer your questions directly. But I can tell you this much: it's highly probable that if Jones jumps off the roof, she'll die.

On the other hand, suppose someone asks you whether you believe that Jones is suicidal. They know that you promised Jones that you wouldn't go around telling people about her psychological state, but they persist in pestering you for information. Suppose that it is common ground that anyone suicidal would likely cut away the safety net and jump off the roof, and that anyone else might jump into the net for fun. It is intuitively fine for you to respond.

(16)   Look, I can't answer your questions directly. But I can tell you this much: it's highly improbable that if Jones jumps off the roof, she'll die.

Hence whether you can assert 'it is highly probable that if Jones jumps, she will die' does not depend only on your credences about Jones and the net, which we may stipulate are the same in the contexts described above. It also depends on features determined by the context of utterance. Expressions of confidence in conditionals are context sensitive. In some contexts, 'it is highly probable that if Jones jumps, she will die' may have a content that you believe just in case you have high conditional credence that Jones will die if she jumps. But in other contexts, this sentence has a different probabilistic content. In the contexts described above, you are considering different questions, and which question you are considering determines whether (13) or (14) says something that you believe.

A second example of the same sort of context sensitivity can be constructed using the Sly Pete story from GIBBARD 1981:

> Sly Pete and Mr. Stone are playing poker on a Mississippi riverboat. It is now up to Pete to call or fold. My henchman Zack sees Stone's hand, which is quite good, and signals its content to Pete. My henchman Jack sees both hands, and sees that Pete's hand is rather low, so that Stone's is the winning hand. At this point, the room is cleared . . . Zack knows that Pete knew Stone's hand. He can thus appropriately assert "If Pete called, he won." Jack knows that Pete held the losing hand, and thus can appropriately assert "If Pete called, he lost." (231)

Suppose that Zack and Jack are your henchmen, and you are collecting information from them. Zack says that if Pete called, he won. Jack says that if Pete called, he lost. As you reflect on your high credence that Zack is trustworthy, you are justified in saying:

(17)   Probably, if Pete called, he won.

On the other hand, as you reflect on your high credence that Jack is trustworthy, you are justified in saying:

(18)   Probably, if Pete called, he lost.

Here again, expressions of confidence in conditionals are context sensitive. As you consider different questions about which of your henchmen is trustworthy, which question you are considering determines whether (17) or (18) says something that you believe.

A number of recent discussions of indicative conditionals aim to account for the sort of context sensitivity exhibited by sentences like (17) and (18). For instance, MORTON 2004 argues that we calculate the intuitive probability of a conditional "by looking for a non-conditional proposition . . . whose probability we are sure is pretty much the same as that of the indicative conditional" (296). KAUFMANN 2004 argues that conditionals have local interpretations that arise only when certain unobserved background variables are especially salient. In short, the context sensitivity of expressions of confidence in conditionals challenges the interpretation of RAMSEY 1931 described at the start of this chapter. According to this interpretation, you believe that a conditional is probable just in case you have high conditional credence in its consequent given its antecedent. The above examples demonstrate that some instances of this biconditional are false at some contexts, namely because their left hand side is context sensitive, whereas their right hand side is not. As a result, the above examples deviate from the alleged pattern of judgments used to motivate Stalnaker's Hypothesis. The same examples also challenge Adams' Thesis. In some contexts, 'if Jones jumps, she will die' has a high degree of assertability, even though you do not have high conditional credence that Jones will die if she jumps.

The context sensitivity of 'it is highly probable that if Jones jumps, she will die' is explained by my semantics for probability operators and indicative conditionals. The expression 'it is highly probable that' is context sensitive, interpreted relative to a contextually determined partition. If you are talking about whether there is a net along the roof, then this partition contains two propositions: that there is a net, and that there is no net. You believe that if there is no net, then if Jones jumps, she will die. Hence the proposition that there is no net accepts the content of 'if Jones jumps, she will die' relative to your credences. In addition, you give more than .5 credence to this proposition. That is why the content of 'it is highly probable that if Jones jumps, she will die' contains your credences. By contrast, say you are talking about whether Jones is suicidal. Then the contextually determined partition for 'it is highly probable that' contains different propositions: that Jones is not suicidal, and that she is suicidal. The former proposition does not accept that Jones will die if she jumps. The latter proposition does accept that Jones will die if she jumps, but you do not give that proposition more than .5 credence. Hence my semantics predicts that the content of 'it is highly probable that if Jones jumps, she will die' does not contain your credences. The context sensitivity of expressions of confidence in conditionals provides a reason to prefer my semantics over theories that fail to account for this context sensitivity. This argument presents a challenge for many existing theories of indicative conditionals.[10] As explained in §2.4, many non-truth-conditional theories of conditionals are designed to vindicate connections between conditionals and conditional probability.

In response to this challenge, advocates of Stalnaker's Hypothesis or Adams' Thesis might try to resist the judgments that I have used to support my semantics. For instance, they might defend an error theory of our judgments about (13):

(13)   It is highly probable that if Jones jumps off the roof, she will die.

According to this line of thought, it is a mistake for you to believe or assert that it is highly probable that if Jones jumps, she will die. As long as you have high credence that Jones will live if she jumps, you will not believe the content of (13) as uttered in any context. As DOUVEN 2008a and others have pointed out, if our assertion of sentences like (13) is a cognitive error, then sentences like these pose no threat to Stalnaker's Hypothesis or Adams' Thesis.[11]

---

[10] For some notable exceptions, see KAUFMANN 2004, ROTHSCHILD 2013, MOSS 2015, and KHOO 2016. KHOO 2016 discusses KAUFMANN 2004 at length, without mentioning that other authors that he cites also defend their theories on the grounds that they can explain the context sensitivity of indicative conditionals.

[11] In addition to raising this objection, Douven criticizes KAUFMANN 2004 for making inconsistent predictions about the probabilities of conditionals. The semantics I defend addresses this sort

To forestall error theories of sentences like (13), I want to introduce a novel problem for the alleged connection between probabilities of conditionals and conditional probabilities, namely a problem concerning probabilistic inferences. Imagine that in the Sly Pete case, you listen to each of your henchmen and you trust them up to a point. On the basis of their reports, you reason:

(19)   a. It is at least .9 likely that if Pete called, he won.
        b. It is at least .9 likely that if Pete called, he lost.
        c. Therefore, it is at least .8 likely that Pete did not call.

The premises of this inference are consistent. As a rational agent, you can consistently believe both (19-a) and (19-b) and thereby come to believe the conclusion. However, you cannot consistently have at least .9 conditional credence that Pete won if he called, while also having at least .9 conditional credence that Pete lost if he called. Hence we have another argument against the biconditional claim that you believe (19-a) just in case you have .9 conditional credence that Pete won given that he called. The conditionals 'if Pete called, he won' and 'if Pete called, he lost' each have high probability in the context of the inference described above, even though the corresponding conditional probabilities cannot both be high for any rational agent. At this point, it does not seem right to object that we should give an error theory of (19-a) or (19-b). The fact that you rationally believe both of these premises explains why it is rational for you to end up with .8 credence that Pete did not call in the Sly Pete case.

The semantics I have defended accounts for the consistency of (19-a) and (19-b), and for the validity of the inference (19). According to my semantics for probability operators and conditionals, (19) is valid as uttered in any context satisfying three modest constraints. The first constraint is that context must supply the same partition to the semantic values of the conditionals in the premises of (19). The second constraint is that context must supply the same partition to the semantic values of the probability operators throughout the inference. These constraints are modest, as it is natural and charitable to read (19) without supposing that the inference equivocates. The third constraint is that context must supply the conditionals in (19) with a partition that is *decisive* with respect to whether Pete called, meaning that each element of the partition entails either that Pete called or that he didn't. This last constraint is an instance of a more general pragmatic rule. As I argue in §4.5, context often supplies indicative conditionals with partitions that are decisive with respect to the traditional propositional

---

of objection, namely by saying that distinct readings of sentences like (13) result from distinct resolutions of context-sensitive expressions.

content of their antecedents. As long as these modest constraints are satisfied, my semantics predicts that the premises of (19) entail its conclusion.[12] Accounting for the validity of the probabilistic Sly Pete inference is another attractive feature of my semantics.

To sum up the big picture: in light of triviality results proved by Lewis and others, many theorists have pursued non-truth-conditional semantic theories of indicative conditionals. Their theories are often designed to vindicate Stalnaker's Hypothesis, Adams' Thesis, or other unqualified connections between conditionals and conditional probability. In this section, I have argued that the connection between conditionals and conditional probability should in fact be qualified. By contrast with many existing theories, my semantics explains intuitive judgments that distinguish probabilities of conditionals from conditional probabilities.

4.4 A semantics for other logical operators

In addition to accounting for the validity of the probabilistic Sly Pete inference, my semantics can account for the *invalidity* of other inferences containing epistemic vocabulary. Suppose that a fair die has been rolled, and you have not yet seen how it landed. The die has three low numbers: 1, 2, and 3. The die has three high numbers: 4, 5, and 6. Consider the following inference about the number rolled:

(20) a. If it is low, it is probably odd.
      b. It is not probably odd.
      c. #Therefore, it is not low.

This inference appears to be an instance of *modus tollens*. But the inference is invalid. The first premise contains your credences, since you believe that two out of three of the low numbers are odd. The second premise contains your credences, since you do not have more than .5 credence that an odd number was rolled. But the conclusion doesn't contain your credences, since you are agnostic about whether a low number was rolled. Additional puzzles arise for other standard inference rules. For instance, constructive dilemma also appears to have invalid instances embedding epistemic vocabulary:

(21) a. If it is low, it is probably odd.
      b. If it is high, it is probably even.
      c. It is either low or high.
      d. #Therefore, either it is probably odd or probably even.

---

[12] See Appendix A.4 for a proof of this result.

Both of the above inferences contain probability operators, but one can generate similar puzzles using epistemic modals, epistemic adjectives, and epistemic comparatives.

A number of authors have used epistemic vocabulary to construct similar apparent counterexamples to standard inference rules.[13] A complete theory of these puzzling inferences should answer at least two questions. First, why are the inferences invalid? And second, are the inferences actually instances of classically valid inference rules, or are they merely apparent instances of these rules? Unfortunately, a number of existing theories of epistemic vocabulary are not equipped to answer these questions. For instance, some theories say little or nothing about the interaction of epistemic modals and disjunction, including the theories of epistemic modals defended in YALCIN 2007, WILLER 2013, and SWANSON 2016a. SCHROEDER 2012 extrapolates a semantics for disjunction from YALCIN 2007 and then goes on to identify several problems for that semantics. In response to examples like (21), KOLODNY AND MACFARLANE 2010 argue that we should accept a semantics for indicative conditionals according to which constructive dilemma is invalid. However, the similar invalidity of apparent instances of De Morgan's laws suggests that the apparent failure of classically valid inference rules is not the responsibility of indicative conditionals alone, but rather something that concerns the interaction of epistemic vocabulary with logical operators more generally.[14] In the rest of this section, I supplement my semantics for conditionals with a semantics for other logical operators. Then I use my semantics to answer the two questions raised above, explaining why the puzzling inferences are invalid and arguing that they are not genuine counterexamples to standard inference rules.

In stating a formal semantics for 'not', 'and', and 'or', it is important to remember that these logical operators embed expressions of various syntactic categories and semantic types. PARTEE AND ROOTH 1983 observe that "virtually every major category can be conjoined with 'and' and 'or'" (334). For example, logical operators can embed sentences, names, predicates, numerical determiners, and quantifiers:

(22) Jones passed the exam and Smith failed it.

(23) Jones or Smith passed the exam.

(24) Jones studied hard and passed the exam.

---

[13] For some recent examples, see CANTWELL 2008, DREIER 2009, KOLODNY AND MACFARLANE 2010, SCHROEDER 2012, YALCIN 2012c, and SALERNO 2016. See also MOSS 2015 for puzzles for other standard inference rules, in addition to those discussed in this section.

[14] See Appendix A.5 for discussion of apparent counterexamples to De Morgan's laws.

(25)   Three or four students passed the exam.

(26)   Some and indeed all students passed the exam.

According to my probabilistic semantics, sentences can denote sets of probability spaces, in which case they have an entirely different semantic type than
the traditional types of the expressions mentioned above. Accordingly, logical
operators can also denote operations on sets of probability spaces. For instance,
the denotation of 'and' in (27) operates on thoroughly probabilistic contents:

(27)   Jones probably smokes, and Smith probably doesn't.

At a first pass, it may appear easy to extend a standard semantics for logical
operators to account for sentences like (27). Just as with other types of arguments,
'and' could be used to denote the intersection of two probabilistic contents,
'or' could be used to denote their union, and 'not' could be used to denote
the complement of a probabilistic content. Just as with sets of any sort, these
operations on sets of probability spaces are indeed well defined.

At a second pass, however, the semantics of logical operators is more complicated in two respects.[15] The first complication is that when logical operators have
sentences as their arguments, those logical operators can have different meanings,
depending on whether or not their arguments contain any epistemic vocabulary.
As applied to simple sentences, logical operators denote operations on propositions, just as they do on a more traditional semantics. In the sentence 'Jones
smokes or Smith drinks', for instance, 'Jones smokes' and 'Smith drinks' both
denote sets of worlds, and the semantic value of 'or' produces the union of those
sets. As discussed in §3.5, this disjunction also contains a covert operator that
shifts its semantic type, producing a sentence that denotes the set of probability
spaces according to which it is certain that either Jones smokes or Smith drinks.
This nominally probabilistic content is the content that you use the disjunction
to assert. Similarly, 'not' can denote operations both on propositions and on
probabilistic contents. The negation in 'Jones does not smoke' operates on a set of
worlds, producing the complement of the set of worlds where Jones smokes. This
sentence also contains a covert type-shifting operator, producing a sentence that
denotes a nominally probabilistic content—namely, the set of probability spaces
according to which it is certain that Jones does not smoke.

The fact that logical operators denote operations both on propositions and on
probabilistic contents helps explain why some apparent instances of classically

---

[15] For a more detailed formal discussion of the ideas presented here, see Appendix A.5.

valid inference rules are invalid. For example, an equivocation in the interpretation of 'not' helps explain the invalidity of the following inference:

(20)   a. If it is low, it is probably odd.
      b. It is not probably odd.
      c. #Therefore, it is not low.

The occurrence of 'not' in (20-b) does not have the same semantic value as 'not' in (20-c). The former denotes an operation on sets of probability spaces, while the latter denotes an operation on sets of worlds. The resulting inference (20) is not appropriately classified as an instance of *modus tollens*, nor should it be considered a counterexample to this standard inference rule.

The foregoing observations do not constitute a complete explanation of the invalidity of (20), but they are sufficiently illuminating for our purposes. They account for the fact that apparent counterexamples to *modus tollens* are limited to inferences containing epistemic vocabulary, since in inferences involving only simple sentences, negation is applied consistently to propositional contents throughout. In addition, my semantics accommodates the fact that some instances of *modus tollens* contain epistemic vocabulary but are nevertheless perfectly valid. For example, consider the following inference about the number rolled:

(28)   a. If it is probably five, then it is probably odd.
      b. It is not probably odd.
      c. Therefore, it is not probably five.

The operator 'not' is used consistently throughout (28), denoting an operation on probabilistic contents in both (28-b) and (28-c). Hence my semantics provides for the fact that (28) has a valid reading, on which it avoids the sort of equivocation exhibited by the apparent counterexample to *modus tollens* given above.

In addition to logical operators between sentences having denotations of multiple types, there is a second complication for our first pass semantics. The content of a disjunction containing epistemic vocabulary is not simply the union of the contents of each disjunct. For instance, consider the following sentence:

(29)   The number rolled is low or it is probably even.

Since you merely have .5 credence that the number rolled is low, your credences are not contained in the content of the first disjunct of (29). Since you believe that the number is only .5 likely to be even, your credences are not contained in the content of the second disjunct either. Hence they are not contained in the union of the contents of these disjuncts. Nevertheless, you believe the content of the disjunction itself. Hence the content of (29) must be more complicated than our first pass semantics predicts.

The lesson of examples like (29) is that disjunctions embedding epistemic vocabulary can be used to express combinations of conditional probabilistic opinions. In this respect, disjunctions embedding epistemic vocabulary are just like sentences containing nested epistemic vocabulary. As you focus on the question of whether the number rolled is high, certain conditional probabilistic opinions are salient, namely your credences conditional on hypotheses about whether the number is high. As argued in chapter 3, you believe that the number *might be likely to be even* because you have a certain conditional opinion according to which the number is likely to be even. The very same conditional credences are relevant not only for the interpretation of nested epistemic vocabulary, but also for the interpretation of sentences like (29). You believe that the number is *low or probably even* because each of your conditional opinions either says that the number is low or says that the number is probably even. In sentences like (29), logical vocabulary exhibits just the same sort of context sensitivity as epistemic vocabulary. An adequate semantics for logical operators should reflect this fact.

According to our second pass semantics for logical operators, certain occurrences of 'or' are context sensitive, namely those denoting operations on probabilistic contents. Their context sensitivity is just like the context sensitivity of epistemic modals, probability operators, and indicative conditionals. The interpretation of an occurrence of 'or' embedding epistemic vocabulary depends on a partition of logical space provided by context. The content of a disjunction contains your credences just in case each proposition in the partition is such that relative to your credences, it accepts the content of the first disjunct or it accepts the content of the second disjunct. In other words, among the various opinions that you are torn between, every opinion is in the content of some disjunct or other. A similar semantics can be given for conjunctions and negated sentences containing epistemic vocabulary. The content of a conjunction containing epistemic vocabulary contains your credences just in case each proposition in the corresponding partition accepts the content of both conjuncts. The content of a sentence formed by negating a sentence containing epistemic vocabulary contains your credences just in case no proposition in the corresponding partition accepts the content of the negated sentence.[16]

---

[16] This informal presentation of my semantics for logical operators is intended for readers without any background in linguistics. Appendix A.5 contains a formal semantics for logical operators, as well as further discussion of motivations for my semantics.

The context sensitivity of logical vocabulary is a second reason why some apparent instances of classically valid inference rules are invalid. In addition to equivocating between different semantic types of logical operators, inferences may be invalid in virtue of equivocating between different resolutions of their context sensitivity. This is a familiar phenomenon. Almost any inference containing context-sensitive vocabulary may fail to be valid when earlier claims are interpreted relative to one context and later claims are interpreted relative to another, and sometimes the most natural reading of a context-sensitive inference will involve just this sort of equivocation. For comparison, consider the following bad inference:

(30)   a. Every human being needs to eat.
  b. Everything that needs to eat is currently alive.
  c. Therefore, every human being is currently alive.

On the most natural reading of this inference, the quantifier 'every human being' ranges over different domains in (30-a) and (30-c). As a result, (30) is invalid in the following straightforward sense: the content that is actually expressed by the conclusion in the context in which it is uttered is not entailed by the intersection of the contents that are actually expressed by the premises. Similarly, the context sensitivity of logical vocabulary helps explain why our initial apparent instance of constructive dilemma is invalid:

(21)   a. If it is low, it is probably odd.
  b. If it is high, it is probably even.
  c. It is either low or high.
  d. #Therefore, either it is probably odd or probably even.

The premises (21-a) and (21-b) sound fine because they are naturally interpreted as expressing your conditional credences. Meanwhile, the conclusion of (21) is naturally interpreted as expressing your all-things-considered credences. In more formal terms, 'if' in (21-a) and (21-b) is interpreted relative to a partition containing two propositions—that the number rolled is low, and that the number is high—while 'or' in (21-d) is interpreted relative to the partition containing just the trivial proposition. Conditional on the trivial proposition, you do not have greater than .5 credence that the number rolled is even or greater than .5 credence that it is odd. Hence you do not believe the content of (21-d).

The inference (30) is an invalid inference to the conclusion that every human being is currently alive. This inference does not constitute a genuine counterexample to the rule of inference by categorical syllogism. The inference (30) equivocates, whereas genuine instances of categorical syllogism do not. According to my semantics, the same goes for other invalid inferences mentioned in this section. All classically valid inference rules remain in good standing. The inferences in this section serve to highlight the fact that many inferences appear to be instances of these rules when in fact they are not. In chapter 7, I discuss several arguments against the thesis that we have probabilistic knowledge. Fortunately, some of these arguments are also merely apparent instances of classically valid inference rules. Arguments that might appear devastating for probabilistic knowledge suffer from the same sort of equivocation as the simple inferences considered here.

4.5 The pragmatics of epistemic vocabulary

The semantics defended in this chapter accommodates the context sensitivity of expressions of confidence in conditionals, as well as facts about the validity and invalidity of inferences containing epistemic vocabulary. The semantics defended in chapter 3 accommodates many intuitive judgments about the interpretation of nested epistemic expressions. These are significant advantages of my probabilistic semantics. However, the semantics defended in these chapters has its limits. My semantics yields concrete predictions about sentences containing epistemic or logical vocabulary only in conjunction with supplementary assumptions about what partitions are contributed by context to the interpretation of that vocabulary. For instance, my semantics alone does not entail that 'it is highly probable that if Jones jumps off the roof, she will die' is interpreted relative to different partitions in different contexts. It does not follow from my semantics that 'if it is low, it is probably odd' expresses your credences conditional on whether a low or high number was rolled, while 'either it is probably odd or probably even' expresses your all-things-considered credences. And it does not follow from my semantics that nested modals are often interpreted relative to distinct partitions, and therefore often have cumulative rather than concord readings. Absent any discussion of pragmatics, one might worry that my semantics can only give ad hoc explanations of the ordinary language judgments I have used to motivate it.

These limits of my semantics are inevitable and appropriate. It would be unreasonable to demand that a contextualist semantics come equipped with rules for deriving the values of context-sensitive expressions from facts about context. To take a very relevant example, consider the contextualist semantics for epistemic modals defended in KRATZER 1981. Kratzer does not equip her readers with rules for determining exactly what evidence is relevant to the interpretation of an epistemic modal as uttered at a particular context. It is not hard to understand why. The interpretation of an epistemic modal may depend on contextual features that are so subtle that is impossible to state rules that specify the interpretation of that modal at an arbitrary context.[17] Instead, as contexts are described, we often make intuitive assumptions about the intended interpretation of various context-sensitive expressions. Just like standard contextualist theories, my semantics for epistemic vocabulary predicts specific ordinary language judgments when supplemented with these sorts of intuitive assumptions.

However, the case for my semantics goes beyond the fact that it delivers useful predictions when supplemented with such assumptions. In addition, my semantics delivers specific predictions when supplemented with independently motivated pragmatic principles. For example, according to my semantics, it is often the case that if multiple nested modals are interpreted relative to the same partition, they are equivalent to a single modal operator. The same goes for probability operators. For instance, suppose 'unlikely' and 'probable' in (31) are interpreted relative to the same partition:

(31)   It is unlikely that Jones is a probable hire.

According to the semantics for probability operators in §3.4, (31) would then have the same content as the following:

(32)   It is unlikely that Jones is a hire.

The maxim of manner dictates that we should charitably interpret (31) as having some meaning that could not have been more succinctly expressed using (32). Hence general pragmatic reasoning familiar from GRICE 1967 will lead us to interpret 'unlikely' and 'probable' in (31) relative to distinct partitions. This sort of pragmatic reasoning is defeasible, since the maxim of manner may be overruled by other conversational priorities. But we have pragmatic reason to expect that in many contexts, nested epistemic modals and nested probability operators will be interpreted as having cumulative readings.

Another supplementary observation is that certain constructions may themselves have a predictable pragmatic effect on the partition that context contributes to their interpretation. For instance, the following sentences predictably call attention to the question of whether it is the case that Jones smokes:

(33)   If Jones smokes, then Smith smokes.

(34)   Jones might smoke.

(35)   Jones probably smokes.

(36)   It is .3 likely that Jones smokes.

---

[17] For a related but more radical view of the limits of semantic and pragmatic theories, see the discussion of *pragmatic particularism* in SWANSON 2017.

In more formal terms, say that a partition is *decisive* with respect to a proposition p just in case each element of that partition entails either p or its negation. If the antecedent of a conditional is a simple sentence, we predictably interpret the conditional using a partition that is decisive with respect to the traditional propositional content of its antecedent. The same goes for epistemic modals and probability operators embedding simple sentences. Given this fact, it follows from my semantics that many sentences containing epistemic vocabulary are used to assert fairly simple probabilistic beliefs. For example, suppose that the probability operator in 'it is .3 likely that Jones smokes' is interpreted relative to a partition that is decisive with respect to whether Jones smokes. Then the content of this sentence will just be the set of probability spaces that assign .3 probability to the proposition that Jones smokes.[18] That is why it is often fine to say that Smith believes it is .3 likely that Jones smokes just in case Smith has .3 credence that Jones smokes. For many sentences in many contexts, my semantics delivers just the same contents as the tempting semantics for epistemic modals and probability operators described in §3.2. The same goes for the first pass semantics for conditionals described in §4.1. In subsequent chapters, sometimes I adopt the simplifying assumption that epistemic expressions embedding simple sentences are interpreted relative to partitions that are decisive with respect to the traditional propositional contents of those sentences, provided that this assumption does not make a difference to my arguments.

In addition to generalizations about the interpretation of nested and single occurrences of epistemic vocabulary, my semantics can be augmented with pragmatic generalizations about the interpretation of context-sensitive expressions. For example, it is hard to hear sentences such as (37) as expressing anything but a contradiction:

(37)   #Nobody danced and somebody danced.

The semantics for quantifiers does not itself entail that 'nobody' and 'somebody' must be interpreted relative to the same domain. Rather, there are pragmatic reasons why quantifier phrases in parallel constructions often share contextual restrictions. The same goes for epistemic and logical expressions. For example, speakers often interpret 'not' and 'might' in (38) relative to the same partition:

(38)   #It is not probably raining, and it might be probably raining.

---

[18]   See Appendix A.2 for a proof of this result.

In addition, speakers naturally interpret both occurrences of 'probably' in (38) relative to the same partition. As a result, it is hard to hear this sentence as expressing anything but a contradiction.

In addition to predictions of particular ordinary language judgments, my semantics is also supported by more general evidence suggesting that epistemic vocabulary is context sensitive. The behavior of epistemic vocabulary resembles the behavior of other context-sensitive expressions. For instance, the invalid inferences in §4.3 resemble inferences containing adverbs of quantification, such as the following:[19]

(39)   a. If Jones and Smith are together, they are usually happy.
       b. If Jones and Smith are not together, they are usually sad.
       c. Jones and Smith are either together or not together.
       d. #Therefore, Jones and Smith are usually happy, or they are usually sad.

The premises of (39) sound fine because they are naturally interpreted as talking about restricted situations, and the conclusion sounds bad because it is naturally interpreted as talking about Jones and Smith in general. A more complete pragmatic theory would derive my diagnosis of invalid inferences containing epistemic vocabulary from a more general explanation of the invalidity of many context-sensitive inferences.

Another argument for the context sensitivity of epistemic vocabulary is more theoretical in nature. I argued in §1.2 that the contents of belief play certain theoretical roles. For instance, you count as changing your mind about something just in case you believe inconsistent contents at different times. Also, subjects count as disagreeing with each other just in case they believe inconsistent contents. These theoretical roles can be used to distinguish the contents of epistemic sentences in different contexts. For example, suppose you assert (13) when talking about whether there is a net along the roof, and you assert (14) when talking about whether Jones is suicidal:

(13)   It is highly probable that if Jones jumps off the roof, she will die.

(14)   It is highly improbable that if Jones jumps off the roof, she will die.

In the later context, you need not have changed your mind about anything. In different contexts, you may use (13) or (14) to express consistent beliefs, namely because you may have high credence that Jones would jump only if there was a net along the roof, while also having high credence that there is no net. Similarly,

[19] See DUMMETT 1964 for a similar example involving tense operators, and see KOLODNY AND MACFARLANE 2010 for an example involving deontic modals.

someone who says (13) in one context and someone who says (14) in another context are not necessarily thereby disagreeing about likelihood facts. They may have consistent beliefs and differ only with respect to which beliefs they would use (13) to express. This intuitive absence of mind changing or disagreement suggests that (13) and (14) can have consistent contents as uttered in different contexts, which provides further evidence for my semantics for these sentences.

There is much left for future research on the pragmatics of epistemic vocabulary. A more complete pragmatic theory would deliver even stronger constraints on the interpretation of epistemic and logical vocabulary, and would derive these constraints from even more general principles. In addition, such constraints might eventually be connected with independently motivated theories of *questions under discussion* developed by GINZBURG 1994, ROBERTS 1996, and others. The semantic value of a question can be identified as the partition of logical space corresponding to its possible answers (cf. HAMBLIN 1973), and so the questions under discussion in a context could easily be related to the partitions supplied by that context to the interpretation of epistemic vocabulary. ROBERTS 2016 argues that facts about questions under discussion restrict our interpretation of probability operators, for instance. Roberts agrees with my observation in MOSS 2015 that certain sentences containing conditionals and probability operators are context sensitive, including sentences that closely resemble (13) and (14). According to Roberts, the interpretation of these sentences at a context may depend in part on the questions under discussion in that context, such as whether there is a net along the roof of your office building, or whether Jones is suicidal.

To sum up the big picture: in the first two chapters of this book, I argued that the contents of belief and assertion can be sets of probability spaces. In chapters 3 and 4, I argued that the semantic contents of sentences are sets of probability spaces. The semantic and pragmatic theories defended in these chapters provide a unified account of many distinctive features of epistemic vocabulary. They also give us a better grasp of exactly what sets of probability spaces are the contents of our ordinary beliefs and assertions. In the remaining chapters of this book, I argue for my third and final central thesis, namely that the contents of our probabilistic beliefs and assertions can also be contents of knowledge.

5

The case for probabilistic knowledge

5.1 The thesis that probabilistic beliefs can be knowledge

The first four chapters of this book argued for theses in the philosophy of mind and language—namely, that we can believe and assert probabilistic contents. The remaining chapters argue for the epistemological thesis that probabilistic beliefs can constitute knowledge. But before arguing for this thesis, I will make it more precise. In this section, I spell out what notions of *belief* and *knowledge* are under discussion, what it is for beliefs and knowledge to be *probabilistic*, what it is for beliefs to *constitute* knowledge, and what sense of possibility is at issue in the claim that beliefs *can* constitute knowledge.

The expressions 'belief' and 'knowledge' are commonly used both for mental states and for their contents. A content constitutes knowledge in the latter sense in virtue of being the content of a state that constitutes knowledge in the former sense. There is a mental state of believing that Jones probably smokes, for instance, and the content of this state can be knowledge. In particular, the state of believing that Jones probably smokes is the state of having credences that are contained in a certain set of probability spaces, such as the set of probability spaces that assign at least .5 probability to the proposition that Jones smokes. According to my first central thesis, this set of probability spaces is the content of your belief that Jones probably smokes. If my third central thesis is also correct, then this same set of probability spaces can be knowledge. Throughout this book, when I discuss my third central thesis, I talk as if probabilistic beliefs have probabilistic contents. But many of my arguments for probabilistic knowledge are independent of this thesis. If probabilistic beliefs turn out to be degreed attitudes toward propositions, the arguments in this chapter support the surprising claim that these degreed attitudes can constitute knowledge, in just the same way that full belief attitudes can.

What does it mean to say that probabilistic beliefs *constitute* knowledge? The short answer: just the same as whatever it traditionally means to say that beliefs constitute knowledge. The long answer: when we say that a belief state constitutes knowledge, we are saying that it is a mental state of a certain type. A belief may be this type of mental state only contingently or temporarily, since further evidence may undermine its content. Compare: "his fear may have once been legitimate, but now that he has more information, it *constitutes* paranoia." Some but not all fears have the property of constituting paranoid fears. Similarly, some but not all beliefs have the property of constituting knowledge.

Finally, what does it mean to say that probabilistic beliefs *can* constitute knowledge? The short answer: again, just the same as whatever it traditionally means to say that beliefs can constitute knowledge. The long answer: relevant contrasting possibility claims concern other types of mental states. The desire that Jones stop smoking cannot constitute knowledge, simply because desires are not the right sort of mental state to constitute knowledge. At most, a desire can have the same content as a belief that constitutes knowledge. By contrast, it is consistent with the nature of probabilistic beliefs that they constitute knowledge.

In this chapter, I argue that we can get probabilistic knowledge in all the familiar ways of getting knowledge, namely by testimony, perception, inference, memory, and *a priori* reflection. We can also fail to have probabilistic knowledge in familiar ways, such as when we are victims of intervening or environmental epistemic luck. Probabilistic beliefs can count as knowledge according to several traditional theories of knowledge. In addition, probabilistic knowledge plays an important role in many philosophical discussions outside epistemology. According to some theories of meaning, for instance, subjects must have probabilistic knowledge in order to grasp the meanings of certain expressions. According to some norms of assertion, subjects must have probabilistic knowledge in order to permissibly assert certain contents. Finally, the notion of probabilistic knowledge plays an important role in discussions about gender and speech, helping us identify problems with misguided conventional advice about how women should use language in ordinary conversation.

Each of my arguments for probabilistic knowledge depends on a pair of claims: that the beliefs under discussion are *probabilistic* and that they are *knowledge*. In some cases, I focus on the latter claim and rely on the reader to identify the beliefs under discussion as probabilistic beliefs. Sentences containing epistemic vocabulary often have multiple readings, including readings on which they express full beliefs about probabilities of some sort. In most examples in this chapter, sentences containing epistemic vocabulary are intended to be read as having *thoroughly probabilistic* contents. A thoroughly probabilistic content is a set of probability spaces that does not correspond to any proposition, and my thesis is that these contents can be knowledge. I assume throughout that the reader is familiar with the test battery for thoroughly probabilistic content described in §2.5, and I count on the reader to apply this test battery in order to identify the intended readings of epistemic sentences throughout.

5.2 Testimony

Given the thesis that we can assert probabilistic contents, testimony is perhaps the most straightforward source of probabilistic knowledge. For instance, consider the following example from VAN FRAASSEN 1981:

> [Judy Benjamin and her soldiers are] hopelessly lost. Using their radio they are at one point able to contact their own headquarters. After describing what they remember of their movements, they are told by the duty officer 'I don't know whether or not you have strayed into Red Army territory. But if you have, the probability is 3/4 that you are in their Headquarters Company Area.' (377)

Suppose that Judy Benjamin knows that the officer is an expert, and she completely trusts his opinion. Then intuitively she learns something when she listens to the radio, namely whatever the officer says. This content is something that she comes to know by testimony, something that she did not know before. Furthermore, the belief that Judy Benjamin thereby comes to share with the officer is not a full belief about her location. It is a probabilistic belief, namely a conditional credence. Given some natural assumptions about context, the content that the officer asserts is the set of probability spaces according to which it is .75 likely that Judy Benjamin is in the Red Army Headquarters Area, given that she is in Red Army territory. When she hears the officer's assertion, this probabilistic content is what Judy Benjamin comes to know. In this example and many others, speakers use epistemic vocabulary to assert thoroughly probabilistic contents, and others come to believe these contents on the basis of their testimony. Intuitively, there is no difference between the epistemic status of these beliefs and beliefs based on testimony stated without epistemic vocabulary. Beliefs conveyed using epistemic vocabulary are capable of constituting testimonial knowledge.

In addition to examining particular examples of testimony, we can derive the existence of probabilistic knowledge from general theories of testimony. For illustration, consider the following "naïve theory" of testimonial knowledge described in LACKEY 2003:

> For every speaker A and hearer B, B knows that p on the basis of A's testimony that p if and only if: (1) B believes that p on the basis of the content of A's testimony that p, (2) p is true, and (3) B has no defeaters for A's testimony that p. (707)

Probabilistic beliefs can straightforwardly satisfy conditions (1) and (3) of the naïve theory. For instance, after talking with her duty officer, Judy Benjamin is justified in having .75 conditional credence that she is in the Red Army Headquarters Area, given that she is in Red Army territory. Her justification for that belief would be defeated if she learned that the officer on the radio was a double agent, or if she overheard some Red Army soldiers saying that their Headquarters Area was far away. But as a matter of fact, she has no defeaters of the sort.

Condition (2) of the naïve theory is less straightforwardly satisfied. Can probabilistic beliefs be true? The short answer: yes, of course. The belief that Jones probably smokes is true just in case Jones probably smokes. The belief that it is .6 likely that Jones smokes is true just in case it is .6 likely that Jones smokes. And so on, for any probabilistic belief.

The long answer: many recent theories in metaethics and the philosophy of language assign non-truth-conditional contents to certain ordinary beliefs and assertions. Such theories often fit naturally with a deflationary theory of truth, according to which asserting that some content is true is nothing over and above asserting that content. The same goes for my probabilistic theory of belief and assertion. In chapter 6, I discuss the truth of probabilistic contents in much greater detail. For the immediate purpose of evaluating whether testimonial probabilistic beliefs can be knowledge, the important point is that ordinary intuitions do not support Lackey's condition (2) any more than they support condition (2′):

(2)   B knows that p on the basis of A's testimony that p only if p is true.

(2′)   B knows that p on the basis of A's testimony that p only if p.

Advocates of probabilistic knowledge may understand condition (2) as being equivalent to condition (2′). Like the conditions (1) and (3) of the naïve theory of testimonial knowledge, condition (2′) is not essentially restricted to propositional beliefs. The naïve theory therefore allows that probabilistic beliefs can constitute knowledge.

LACKEY 2003 challenges the naïve theory of testimonial knowledge with several counterexamples, each of which motivates an additional necessary condition on testimonial knowledge. Her additional necessary conditions also naturally extend to probabilistic beliefs. For example, Lackey argues that you can fail to get testimonial knowledge in virtue of being bad at distinguishing reliable sources of information from unreliable sources. In addition, you can fail to get testimonial knowledge from a reliable source in virtue of being in an environment where you could easily have received information from an unreliable source instead. Lackey concludes that in order to get testimonial knowledge, you must be appropriately sensitive to defeaters as you identify reliable sources of information, and your environment must be suitable for the reception of reliable testimony. These necessary conditions can be satisfied when you come to have probabilistic beliefs by testimony, provided that sources of probabilistic testimony can count as being reliable or unreliable. I develop relevant probabilistic analogs of traditional notions of reliability in §5.7. To sum up, some traditional theories of testimony regard certain features as necessary and sufficient for testimonial knowledge, and these features are indeed features that probabilistic beliefs can have.

5.3 Perception

According to a widely held view of testimony, testimony is merely a way of transmitting knowledge, never a way of generating it.[1] If that is correct, then saying that we can have testimonial probabilistic knowledge is just pushing the bump in the carpet. How does anyone get any probabilistic knowledge in the first place? The short answer is that you can get probabilistic knowledge in all the same ways you can get propositional knowledge. For instance, you can know probabilistic contents by perception. There are many theories about the contents of your perceptual experiences, including theories that say that these experiences have propositional contents, that they have probabilistic contents, or that they have no contents at all. According to any of these theories, perceptual experience can be a source of probabilistic knowledge.

Suppose that perceptual experiences do not have representational content. When you see a green piece of cloth under a white light, your visual experience does not represent it as being green. However, you may nevertheless come to believe that it is green on the basis of your experience. For instance, perhaps you believe a content on the basis of your perceptual experience just in case that content is *the way you take your environment to be* when your experience presents you with it. TRAVIS 2004 uses an analogy to spell out this sort of account of the cognitive role of perception. If you see Sid and Pia whispering together, you may take them to be trysting and thereby come to know that they are trysting, though your experience merely presents you with your environment, rather than with this content. Analogously, if you see a green piece of cloth, you may take it from your experience that the cloth is green and thereby come to know that it is green, though the content that it is green is not part of the content of your

---

[1] LACKEY 2008 provides an overview of recent literature endorsing this view of testimony, before going on to develop several dissenting arguments.

experience. This explanation of the cognitive role of perception extends equally well to perceptual beliefs with probabilistic content. Just as you may take Sid and Pia to be *trysting*, you may take them to be *probably trysting but possibly just flirting*. Analogously, just as you may take it from your visual experience that the cloth is *green*, you may take it that the cloth is *probably green*. Hence in just the same way that you come to know that the cloth is green, you may come to know that it is probably green on the basis of your perceptual experience.

On the other hand, suppose that perceptual experiences do have representational content. Following Siegel 2012, let us restrict our attention to visual perceptual experiences, and let us identify the *Content View* as the claim that these experiences have representational content. What should the Content View say about cases where you believe probabilistic contents on the basis of your perceptual experiences? According to one version of the Content View, perceptual experiences can only have propositional contents. Call this the *propositional content view*. If this view is correct, then the probabilistic contents that you believe on the basis of perception fall into two categories. First, you believe probabilistic contents that are logically entailed by the propositional contents of your perceptual experiences. For example, if you know by perception that a piece of cloth is green, you may thereby come to know by perception that it is probably green. Second, you believe probabilistic contents that are entailed by the contents of your perceptual experiences together with certain contents that you believe independent of any experience. To modify an example from Siegel 2017: if you see a ripe banana and know by perception that it has a certain shape and texture, and you antecedently know that it is probably yellow if it has that shape and texture, then intuitively you can know by perception that the banana is probably yellow. At first, one might be tempted to object that your knowledge that the banana is probably yellow is not true knowledge by perception, but merely knowledge by some combination of perception and other faculties. However, as Siegel 2017 puts it, "experiences that result from resolving ambiguities in pre-perceptual processing might be as direct as perception gets" (9). If your knowledge that the banana is probably yellow does not count as perceptual knowledge, then it may well turn out that you do not have very much perceptual knowledge at all. The natural conclusion of the propositional content view is that whether the content of your experience directly or indirectly entails that the cloth is probably green, your resulting belief that the cloth is probably green can constitute perceptual knowledge.

According to a second version of the Content View, perceptual experiences can have probabilistic contents. Call this the *probabilistic content view*. John Morrison introduces and defends the spirit of this view in Morrison 2014, in which he argues for the central thesis that "perceptual experiences assign degrees of confidence" (1). Strictly speaking, I do not want to attribute the view that experiences have probabilistic contents to Morrison, as his view is consistent with the claim that we should instead "replace the perceptual entertaining relation with a series of relations indexed to various degrees of confidence, such as perceptually-entertains-with-fifty-percent-confidence and perceptually-entertains-with-forty-percent-confidence" (33). According to Morrison, it may turn out that both perception and belief are degreed relations to propositional contents, rather than simple relations to probabilistic contents as described in §1.2. Although he doesn't endorse the probabilistic content view of perception, I still want to give credit to Morrison for introducing and defending the central insight behind it, namely that experiences can be probabilistic in the same way that beliefs are. In what follows, I simplify my discussion by assuming that such probabilistic experiences are best understood as experiences with probabilistic contents, just as probabilistic beliefs are best understood as beliefs with probabilistic contents.[2]

For illustration, consider the claim in JEFFREY 1968 that "in examining a piece of cloth by candlelight one might come to attribute probabilities .6 and .4 to the propositions G that the cloth is green and B that it is blue, without there being any proposition E for which the direct effect of the observation is anything near changing the observer's degree of belief in E to 1" (172). The probabilistic content view provides one simple account of what happens when you see the cloth, namely that your experience has the content that the cloth is probably green and thereby directly constrains you to have high credence that it is green. In other words, you do not end up with high credence that the cloth is green as a result of coming to believe some propositional content of your experience. It is not that the cloth looks as if it is some very specific shade of blue-green and you infer from how the cloth looks that it is probably green. It simply looks to you as if the cloth is probably green.

The probabilistic content view raises an important question: how are you supposed to learn from your experiences, if not by conditionalizing on their propositional contents? If the content of your experience is that the cloth is .6 likely to be green, you could update your credences by Jeffrey conditionalizing on that content, as suggested in JEFFREY 1968. If the content is an arbitrary set of probability spaces, you could update your credences on that content using generalizations of Jeffrey conditionalization.[3] There are many open questions

---

[2] Aligning herself with Morrison, MUNTON 2016 provides additional arguments for the claim that "our visual experience . . . assigns degrees of confidence" (17). For further discussion, see also the penultimate paragraph of PAUTZ 2016.

[3] See DIACONIS AND ZABELL 1982 for an introductory discussion of procedures for updating your credences on arbitrary probabilistic contents.

about procedures for rationally updating your credences on arbitrary probabilistic contents. But these questions are mostly orthogonal to the conclusion of our present discussion, namely that however you come to have knowledge by perception, you can thereby come to have perceptual probabilistic knowledge.

5.4 Arguments for probabilistic contents of experience

The claim that you have probabilistic knowledge by perception does not depend on the claim that perceptual experiences have probabilistic contents. To reiterate, just as you may know by perception that a banana is yellow in virtue of knowing related facts about its shape and texture by perception, you may know by perception that a banana is probably yellow in virtue of knowing related propositional contents by perception. However, it would be especially nice for advocates of probabilistic knowledge if some perceptual experiences did have probabilistic contents, since then an experience could ground your knowledge of its content directly, without the help of any antecedent knowledge. In addition, the probabilistic content view of perception fits naturally with the central theses of this book. If contents of belief and assertion can be probabilistic, why not also contents of experience? In light of these connections, it is worth considering arguments for the probabilistic content view. In this section, I describe several arguments favoring the probabilistic over the propositional content view of perception.[4]

A couple of arguments for the probabilistic content view are conditional in nature. Some traditional arguments for the view that *experiences have contents* also support the view that *some experiences have probabilistic contents*. If these traditional arguments are good arguments for the Content View, then they are equally good arguments for the probabilistic content view. For instance, one might argue for the Content View on the grounds that it provides the best explanation of perceptual illusions. The first line of the Müller-Lyer illusion looks shorter than the second when you don't know that the case is a visual illusion. But in addition, the first line continues to look shorter even after you learn that the case is illusory. In his critical discussion of the argument from illusion, BYRNE 2009 sums up the argument as follows: even once you believe the lines have equal length, "the (mis-)information that the lines are unequal is perceptually available, and [the Content View] apparently has a neat diagnosis of the situation" (438), namely that the proposition that the first line is shorter continues to be part of the content of your visual experience.

---

[4] As I see it, these arguments are not conclusive. Because the arguments play a limited dialectical role in my overall project, I merely record them here without evaluating their merits.

If this argument for the Content View succeeds, one might equally well argue for the probabilistic content view on the grounds that it provides the best explanation of probabilistic perceptual illusions.[5] For instance, suppose that you are looking at the standard Müller-Lyer illusion, and imagine that you don't know that the case is a visual illusion. The first line looks shorter than the second, and so you believe it is shorter. Now suppose that we start to modify the illusion by gradually increasing the length of the first line. At some point, you will start to have merely some fairly high credence that the first line is shorter on the basis of your visual experience. In more colloquial terms, it can look to you like the first line is *probably* shorter than the second, though not *definitely* shorter. The argument for the probabilistic content view proceeds as follows: in the same sense as before, the first line will *continue* to look probably shorter even once you have been informed that it is actually longer than the second line. The content that the first line is probably shorter is a probabilistic content. This content continues to be perceptually available to you, even after you no longer believe it. The best explanation of this informational remainder is that the content that the first line is probably shorter is part of the content of your visual experience.

A second conditional argument in favor of the probabilistic content view concerns ordinary talk about the way things look. Following CHISHOLM 1957, JACKSON 1977 pulls apart three senses of 'looks' in ordinary language, distinguishing its phenomenal use from its comparative and epistemic uses. According to Jackson, saying that things look some way does not always mean we should infer from how they look that they are that way, or that they look the way things normally look when they are that way. The Content View is attractive insofar as it helps us make sense of the claim that things look some particular way in a distinctive phenomenal sense, namely by interpreting it as the claim that it is part of the content of your visual experience that things are that way.[6]

If this argument for the Content View succeeds, one might equally well argue for the probabilistic content view on the grounds that it makes sense of ordinary uses of 'looks' that embed epistemic vocabulary. In our modified illusion case, saying that it looks like the first line is probably shorter than the second does not mean that we should infer from how it looks that it is probably shorter, since we may well know that we are experiencing an illusion and that we should not infer conclusions about the length of the lines from how they look. Also, saying that it looks like the first line is probably shorter does not mean that the lines look

---

[5] MORRISON 2014 also defends this claim, although not using the sort of argument I give here.
[6] SCHELLENBERG 2011 and BROGAARD 2011 defend the Content View using arguments roughly in this spirit.

the way lines normally look when one is probably shorter than the other, since it may well be that when one line is probably shorter than another, normally neither line is flanked by illusion-inducing line segments. The probabilistic content view is attractive insofar as it helps us make sense of the claim that *it looks like the first line is probably shorter*, namely by interpreting it as the claim that *it is part of the content of your visual experience that the first line is probably shorter*. To sum up, the contents of experience have been assumed to play various theoretical roles, such as explaining perceptual illusions and grounding facts about the way things look, and these roles can just as well be played by probabilistic contents.

In addition to extending traditional arguments for the Content View to argu-ments for the probabilistic content view, one can argue for the latter on its own merits. For instance, MORRISON 2014 defends the spirit of the probabilistic content view using examples in which you form probabilistic beliefs by *completely trusting* your perceptual experiences. For example, say you see someone walking toward you in the distance. As the person approaches, you gradually increase your credence that it is your friend Isaac. According to Morrison, you may completely trust your experience with respect to whether it's Isaac and thereby "end up with slightly more doxastic confidence that it's Isaac than not. Say: fifty-five percent" (19), and the best explanation of your .55 credence is that your experience assigns .55 probability to the proposition that the approaching person is Isaac.

As I understand it, the central argument of MORRISON 2014 rests on an analogy between perceptual experience and testimony. Morrison spells out the analogy as follows:

> What is it to *completely trust* your experience? When you completely trust a doctor, plumber, or rabbi, you follow her advice . . . Continuing this pattern, when you completely trust an experience you endorse the way it presents objects . . . We regularly trust our experiences to lesser and greater extents, making this a limit case of a familiar phenomenon. (17)

The upshot of this passage is that by comparing the content of perception with the advice of experts, we may see that a theory of the latter may provide a model for a theory of the former. Assume that when you get expert testimony that something is .55 likely, you may completely trust that testimony and thereby end up with .55 credence in some proposition. According to the theory of assertion defended in the first four chapters of this book, the content that you believe on the basis of the testimony is in fact the probabilistic content of the testimony itself. If the analogous claim holds for perceptual experience, we may conclude that the content that you believe when you completely trust your experience is in fact the probabilistic content of your experience. Hence some perceptual experiences have probabilistic contents.

According to the opposing propositional content view, you come to have .55 credence that the approaching person is Isaac because you come to believe the propositional content of your experience, perhaps something about the shape and color of the approaching figure, and you adjust your credences in light of that information and your antecedent probabilistic beliefs about what Isaac looks like. Morrison rejects this opposing view on the grounds that "it doesn't seem as though you're relying on an antecedent belief. All other things being equal, that's a reason to think you're not . . . Introspection is fallible, but it still provides valuable evidence about why we form certain beliefs" (23–4). As I see it, this argument for the probabilistic content view is unfortunately not very decisive. Advocates of the propositional content view may concede that it does not seem to you that you are deriving your .55 credence from any standing beliefs, while maintaining that this merely demonstrates that you do not have introspective access to the sub-personal derivation of your perceptual beliefs. By analogy, it may simply seem to you that a sentence is ungrammatical, without seeming as if you are deriving this conclusion from general principles of grammar—but roughly speaking, that is only because you do not have introspective access to the rules represented in the language module, despite their active role in determining your syntactic judgments.

That being said, even if the propositional content view of your Isaac experience is not motivated by introspection, it might be motivated by theoretical claims about the nature of the objects and properties represented in experience. For some theorists, it might be a theoretical virtue or an operational constraint that the contents of experience concern ordinary objects and properties. If the contents of your perceptual experience in the Isaac case are propositions, what sorts of properties could they concern? At best, they might be conjunctions of demonstrative propositions to the effect that the approaching object has *exactly that three-dimensional shape* and *exactly that arrangement of surface colors* and *exactly that motion pattern*. By contrast, probabilistic contents may directly concern whether the object is *Isaac*. To give another example, suppose an infant is watching as an object approaches. On the probabilistic content view, the object may look as if it *might be Mama*, as opposed to looking as if it has some particular arrangement of surface colors. This argument turns one potential consideration in favor of the propositional content view on its head. The propositional content view might at first appear to be supported by the thought that probabilistic contents are too complex to be contents of experience. But in certain conceptual respects, the contents assigned by the probabilistic content view are in fact simpler than those assigned by the propositional content view.

A final potential argument favoring the probabilistic over the propositional content view concerns the best interpretation of scientific theories of perception.

Suppose that there is a noisy bright object nearby. How do you integrate the visual and auditory features of the object when you form opinions about where it is located? According to one compelling Bayesian approach to human visual perception, you rely on your prior conditional credences that you will receive various visual and auditory signals, conditional on hypotheses about the location of the object.[7] There are three sorts of contents that play a role in this approach to multisensory integration. Any of these contents could in principle be identified as contents of your perceptual experience. First, there are propositional contents corresponding to your separate visual and auditory signals. Second, there is the probabilistic content corresponding to the posterior credence distribution that integrates these signals. Finally, according to some theories, there is another propositional content intended to represent the state of the world that most closely corresponds to your posterior credences about where the object is located. This third content is supposed to play an important role in your practical reasoning, such as your forming an intention to reach for the object in one location rather than another.

To give a simple example, suppose that you see and hear an object that is just out of reach. As it happens, your senses conflict: you see the object as being ten inches away from your hand, but you hear it as being four inches away. As a result, you would say that the object is possibly four inches but probably closer to ten inches away, and you reach for the object by moving your hand exactly eight inches. There are three sorts of contents that might count as being the content of your perceptual experience. The contents of your experience might include the proposition that the object is ten inches away and the proposition that it is four inches away, or the probabilistic content that the object is possibly four but probably closer to ten inches away, or the proposition that the object is eight inches away. As you move your hand, one might say that you are acting as if this third propositional content is true.

At first glance, the third sort of content might appear to be a good candidate for the content of your perceptual experience. And indeed, this interpretation of theories of multisensory integration is suggested by ROTHKOPF ET AL. 2010 in the following passage:

> Given that *perceptually we experience a single state of the world* instead of a posterior distribution over possible scene parameters, the posterior distribution has to be utilized to come to a single estimate corresponding to the perceived scene. Similarly,

---

[7] For an introductory discussion of this Bayesian approach to visual perception, see MAMASSIAN ET AL. 2002.

when an action is required such as reaching for a point in the scene, a single direction of motion of the hand has to be obtained from the entire probability distribution.

(34, my emphasis)

Applying a loss function to your posterior credence distribution collapses that distribution into a hypothesis with propositional content, such as the proposition that a certain object is eight inches away. According to Rothkopf et al., this propositional content is the single state of the world that you perceptually experience.

However, on closer inspection, the practice of deriving propositions from posterior credence distributions seems to be an artifact of the perceived need for perceptual experience to deliver propositional contents, rather than the other way around. According to Rothkopf et al., you reach for an object on the basis of some propositional belief about its location. But suppose that in fact, you act on the basis of *credences* rather than propositional beliefs. Then you do not act on the basis of any proposition to the effect that the object is at a certain location. This criticism of Rothkopf et al. is suggested by KNILL AND POUGET 2004 as they argue that "the brain represents sensory information probabilistically" (712). According to Knill and Pouget, the opposing propositional content view is "intuitive but also misleading. This intuition might be due to the apparent 'oneness' of our perceptual world and the need to 'collapse' perceptual representations into discrete actions, such as decisions or motor behaviors" (712). A naïve experimental model of how you integrate sensory information might identify hypotheses about where you fully believe an object is located, and then use these hypotheses together with a generic loss function to make predictions that are confirmed or disconfirmed by the motion of your hand. But this sort of model neglects the fact that whether you reach for an object in one location or another depends not only on your opinions about where the object is located, but also on your utility function. A more sophisticated experimental model would instead identify hypotheses about your credences about where an object is located, and then use these hypotheses together with information about your utility function to predict the motion of your hand. The content of your experience should not then be identified with any proposition corresponding to the predicted motion of your hand, since the latter depends on your utility function while the former intuitively does not.[8]

To return to our simple example, the fact that you move your hand exactly eight inches toward an object may depend on facts that have nothing to do with where you perceive the object to be. Suppose that the object is a whirring desktop fan that you would like to adjust. If you would say that the fan is possibly four but

---

[8] See MALONEY 2002 for sympathetic discussion of this sort of argument, as well as further discussion of alternative candidate contents of perceptual experience.

probably closer to ten inches away, then you might move your hand only a fraction more than four inches closer to it. But if the object is a dollar bill being carried away by the wind, then you might well move your hand much farther. Does this mean that you perceive the dollar bill as being farther away than the desktop fan? The intuitive answer is that it does not. The content of your experience is not best identified with the proposition corresponding to the predicted motion of your hand. The motion of your hand is the product of your credences and utilities, and the content of your experience is independent of the latter.

In light of these observations, there are two remaining candidates for the contents of experience: propositional contents corresponding to your separate visual and auditory signals, and the probabilistic content corresponding to the posterior distribution that integrates these signals. An empirical argument for the probabilistic content view emerges. Suppose that a single content of perception can include integrated information from multiple sensory modalities.[9] Then this content is not the propositional content of just one visual or auditory signal, and so the perceptual content must be probabilistic. To put it roughly, if you can not only perceive that something is a noisy object and perceive that it is a bright object, but also perceive the content that it is a noisy and bright object, then features of the posterior distribution that integrates auditory and visual signals are good candidates for the contents of your experience. The same goes not just for the integration of auditory and visual signals, but also for the integration of signals from one sensory modality, such as the integration of visual features like color and shape. Assuming you can perceive that something is a red triangle, for instance, then the contents of your experience are best understood as being fundamentally probabilistic in character. These probabilistic contents may often correspond to full beliefs that you have on the basis of your experiences. But just like contents of belief and assertion, the contents of perceptual experience can also include thoroughly probabilistic contents.

The foregoing empirical argument for the probabilistic content view is modest, since it depends on two controversial premises. First, the argument assumes that the contents of perceptual experience play some role in psychological theories of perceptual experience. Against this premise, one might argue that when psychologists talk about "perceptual representation" or what "we perceptually experience," as in the passages quoted above, they are not talking about the contents of

---

[9] For further discussion of this assumption, see TYE 2003. As Tye puts it, "phenomenal unity is a matter of simultaneously experienced perceptual qualities entering into the same *phenomenal content*" (36).

perceptual experience.[10] Second, the argument assumes that the contents of perceptual experience are rich enough to include integrated features of objects. If both of these controversial premises are correct, though, then there is some empirical support for the view that perceptual experiences can have probabilistic contents—namely, the contents corresponding to properties of probabilistic distributions that integrate signals received by one or more of your sensory modalities.

5.5 Other sources of knowledge

In addition to testimony and perception, you can get probabilistic knowledge from inference, memory, and *a priori* reflection. For instance, probabilistic knowledge can be based on inferences from premises without any epistemic vocabulary:

(1) a. Jones smokes.
     b. Therefore, it is not less than .5 likely that Jones smokes.

The same goes for inferences from premises containing epistemic vocabulary:

(2) a. If it is almost certainly raining, it is unlikely that Jones is skiing.
     b. It is almost certainly raining.
     c. Therefore, it is unlikely that Jones is skiing.

And the same goes for mixed inferences from premises of both sorts:

(3) a. If it is raining, it is unlikely that Jones is skiing.
     b. It is raining.
     c. Therefore, it is unlikely that Jones is skiing.

Each of these inferences has a valid reading with a thoroughly probabilistic conclusion.[11] Furthermore, there is no intuitive epistemic difference between these inferences and inferences that do not contain epistemic vocabulary. Just like inferences that conclude with simple sentences, each of the above inferences is capable of yielding inferential knowledge.

Probabilistic knowledge can also be based on inferences from knowledge of facts about various sorts of probability functions. For example, probabilistic knowledge can be derived from knowledge of facts about objective chances.

---

[10] MORRISON 2014 rejects empirical arguments for the probabilistic content view on roughly these grounds.

[11] For further discussion of the probabilistic contents of the sentences in these inferences, see my semantics for probability operators in §3.4 and my semantics for indicative conditionals in §4.2.

Suppose you have .9 conditional credence that it will rain, given that the objective chance of rain is .9. If your conditional credence constitutes knowledge, and you know that the objective chance of rain is .9, then you can know by inference that it is .9 likely to rain. Similarly, probabilistic knowledge can be derived from knowledge of facts about the subjective probabilities of experts, and even derived from knowledge of facts about statistical frequencies. If you know that the next canary you see is just as likely to be yellow as an arbitrary canary, and you know that an arbitrary canary is highly likely to be yellow, then you may know by inference that it is highly likely that the next canary you see will be yellow.[12]

Just like full beliefs, probabilistic beliefs constitute inferential knowledge only under certain conditions. For starters, you must know the premises of an inference in order to have inferential knowledge of its conclusion. In addition, gaining knowledge by inference may require that you know that the premises of the inference entail its conclusion, or that you knowingly validly infer the conclusion from the premises. Whatever extra conditions apply, they can be satisfied when the result of your inference is a thoroughly probabilistic belief, in which case that belief will be inferential probabilistic knowledge.

In addition to inference, memory is a source of probabilistic knowledge. A lot of recent literature on the rational updating of credences simply takes it as a starting assumption that memory preserves credences, just as it preserves full beliefs. The theory of updating that I defend in Moss 2012c reinforces this starting assumption by defending a detailed analogy between memory and testimony. According to my preferred theory of *de se* updating, having beliefs based on memory is like having beliefs based on a hypothetical conversation with your former self, where this hypothetical conversation includes probabilistic contents of assertion. Insofar as there are deep analogies between beliefs based on memory and beliefs based on testimony, it is natural to accept that the former can include the same sort of knowledge as the latter.

Finally, probabilistic beliefs can constitute *a priori* knowledge. The simplest examples are beliefs in trivial contents. Just as you can know from the armchair that either Jones smokes or Jones doesn't smoke, you can know from the armchair that either it is at least .6 likely that Jones smokes or it is less than .6 likely that Jones smokes. Just as the theorems of propositional logic are trivial propositional contents, the consequences of the probability axioms are trivial probabilistic contents. Whether they are propositional or probabilistic, beliefs with trivial contents can have just the same intuitive epistemic status.

---

[12] For further discussion of the relation between probabilistic knowledge and knowledge of objective chance facts, see §6.5. For further discussion of probabilistic knowledge by statistical inference, see §8.4.

In addition to trivial contents, certain substantive probabilistic contents might also constitute *a priori* knowledge. For instance, suppose you have observed hundreds of emeralds, and all of these emeralds have been green. On the basis of your observations, you are intuitively justified in having high credence that the next emerald you find will be green. Why is your high credence justified? After all, your observations are consistent with the hypothesis that all emeralds are *grue*, in which case the next emerald you find will be blue (cf. GOODMAN 1955). According to the objective Bayesian, the answer is that there are substantive constraints on the prior probability distributions of rational agents. As a result, you may be *a priori* justified in believing that the hypothesis that all emeralds are green is more likely than the hypothesis that all emeralds are grue. Intuitively, this probabilistic belief is not merely justified. It has just the same epistemic status as full beliefs that are known by induction. For objective Bayesians, the natural conclusion is that some rational constraints on prior probability distributions can be *a priori* knowledge.

5.6 Justified true belief without knowledge

It is important to distinguish *justified degrees of belief* and *degrees of justification of belief*. Even if you are perfectly rational, your credence in a proposition may not match the degree to which you are justified in believing it. To take a simple example from WEATHERSON 2014, suppose you are about to flip a fair coin, and you form the outright belief that it will land heads. Although you do not have any justification at all for your outright belief, you are justified in having some credence that the coin landed heads. Justified credences are not degrees of justification of anything.

The proper relationship between credences and degrees of justification is in fact the same as the relationship between full beliefs and degrees of justification. Some of your full beliefs are justified to a greater extent than others, and the same goes for credences and other probabilistic beliefs. For example, suppose that the soldier Judy Benjamin enters the jungle with an unjustified hunch that it is .75 likely that she is in the Red Army Headquarters Area if she is in Red Army territory. She might then see several flags on nearby trees, and remember that such markers are about three times as likely to be seen in the Red Army Headquarters Area as in the rest of the Red Army territory. These observations would provide Benjamin with some justification for her conditional credences. If Benjamin also calls her duty officer on the radio, and he asserts the probabilistic content of her belief, then his testimony will provide her with further justification for her belief in that content.

Among the intuitive parallels between justified full beliefs and justified probabilistic beliefs, one is especially important for our purposes. There are cases in which justified probabilistic beliefs fail to be epistemically good, and they fail in just the same way that justified full beliefs fail to constitute knowledge. Consider the following example adapted from Moss 2013:

> _Nerves_: Alice enters a psychology study with her friend Bert. As part of the study, some participants are injected with a heavy dose of adrenaline, while the others are injected with a saline solution. All participants are then sent to meet their friends. Alice is not told anything about the nature of the injection or the experiment. As it happens, Alice receives the adrenaline injection. As she meets Bert, Alice reflects on her fluttering nerves and comes to have high credence that she finds Bert attractive. And indeed, she probably does find Bert attractive.[13]

Alice's high credence that she finds Bert attractive is justified on the basis of her inference to the best explanation of her fluttering nerves. In addition, since Alice probably finds Bert attractive, her credences are the correct ones to have. But intuitively, her high credence that she finds Bert attractive is still deficient in some respect. As a symptom of this deficiency, notice that the following is intuitively false:

(4)   Alice knows that she probably finds Bert attractive.

After all, we may stipulate that Alice could easily have received an injection that would have left her without any fluttering nerves, and hence without the belief that she probably finds Bert attractive. Like the full beliefs of subjects in GETTIER 1963, Alice's justified high credence is the result of epistemic luck.

To give another example, suppose that when Judy Benjamin calls for information about her location, the officer on the radio is in fact a double agent. The agent is trying to lead her into danger by talking as if the Red Army Headquarters Area is located where the Green Safe Zone is actually located, and vice versa. But the double agent is color-blind and has misread the original map that indicates which area is the Red Army Headquarters Area and which is the Green Safe Zone. As a result, the double agent ends up telling Benjamin just what she would have heard from a friendly officer. Benjamin is justified in having .75 conditional credence that she is in the Red Army Headquarters Area if she is in Red Army territory. Suppose that it is indeed .75 likely that she is in the Red Army Headquarters Area if she is in Red Army territory. Intuitively, her probabilistic belief is still deficient in some respect. Although her belief is true and justified, it does not

---

[13] For a famous real-life experiment demonstrating the misattribution of arousal by study participants, see DUTTON AND ARON 1974.

constitute probabilistic knowledge. Like Alice, Judy Benjamin has gotten lucky. As PRITCHARD 2006 would put it, both Alice and Judy Benjamin have true probabilistic beliefs as a result of *intervening* epistemic luck.

In addition to intervening luck, justified probabilistic beliefs may result from *environmental* epistemic luck.[14] Consider the following variation on the example described above:

> *Fake Letters*: Alice enters a psychology study with her friend Bert. As part of the study, each participant is given a detailed survey of romantic questions about their friend. After the study is over, each participant is informed of the probability that they find their friend attractive. Several disgruntled lab assistants have started mailing out fake letters, telling nearly every participant that they probably find their friend attractive. Alice happens to receive a letter from a diligent lab assistant. Her letter correctly reports that she probably does find Bert attractive. Alice reads the letter and comes to have high credence that she finds Bert attractive.

Again, Alice's probabilistic belief is justified, but it does not constitute knowledge. The same goes for many probabilistic beliefs held by subjects in traditional counterexamples to the justified-true-belief analysis of knowledge. Consider the case of Henry from GOLDMAN 1976. Henry is driving through fake barn country, surrounded by barn facades that look like real barns when viewed from the road. As it happens, Henry is looking at a real barn. His high credence that he is looking at a barn is justified. But since almost all the apparent barns around him are fake, his high credence isn't knowledge. The same goes for Smith from GETTIER 1963. Smith has a justified false belief that Jones owns a Ford and a justified false belief that Brown is not in Barcelona. Smith is justified in having high credence that either Jones owns a Ford or Brown is in Barcelona, on the basis of his justified high credence in the first disjunct. But Smith doesn't know that this disjunction is likely, even though the disjunction is likely and Smith has a justified belief that it is likely. In many traditional cases of mere justified true belief, subjects have accompanying probabilistic beliefs that fail to constitute knowledge. At the same time, the examples of Alice and Judy Benjamin demonstrate that probabilistic Gettier cases need not have this structure. Alice may not fully believe that she finds Bert attractive, and Judy Benjamin may not have any full belief corresponding to her conditional credence about where she is located if she is in Red Army territory. Failures of probabilistic knowledge are not always directly parasitic on failures of propositional knowledge.[15]

---

[14] For discussion of the distinction between intervening and environmental luck, see PRITCHARD 2008.

[15] For further discussion of probabilistic Gettier cases, see KONEK 2016 and NISSAN-ROZEN 2016.

To sum up so far, some probabilistic beliefs are perfectly justified but still epistemically deficient. The third central thesis of this book provides an intuitive explanation of their deficiency: these beliefs fail to constitute knowledge. This explanation is not only intuitive, but is also entailed by general theories about why beliefs fail to constitute knowledge in Gettier cases. To give just one example, PRITCHARD 2005 argues that epistemic luck is incompatible with knowledge because lucky beliefs fail to meet *safety* conditions on knowledge. In particular, Pritchard argues that if you know that *p*, then in all nearby possible worlds where you form your belief about whether *p* in the same way, if you believe that *p* then it is true that *p* (163). This safety condition may be applied to probabilistic beliefs. For instance, in the case of *Nerves* described above, there are nearby worlds where Alice probably does not find Bert attractive, but where she still believes that she probably finds him attractive on the basis of her fluttering nerves. Hence it follows from the safety condition that her probabilistic belief does not constitute knowledge.

Applying the safety condition to probabilistic beliefs raises an important question: what does it mean to say that probabilistic beliefs are true at a world? I address this question in detail in §7.5. For present purposes, it is enough that we have an ordinary understanding of various modal constructions embedding epistemic vocabulary. For instance, it is perfectly intelligible to suppose that Alice could have easily believed that she probably found Bert attractive even if she hadn't probably found him attractive, and vice versa. In extending the safety condition for knowledge to probabilistic beliefs, we may rely on intuitions stated in natural language without giving a formal semantics for that language, and the same goes for other modal conditions on probabilistic knowledge.

5.7 Traditional theories of knowledge

As argued in §5.2–3, probabilistic beliefs can be knowledge according to traditional theories of testimony and perception. Probabilistic beliefs can also be knowledge according to more general theories of knowledge. JOYCE 2005 defends a similar sort of conclusion about evidence. Although Joyce does not discuss knowledge, he suggests that many traditional theories of evidence can easily be extended to probabilistic contents:

> [Some Bayesians] might go reliabilist and argue that a person's evidence is found in those invariant features of her credal state that were produced by belief-forming mechanisms that assign high credences to truths and low credences to falsehoods. Others might claim that some constraints are just 'given' in experience. There are

other options as well: indeed, almost everything epistemologists have had to say about the nature of evidence can be imported into the Bayesian framework. (157)

This section surveys a handful of traditional theories of knowledge, one from each of the last four decades. Each theory can be applied to probabilistic beliefs as well as propositional beliefs. In this sense, probabilistic knowledge bridges a deep schism between traditional and formal epistemology. As described by SPOHN 2012, the schism arises because "Bayesianism misses beliefs [and hence] misses all the things related to belief and, worst of all, knowledge. Small wonder that the traditional epistemologist finds Bayesianism useless" (44). The apparent impossibility of bridging this schism provides the central motivation for the development of ranking theory in SPOHN 2012. But if probabilistic beliefs can be knowledge, ranking functions are not essential to the reconciliation of traditional and formal epistemology. The very same useful features of knowledge are held in common by propositional and probabilistic beliefs.

To begin our survey, consider the reliabilist theory defended in GOLDMAN 1976. According to Goldman, beliefs constitute knowledge only if they are produced by reliable cognitive mechanisms, where "to be reliable, a cognitive mechanism must enable a person to *discriminate* or *differentiate* between incompatible states of affairs" (771). This account can be used to explain why some probabilistic beliefs constitute knowledge and others do not. For example, Alice does not know on the basis of her fluttering nerves that she probably finds Bert attractive, because her nerves do not enable her to discriminate her actual state of affairs from relevant alternatives, such as the state of affairs where her nerves are fluttering merely as a response to an adrenaline injection that she receives even though she probably does not find Bert attractive at all. By contrast, suppose your color vision is reliable. As you look at a cloth that is probably green, your visual experience enables you to discriminate the cloth being probably green from relevant alternatives, such as the cloth being probably red. That is why you can know that the cloth is probably green just by looking at it. As a result of your ability to visually discriminate various states of affairs, your color vision is reliable in the following sense: it generally produces probabilistic beliefs that are *true*.

The passage from JOYCE 2005 quoted at the start of this section suggests a second definition of reliability for cognitive mechanisms producing credences. A mechanism that produces credences could also count as reliable in virtue of generally producing credences that are *accurate*. According to this second definition, your color vision is reliable not because you generally believe that something is probably green whenever it is probably green, but because you generally believe that something is probably green whenever *it is green*. This second definition of reliability is not the same as the first. The most significant difference is that the truth-based condition is thoroughly probabilistic, whereas the accuracy-based condition is not. There is no set of worlds corresponding to the claim that a certain piece of cloth is probably green if and only if you believe that it is probably green, namely because there is no set of worlds corresponding to the claim that the cloth is probably green. Similarly, there is no set of worlds corresponding to the claim that *your probabilistic beliefs are generally true*. By contrast, the claim that *your probabilistic beliefs are generally accurate* corresponds to the set of worlds where you generally have high credences in true propositions and low credences in false propositions. For present purposes, I will not take a stand on which definition of reliability should be preferred. Either definition could in principle be used to extend reliabilism to probabilistic belief.

Nozick 1981 defends another necessary condition for knowledge, namely the following *sensitivity* condition: S knows, via method (or way of believing) M, that p only if "if p weren't true and S were to use M to arrive at a belief whether (or not) p, then S wouldn't believe, via M, that p" (179). As discussed in §5.2, one can eliminate 'true' from this sort of condition on the basis of a deflationary theory of truth. For example, one can say that Alice does not know that she probably finds Bert attractive, because she would have believed that she probably found him attractive on the basis of her fluttering nerves, regardless of whether she probably found him attractive. By contrast, you can know by perception that a piece of cloth is probably green, as long as the following condition holds:

(5) If you looked to see whether the cloth was probably green and it wasn't probably green, then you wouldn't end up believing that it was probably green.

The sentence (5) has several readings, including readings on which it merely concerns facts about the objective chance function, or facts about what is probable given some contextually determined body of evidence. For present purposes, the intended interpretation of (5) is one on which its antecedent has a thoroughly probabilistic content. For instance, you might encounter the intended interpretation of (5) in an argument used to justify having high credence that the cloth is green. "It must be probable that the cloth is green, because you believe it's probable, and if it weren't probable, then you wouldn't believe that it was." If this argument is interpreted as supporting the thoroughly probabilistic content that the cloth is probably green, then in the context of this argument, (5) states a sensitivity condition for thoroughly probabilistic knowledge. By comparison, it may be useful to note that sensitivity conditions such as (5) resemble a condition for moral knowledge defended by Blackburn 1996. Just as I use epistemic vocabulary to state the above sensitivity condition for probabilistic knowledge, Blackburn uses moral vocabulary to state his reliability condition: "Am I reliable? If Alaric had not behaved well I should not be going around thinking that he did" (88). In both cases, one states necessary conditions for knowledge of certain contents by using the same sort of vocabulary used to assert those very contents themselves.[16]

PLANTINGA 1993 defends necessary and sufficient conditions for a belief to be warranted, where sufficiently warranted true beliefs constitute knowledge:

> B has warrant for you if and only if (1) the cognitive faculties involved in the production of B are functioning properly... (2) your cognitive environment is sufficiently similar to the one for which your cognitive faculties are designed... [(3)] the design plan governing the production of the belief in question involves, as purpose or function, the production of true beliefs... (4) the design plan is a good one. (194)

The first and second of these four conditions straightforwardly apply to the production of probabilistic beliefs. The third condition can be restated without mentioning truth, so that it simply requires that the design plan governing the production of the belief B involves, as purpose or function, the production of an arbitrary belief that p only if it is indeed the case that p. As for the fourth condition, Plantinga himself extends this condition to design plans governing the production of credences. According to Plantinga, when it comes to the production of degrees of confidence invested in A on the basis of B, a good design plan is one such that "there is a substantial statistical probability that a propositional attitude formed in accordance with [the plan] (in a favorable cognitive environment) toward a proposition A, on the basis of a proposition B, will match the objective probability of A on B" (166). This passage suggests an additional necessary condition that probabilistic beliefs must satisfy in order to be knowledge. Like the accuracy condition proposed by JOYCE 2005, this necessary condition is a nominally probabilistic content, rather than a thoroughly probabilistic content.

SOSA 2007 distinguishes two kinds of knowledge, namely reflective knowledge possessed only by creatures capable of theorizing, and a more basic animal knowledge that humans share with other creatures. According to Sosa, there are three necessary conditions that are together sufficient for your belief to constitute animal knowledge: (1) your belief must be *accurate*, (2) your belief must be *adroit*, i.e. resulting from your exercise of an epistemic competence, and (3) your

---

[16] For further details, see my discussion of epistemic vocabulary under intensional operators in §7.5.

belief must be *apt*, i.e. accurate precisely because it is adroit. Just like full beliefs, probabilistic beliefs can be accurate, adroit, and apt. They can also fail to be knowledge in virtue of failing to meet these conditions. For example, Alice has an accurate belief that she probably finds Bert attractive in *Nerves*. Her belief is adroit, since it results from her competent inference to the best explanation of her fluttering nerves. But she fails to know that she probably finds Bert attractive, namely because her belief is not apt. The accuracy of her belief is not explained by her competent inference, but by the fact that the experimenters decided to inject her with adrenaline. By contrast, your high credence that a certain piece of cloth is green may indeed be knowledge, as long as the accuracy of your credence may be explained by the fact that it results from your competent exercise of your color vision.

To give another example, suppose that Jones and Smith watch as a coin is tossed nine times. The coin lands heads each time. The coin is then tossed for a tenth time, with the result hidden from Jones and Smith. Suppose that both Jones and Smith end up with the accurate belief that the coin probably landed heads. But Jones and Smith arrive at this probabilistic belief in different ways. Jones starts out believing that the coin might just as well land tails as opposed to heads, and then comes to believe that the coin is probably biased toward heads because that hypothesis is confirmed by the repeated heads outcomes. Meanwhile, Smith starts out with a strong hunch that the coin is biased toward heads. Smith is also convinced of a conspiracy theory, according to which regardless of how the coin actually lands in the nine observed tosses, someone will use a smoke and mirrors trick to make it seem like it landed heads. Intuitively speaking, when the coin is tossed for a tenth time, Jones knows that the coin probably landed heads, and Smith doesn't. The virtue epistemology defended by Sosa 2007 explains this result: for Jones but not for Smith, the accurate belief that the coin probably landed heads results from the exercise of an epistemic competence.

As the above examples illustrate, we have some intuitive grasp on aptness as applied to probabilistic beliefs. Konek 2016 spells out a much more detailed account of what it takes for your credences to be accurate as the result of cognitive ability or skill. In addition to defending this innovative account, Konek uses it to articulate a necessary condition on probabilistic knowledge. Accepting my defense of probabilistic knowledge in Moss 2013, Konek argues that "probabilistic knowledge requires cognitive ability, in the following sense: if some of your credences constitute knowledge, then your evidence explains their success (accuracy) to the greatest degree possible" (14). According to Konek, Jones knows that the coin probably landed heads because the procedure of updating on observed tosses yields accurate credences regardless of which way the coin is biased. By contrast, Smith ends up with accurate credences only when the coin is biased toward heads. More precisely, Konek says that "the statistic that will help us sift credal states that satisfy the probabilistic ability condition from ones that do not . . . is: variance in objective expected posterior accuracy across theoretical hypotheses" (14). There are many possible objective chance functions corresponding to possible biases of the coin that Jones and Smith observe. These functions agree that Jones will probably end up with accurate credences. That is, according to each function, the objective chance that Jones will end up with accurate credences is high. But these same functions do not agree about whether Smith will probably end up with accurate credences, since Smith ends up with accurate credences when the coin is biased toward heads, but inaccurate credences when it is biased toward tails. That is roughly what it means for Smith's credences to have a large variance in objective expected posterior accuracy, which is why his credences fail the ability condition that Konek introduces. According to the probabilistic virtue epistemology that Konek defends, that is why Smith's credences fail to constitute probabilistic knowledge.

5.8 An alternative mental state?

In this chapter so far, I have argued that probabilistic beliefs can exhibit many of the epistemic virtues commonly attributed to knowledge. They can be factive, safe, reliable, sensitive, apt, and so on. In addition, probabilistic beliefs with these virtues can be ascribed using 'knows' and other factive attitude verbs. Here are some naturally occurring examples:

(6)   The report was made public, and it was at this juncture that the residents of Triana learned that they might be contaminated with DDT.[17]

(7)   The Fellahs advanced till they saw that it was probably a large tomb.[18]

(8)   If you give a clear, understandable direction . . . and the child does not comply, then you know that it is more likely due to compliance issues than lack of understanding.[19]

(9)   She moved to get her cell phone then remembered it was probably in the Lexus.[20]

(10)   I sensed that I might be losing my capacity to ever be surprised again.[21]

---

[17] TAYLOR 2014, p.9–10.   [18] PHILLIPS 1822, p.108.   [19] WEBB ET AL. 2007, p.113.
[20] HANSEN 2007, p.384.   [21] THORP 2002, p.xiii.

As I see it, these sentences can be used to ascribe probabilistic knowledge based on testimony, perception, inference, memory, and introspection, respectively.

However, the arguments in this chapter leave room for an alternative conclusion. For all I have argued, probabilistic beliefs could be everything but knowledge. That is, probabilistic beliefs could merely share the epistemic virtues of full beliefs that constitute knowledge. Traditional theories of knowledge could be implicitly restricted to full beliefs. Ordinary speakers could be in error when they apply 'knows' to probabilistic beliefs, or they could use 'knows' to ascribe something other than knowledge. To borrow a term used by GIBBARD 2003 in discussing moral knowledge, probabilistic beliefs could constitute mere *quasi-knowledge*.

To the extent that knowledge is a natural kind, we have some reason to reject the conclusion that probabilistic beliefs are mere quasi-knowledge. By comparison, if we encounter some novel species of warm-blooded animals with fur and mammary glands, there is room in logical space for the conclusion that they are merely quasi-mammals, but it is hard to motivate such an unnatural restriction of our explanatory theories. In earlier chapters, I argued that the contents of full beliefs and thoroughly probabilistic beliefs form a natural kind, insofar as they are equally suited to be contents that we assert and believe. The natural unification of these contents is further supported by the arguments of this chapter, and by my probabilistic theory of full belief in §3.6.

If knowledge is not a natural kind, then there is a greater risk that whether probabilistic beliefs can constitute knowledge is a merely verbal question.[22] But if this question is merely verbal, there are still substantive claims in the neighborhood, namely that probabilistic beliefs can be just as good as knowledge in many substantive respects. I have assumed for ease of exposition that if probabilistic beliefs can be just as good as knowledge, then they can be knowledge. Strictly speaking, my opponent could agree that probabilistic beliefs and propositional beliefs can exhibit exactly the same epistemic virtues, and yet insist that probabilistic beliefs have merely separate but equal epistemic status, namely the status of quasi-knowledge. But once the substantive similarities have been established, why legislate that only propositional beliefs can be knowledge? Aren't both sorts of beliefs equally deserving of the name? It is not clear that there are any good reasons for insisting that knowledge is, by definition, a relation between a subject and a proposition. On the contrary, we can strengthen the institution of traditional epistemology by recognizing probabilistic contents as knowledge.

---

[22] See chapter 5 of SIDER 2011 for relevant discussion of the relation between naturalness and verbal disputes.

Hopefully, even the term 'probabilistic knowledge' will fall by the wayside in time. As I see it, the term 'probabilistic knowledge' is like the term 'gay marriage'. The fact that some contents are probabilistic is not significant when it comes to whether or not those contents are knowledge, except insofar as philosophical tradition has unfairly failed to count them as such. If my arguments for probabilistic knowledge are successful, then hopefully this book will one day manage to undermine its own title.

5.9 Applications

Although it is not often recognized as such, probabilistic knowledge plays an important role in many philosophical theories, including many theories in areas outside epistemology. Indicative conditionals provide one especially abundant source of examples. For instance, the armchair knowledge argument against externalism concerns our knowledge of the contents of indicative conditionals:[23]

(11)   If I am thinking that water is wet, then water exists in my environment.

The same goes for debates about contingent *a priori* knowledge of certain contents:

(12)   If anyone uniquely invented the zipper, Julius invented the zipper.[24]

(13)   If some planet is the unique cause of the perturbations in planetary orbits observed by Leverrier, then that planet is Neptune.[25]

The same goes for debates about knowledge of certain allegedly analytic truths:

(14)   If 'if' means what it does, then *modus ponens* has to be valid.[26]

(15)   If 'bachelor' has a meaning, then 'bachelors are unmarried men' is true.[27]

If the content of an indicative conditional is not a proposition, then our knowledge of the above conditionals is not propositional knowledge. Anyone engaged in debates about these conditionals could stipulate that for their purposes, the conditional in question must be understood as a material conditional. But in the absence of any such stipulation, the material conditional interpretation of the conditionals in these theories is just as unnatural as for any other conditional

---

[23] For instances of this argument, see McKINSEY 1991, BROWN 1995, and BOGHOSSIAN 1997.
[24] EVANS 1979, p.50.   [25] Adapted from KRIPKE 1980, p.79.
[26] This is roughly an instance of a schema discussed by BOGHOSSIAN 1996, p.386.
[27] If 'bachelors are unmarried men' is used to implicitly define 'bachelor', then this is an instance of a schema discussed by HORWICH 2001 in his critique of Boghossian's account of *a priori* knowledge.

in natural language. Arguments about content externalism, *a priori* knowledge, and analyticity are most naturally interpreted as arguments about knowledge of probabilistic contents.

Probabilistic knowledge also plays an important role in several central arguments in CHALMERS 2012. Chalmers argues that there is a certain class of truths from which all truths are "conditionally scrutable," where conditional scrutability essentially involves knowledge of indicative conditionals with antecedents in that class of truths. For instance, you have knowledge of the following conditional:

> (16) If "in front of me is a substance that looks watery, that behaves in a certain fluid way, and that has a certain molecular structure . . . [where] the same molecular structure is present in most other substances that look watery in my environment" (122–3), then the substance in front of me is water.

The claims in the antecedent of (16) belong to a special class of truths *PQI* such that "for all ordinary true sentence tokens *M*, the speaker is in a position to know (on ideal reflection) that *if PQI* is true, then *M* is true" (138). Chalmers intends for our knowledge of (16) and similar conditionals to vindicate a broadly internalist theory of content. The idea is that even if the referent of 'water' depends on facts about your environment, (16) is an important fact related to meaning and content that you can know from the armchair. Chalmers himself observes that "using material conditionals would trivialize conditional scrutability" (59). He concludes that the knowledge relevant for conditional scrutability is knowledge of an indicative conditional, where this conditional knowledge is not propositional knowledge. Chalmers refers to Moss 2013 for a relevant proposal for understanding knowledge of indicative conditionals. The upshot of adopting that proposal is that probabilistic knowledge is essential to Chalmers' conditional scrutability thesis.

If there were no such thing as probabilistic knowledge, Chalmers could still endorse conditional scrutability theses about justified beliefs. For instance, Chalmers could argue that you are in a position to have a justified belief in conditionals such as (16). However, it is not clear that this revised conditional scrutability thesis could still be used to argue for *a priori* scrutability theses that could be "used to deflate many traditional skeptical arguments about *knowledge*" and to "analyze notions of meaning and content that are tied to thought and *knowledge*" (xvi–xvii, my emphases). Insofar as we care about these applications of the knowledge that Chalmers sets out to ground, the central project of CHALMERS 2012 depends on the existence of probabilistic knowledge.

Another application for probabilistic knowledge is the explanation of intuitive distinctions between epistemic states. For instance, there is an intuitive distinction between merely *being sure of something you know* and *knowing it for sure*. Suppose that Bobby knows by testimony from his parents that Santa Claus does not exist. In addition, suppose that young Bobby is going through an extremely confident phase, assigning credence 1 to every proposition that he believes. Bobby is intuitively not justified in having such an extremely high credence that Santa does not exist. His youthful overconfidence does not warrant his betting against the existence of Santa Claus at any odds. When it comes to the fact that Santa Claus does not exist, Bobby knows it, and he is sure of it, but he does not know it for sure.[28] Probabilistic knowledge allows us to make sense of Bobby's epistemic situation. Loosely speaking, the full belief that Santa Claus does not exist does constitute knowledge for Bobby, but some of his more extreme probabilistic beliefs do not.

Exactly what does it mean to know something for sure? If you know something for sure, then you are certain of some proposition, and your certainty in that proposition constitutes knowledge. To build on the theory of full belief defended in §3.6, knowing something *for sure*, as opposed to just knowing it, is like knowing that it is *exactly* 3:00, as opposed to just knowing that it is 3:00. In more technical terms, 'for sure' is a *slack regulator* in the sense of LASERSOHN 1999. This slack regulator not only appears in ordinary language, but also in the context of philosophical arguments. For example, in addition to assuming that we can know conditionals, CHALMERS 2012 also appeals to the idea that the attitude of certainty can constitute knowledge in his discussion of "*conclusive* knowledge and scrutability, involving knowledge with certainty" (56). Here again, probabilistic knowledge plays an indispensable role in defining precise scrutability theses.

Another philosophical application of probabilistic knowledge concerns the relation between knowledge and assertion. According to the second central thesis of this book, we can assert probabilistic contents. WILLIAMSON 2000 defends the norm that you may assert something only if you know it. If some subjects permissibly assert probabilistic contents, it follows from the knowledge norm of assertion that some subjects know probabilistic contents. This is no doubt one of the fastest arguments from the second central thesis of this book to the third. Together with my second central thesis, the knowledge norm of assertion requires probabilistic knowledge.

In addition to the foregoing applications, the relationship between probabilistic knowledge and assertion also has implications for feminist thinking about gender and speech. Prompted by the pioneering discussion of gender and language in

---

[28] The column "What I Know For Sure" in *O, The Oprah Magazine* contains many naturally occurring instances of 'knows for sure' (cf. WINFREY 2014).

LAKOFF 1975, many empirical studies have investigated gendered patterns of speech, including gender differences in speakers' use of epistemic vocabulary. According to some studies, women are more likely than men to hedge their assertions using epistemic vocabulary. For instance, after observing the use of modals such as 'could', 'may', and 'might' by male and female subjects in experimental settings, MCMILLAN ET AL. 1977 conclude that women use "modal constructions almost twice as often" as men (551). Empirical studies have also suggested that stereotypically female speech patterns are associated with ignorance. For instance, according to BRADLEY 1981, "women who argued without qualifiers . . . were rated as being more *knowledgeable*" when arguing for an unpopular position (83, my emphasis). According to a study of hedges such as 'maybe' in CARLI 1990, "both male and female speakers judged a woman who spoke tentatively to be less competent and *knowledgeable* than a woman who spoke assertively" (948, my emphasis). Finally, women are routinely advised to change the way they talk, namely by adopting more stereotypically male speech patterns. For example, in her recent article titled "The Communication Style You Need To Break Into the Boys' Club," communication consultant Judith Humphrey instructs women: "Make your point with strong, plain words and straightforward declaratory sentences. Avoid weak modifiers like 'probably'."[29] To sum up, academic and popular articles have advanced claims to the effect that female speech involves a comparatively heavy use of epistemic vocabulary, that this speech is perceived as ignorant, and that it stands in need of correction. Connecting the dots, we arrive at the following simple argument: women should use epistemic vocabulary less often, because using epistemic vocabulary makes women sound like they do not know what they are talking about.

Now that we have spelled out the simple argument, the flaw in it should be obvious. The assertions that women make using epistemic vocabulary have probabilistic contents. But these contents can nevertheless constitute knowledge, just as much as the contents of simple unhedged sentences. The simple argument is undermined by the existence of probabilistic knowledge. Women should not change the way they talk. We should change how we evaluate the way they talk. What needs revision is the conventional association of epistemic vocabulary with ignorance.

Having aimed my theory of probabilistic knowledge at some conventional conclusions about gender and speech, let me be explicit about its target. By pointing out one flaw in the simple argument given above, I do not mean to suggest that the argument is otherwise flawless. In fact, the argument itself is not

---

[29] HUMPHREY 2015, §3.

obviously supported by empirical research. Epistemic modals are only one sort of hedged vocabulary, hedged vocabulary is only one element of characteristically female speech, and failing to have knowledge is only one negative feature that is generally associated with using characteristically female speech. The empirical studies cited above do not isolate the use of epistemic modals from other features of female speech. In addition, some studies suggest that the mere use of epistemic vocabulary is not responsible for the extent to which women sound ignorant to others. For instance, it may be that epistemic vocabulary conveys ignorance when used by women but not when used by men: "linguistic devices used by women are often mistakenly devalued . . . perceived as indicators of uncertainty and nonassertiveness when used by women but as tools of politeness . . . when used by men" (BRADLEY 1981, 90).[30] The target of my argument is circumscribed. Insofar as normative conclusions about speech are implicitly motivated by the simple argument spelled out above, the existence of probabilistic knowledge undermines those conclusions.

Probabilistic knowledge not only undermines the simple argument, but turns it on its head. Probabilistic beliefs often constitute knowledge when stronger propositional beliefs do not. Hence speakers can often use epistemic vocabulary to assert knowledge that they could not assert without it. The practical importance of this observation depends on some complicated empirical questions—for instance, how often does adding the expressive power of epistemic vocabulary allow women to assert something stronger than they could have otherwise asserted, and how much stronger are their probabilistic assertions? But however we answer these questions, the simple argument is opposed by the thought that women should use epistemic vocabulary because it *enables* them to assert knowledge.

Alongside this thought, we should also consider a second potential argument against the use of epistemic vocabulary by women. The second argument depends on a generalization about what women assert and what they know, namely that women are more likely to use epistemic vocabulary to assert thoroughly probabilistic contents when they could have instead used simple sentences to assert strictly stronger contents of knowledge. The argument concludes with a normative claim: in such cases, women should refrain from using epistemic vocabulary, namely because they should assert the strongest contents that they

---

[30] The claim that women should avoid using epistemic vocabulary because it is *unassertive* may implicitly presuppose that epistemic vocabulary is not used to make genuine assertions, in which case this claim may be challenged on similar grounds as the simple argument given above. As argued in chapter 2, the contents of sentences containing epistemic vocabulary are just as fit to be the contents of assertion as the contents of simple sentences.

know.[31] For example, say that Alice asserts that Jones probably smokes, when in fact she knows that Jones smokes. In this case, Alice should refrain from using 'probably' because she should assert the content that Jones smokes. This example invites a tempting generalization, namely that relative to men, it is more likely that a woman is deficient in her use of an epistemic expression, because she should instead be asserting a simple content that entails what she actually asserted. To borrow some vocabulary defined in §7.3, the tempting generalization states that women who assert thoroughly probabilistic contents should instead be asserting nominally probabilistic contents, namely *propositional closures* of the contents they actually assert.

This tempting generalization is not easy to define or defend. The second argument rests on a claim about the relative frequency with which men and women use epistemic vocabulary when they could have instead used simple sentences to assert some stronger content that they knew. This claim is not confirmed or disconfirmed by facts about the relative frequency with which men and women assert probabilistic contents, since it also depends on facts about what contents could have been asserted but weren't. To make matters worse, it is not even clear that advocates of the second argument could define what simple content could have been asserted in place of an arbitrary probabilistic content. The content of 'Jones probably smokes' is entailed by the content that Jones smokes, for instance, and so it is natural enough to fault someone for asserting the former when they could have asserted the latter. But the content of 'Jones might smoke, and she might not' is not entailed by the content of any consistent simple sentence. Again borrowing some vocabulary defined in §7.3, one cannot extend the tempting generalization to assertions of *heretical* probabilistic contents, since heretical contents have empty propositional closures. These observations are not intended to refute the second argument, but simply to raise difficult questions that its proponents must address. However the dialectic unfolds from here, notions of probabilistic assertion and knowledge are likely to be useful in framing the questions and results of further research on gender, speech, and epistemic vocabulary.

---

[31] I first encountered this objection in conversation with Tim Williamson, though it has been echoed by others since, and I am grateful to all who have raised it.

6

Factivity

6.1 Alternatives to probabilistic knowledge?

There are plenty of familiar connections between knowledge and notions of possibility and probability. For instance, something is often said to be an *epistemic possibility* for you just in case it is consistent with everything that you know. Another familiar epistemic notion is the *evidential probability* of a proposition given your total evidence, where your evidence may include your knowledge—or even coincide with it, as argued by WILLIAMSON 2000. Can we use these more conventional notions to respond to the case for probabilistic knowledge presented in chapter 5, without adopting the revisionary thesis that probabilistic beliefs can constitute knowledge? It is prudent to consider and reject conventional proposals before embracing revisionary ones. This section discharges that responsibility, proposing some conventional analyses of probabilistic knowledge and then spelling out their shortcomings. For ease of exposition, I frame the conventional proposals in this section as reductive theories, analyses of probabilistic knowledge in terms of propositional knowledge. Strictly speaking, conventional proposals might instead deny that you have any probabilistic knowledge, insisting that knowledge ascriptions embedding epistemic vocabulary concern only mental states with propositional contents.

Let us start with a simple conventional proposal about what it takes to know that something might be the case. According to the semantics for attitude verbs introduced by HINTIKKA 1969, 'Smith believes that Jones smokes' is true just in case Jones smokes in every world compatible with everything that Smith believes. According to STEPHENSON 2007 and YALCIN 2007, among others, we should extend this semantics by saying that 'Smith believes that Jones *might* smoke' is true just in case Jones smokes in *some* world compatible with everything that Smith believes. Yalcin goes on to argue that it is also "very natural to extend a domain semantics of this type to other attitude verbs, such as . . . 'know'" (996). According to this simple proposal, 'Smith *knows* that Jones might smoke' is true just in case Jones smokes in some world compatible with everything that Smith *knows*.

Knowing that something might be the case does not amount to your knowing any particular proposition, but it can nevertheless be analyzed in terms of the propositions that you know.

As an alternative theory of knowledge ascriptions embedding epistemic vocabulary, this simple proposal is incomplete. In addition to saying what it takes to know that Jones might smoke, the proposal should also say what it takes to know that Jones probably smokes, what it takes to know that Jones is more likely to smoke than Brown, and so on. Fortunately, the simple proposal can be naturally extended to arbitrary probabilistic contents. Assume Epistemic Uniqueness, namely the thesis that your total evidence determines exactly what credence you should assign to any proposition. According to a natural extension of the simple proposal, you know some content just in case that content contains the probability space that represents what you should believe in light of your evidence. For example, you know that Jones probably smokes just in case the proposition that Jones smokes has high probability given your evidence. You know that Jones is more likely to smoke than Brown just in case Jones smoking has higher evidential probability for you than Brown smoking. And so on for any knowledge ascription embedding epistemic vocabulary.

Unfortunately, the simple proposal has several fatal flaws. For instance, the proposal entails that for every probabilistic content, you either know it or know its complement. As a result, the proposal fails to account for intuitive cases of probabilistic ignorance. The simple proposal also fails to account for the possibility of false probabilistic beliefs. When you falsely believe some probabilistic content, neither that content nor its complement constitute knowledge for you, since the former is not true and the latter is not something that you believe. This problem for the simple proposal is especially vivid when it comes to knowing that something might be the case. Whenever Jones smokes, it is false that Jones must not smoke, and hence the simple proposal entails that any subject will automatically count as knowing that Jones might smoke. YALCIN 2012b mentions this result and cites it as a decisive reason for rejecting the simple proposal as applied to knowledge ascriptions embedding epistemic possibility modals.[1]

The simple proposal entails that subjects know too many probabilistic contents. Is there a more modest alternative? Assume Epistemic Permissivism, namely the thesis that your total evidence does *not* determine exactly what credence you should assign to every proposition. Then there are multiple probability spaces that represent what you may rationally believe in light of your evidence. According to a more modest conventional proposal, you know a probabilistic content just in

---

[1] For further discussion, see fn. 7 of DORR AND HAWTHORNE 2012.

case that content contains *every* probability space that represents what you may rationally believe in light of your evidence. This second proposal leaves room for probabilistic ignorance. In particular, you may fail to know some content and also fail to know its complement, namely whenever belief in that content and belief in its complement are each rationally permissible given your evidence.

Although it is an improvement on our first proposal, our second analysis of probabilistic knowledge still fails on several counts. For instance, the second proposal incorrectly predicts that knowledge does not entail belief. Suppose your actual credences are not among the credences that are rationally permissible given your evidence. Then there will be contents that contain all the latter credences without containing the former. According to the second proposal, you know these contents, even though you do not believe them. For example, suppose you have a lot of evidence that you have cancer, but wishful thinking leads you to ignore this evidence and to believe that you are probably healthy. The second proposal predicts that you know that you probably have cancer, even though you do not believe it.

Here is a third proposal: you know a content just in case it contains every probability space that represents what you may rationally believe, *and you believe that content*. Unfortunately, this third proposal retains another flaw of the first two proposals—namely, it conflates knowledge and justification. As a result, the third proposal incorrectly predicts that subjects have knowledge in probabilistic analogs of Gettier cases. Recall the case of *Nerves* described in §5.6. Alice has high credence that she finds Bert attractive on the basis of her fluttering nerves. Her fluttering nerves are actually not caused by Bert, but by a recent injection of adrenaline that she does not know about. Alice has plenty of evidence that she finds Bert attractive. Her evidence is misleading, but it would nevertheless be irrational for her to ignore it. Alice's total evidence may well demand that she have high credence that she finds Bert attractive. According to the third proposal, it follows that she knows that she probably finds Bert attractive. But intuitively, Alice does not know that she probably finds Bert attractive, as her high credence is the result of intervening epistemic luck.

In addition, the third proposal fails to predict that knowledge entails truth. For example, suppose that Smith has a lot of evidence that Jones drinks. But suppose that his evidence is misleading—in fact, Jones has recently quit drinking. According to the third proposal, Smith knows that Jones probably drinks, even though it is not the case that Jones probably drinks. In other words, the content that Jones probably drinks is known by Smith, even though it is false. According to the third proposal, it is perfectly consistent to say that Smith knows that Jones probably drinks, and that Brown knows that she probably doesn't. It is consistent to say that Smith believes that Jones probably drinks, that Brown disagrees, and that both of their beliefs constitute knowledge. These results are unacceptable. Knowledge is not false. Knowledge is not inconsistent. The intended subject of this book is a factive attitude, namely the attitude that is absent in probabilistic analogs of Gettier cases, that could be safe or sensitive according to traditional theories of knowledge, and so on. The intended subject of this book is probabilistic knowledge—and like propositional knowledge, it cannot be easily analyzed in more basic terms.

6.2 The contents of knowledge ascriptions

There is plenty to discuss about probabilistic knowledge, without giving an analysis of it. The remainder of this chapter will discuss exactly what it means to say that probabilistic knowledge is a *factive* attitude. At a first pass, to say that probabilistic knowledge is factive is just to say that the contents of knowledge are true. On first consideration, one might naturally object that the contents of probabilistic beliefs do not appear to be truth apt. The belief that Jones smokes can be true or false, but it is not clear whether the same can be said for credences, conditional credences, and so on. What does it mean to say that these beliefs are true?

The content of a probabilistic belief is a set of probability spaces rather than a set of worlds, and so it is not true at a world simply in virtue of containing that world. However, there is still a very plain sense in which probabilistic beliefs can be true or false. For instance, say that Smith believes that Jones probably smokes. The content of his belief is true just in case Jones probably smokes. The probabilistic theory of content defended in the first four chapters of this book fits naturally with a deflationary theory of truth, according to which these sentences have just the same content:

(1)   Jones probably smokes.

(2)   It is true that Jones probably smokes.

Recall from §1.4 that a set S of probability spaces is *nominally probabilistic* just in case there is some proposition such that S contains all and only the probability spaces that are certain of that proposition. A set of probability spaces is *thoroughly probabilistic* just in case there is no such proposition. The shared content of (1) and (2) is a thoroughly probabilistic content, namely the set of probability spaces according to which Jones probably smokes.

In addition to ascriptions of truth, ascriptions of knowledge can also have thoroughly probabilistic contents. Say that Smith asserts that Jones probably smokes, and also asserts that he himself knows that Jones probably smokes. For sake of argument, suppose that Smith later finds out that Jones does not smoke. In addition to retracting his assertion of the content that Jones probably smokes, Smith should retract his assertion that he knew that content. The content that Smith knows that Jones probably smokes entails the content that Jones probably smokes. If the latter content is false, then so is the former. Both contents are sets of probability spaces. The set of probability spaces according to which Smith knows that Jones probably smokes is a subset of the set of probability spaces according to which Jones probably smokes, and that is why the former entails the latter. The same goes for any subject S and any probabilistic content p. The probabilistic content that S knows p is a subset of the content p itself. At a second pass, that is what it means to say that probabilistic knowledge is a factive attitude.[2]

There is a clear affinity between my claims about truth and knowledge and claims defended by some ethical expressivists. At a first pass, expressivists say that ethical sentences express different sorts of attitudes from the beliefs expressed by ordinary simple sentences. As developed by quasi-realists such as BLACKBURN 1984 and GIBBARD 1990, ethical expressivism is nevertheless consistent with the existence of moral truths and moral knowledge. Ascriptions of moral knowledge can be used to express the same sort of attitude as the sentences containing ethical vocabulary that they embed. For instance, GIBBARD 2003 argues that ascriptions of ethical knowledge are plan-laden, expressing acceptance of various ethical norms, in addition to factual beliefs. In short, it is not an obvious conceptual truth that knowledge ascriptions must have just the same sort of contents that simple sentences are traditionally taken to express.[3]

I have proposed that ascriptions of probabilistic knowledge can have thoroughly probabilistic contents. In this respect, ascriptions of probabilistic knowledge are unlike, say, ascriptions of probabilistic belief. The content that Smith believes that Jones probably smokes is nominally probabilistic, for instance, as it corresponds to the set of worlds where Smith has high credence that Jones smokes. This nominally probabilistic content is entailed by the thoroughly probabilistic content that Smith knows that Jones probably smokes. To sum up the big picture: you believe a probabilistic content just in case that content contains the probability space that represents your total belief state. Whether you also know the content is just a further probabilistic fact, not reducible to any other facts about your

---

[2] See §7.5 for discussion of an additional interpretation of factivity, namely as the modal claim that it is *necessarily* the case that something is true if known.

[3] For further discussion of ethical quasi-realism and how it is ultimately disanalogous to my view, see §7.5.

belief. By contrast with some of the conventional proposals discussed in §6.1, my non-reductionist proposal allows that probabilistic knowledge entails belief. The proposal correctly predicts that subjects can be ignorant about probabilistic contents, and that probabilistic knowledge is more than mere justified true belief. These facts about probabilistic knowledge are not corollaries of any analysis of probabilistic knowledge, but rather facts about the nature of knowledge that hold equally for knowledge of propositional and probabilistic contents.

6.3 Frequently asked questions

The fact that some knowledge ascriptions have thoroughly probabilistic contents raises several questions. Recall that in the case of *Fake Letters* described in §5.6, the experimenters know that Alice probably likes Bert in a romantic way, on the basis of her answers to a survey. What if it turns out that in fact, Alice doesn't like Bert? Then do the experimenters still know that she probably likes him? Suppose for sake of argument that we think that Smith knows that it is at least .6 likely that Jones smokes, but then we learn that Jones doesn't smoke. Does Smith stop knowing that it is at least .6 likely that Jones smokes when we gain information about Jones? Does the fact that someone knows a probabilistic content depend partly on the fact that we ourselves believe that content?

Advocates of probabilistic knowledge have straightforward answers to these questions. If Alice *doesn't* like Bert, then it isn't *more than .5 likely* that she likes him. She doesn't probably like him, and the experimenters don't know that she probably likes him. If Jones doesn't smoke, then it isn't at least .6 likely that she smokes, and Smith doesn't know it is at least .6 likely that she smokes. The same reasoning holds not only for contents that are currently true and known, but also for contents that are true and known at earlier times. For example, imagine someone saying the following in the time of the Babylonians:

(3)   #The Earth is round, and the Babylonians know that it is probably flat.

This sentence sounds bad because it is a contradiction. If the second conjunct of (3) ascribes thoroughly probabilistic knowledge, then it is inconsistent with the first conjunct. The Babylonians believed that the Earth was probably flat. Their belief failed to be knowledge because it was false, and it was false because the Earth is round. The fact that we ourselves believe that the Earth is round is irrelevant. Ascriptions of thoroughly probabilistic knowledge have thoroughly probabilistic contents. But that does not mean that whether someone else knows some content depends on whether we believe it, any more than whether the Earth itself is probably flat depends on what we believe.

Another frequently asked question: "But isn't there some sense in which whether the Earth is probably flat depends on what we believe?" As explained in §2.5, sentences such as (4) and (5) often have multiple readings:

(4)   The Earth is probably flat.

(5)   The Babylonians know that the Earth is probably flat.

For all I have argued, (4) may have a reading that is true just in case the Earth is probably flat according to our total evidence. Whether this reading of (4) is true could indeed depend on what we believe. Relatedly, (5) may have a reading that is true just in case the Babylonians knew that the Earth was probably flat according to their total evidence. This reading of (5) could turn out to be true even if the Earth is round. However, in the context of the present discussion, the intended readings of (4) and (5) are not these readings, but rather thoroughly probabilistic contents.

"Isn't there some sense in which the Babylonians knew that the Earth was probably flat, though they turned out to be wrong?" Again, the Babylonians may have had some knowledge that is ascribed by one reading of (5), such as knowledge of the fact that the Earth was probably flat according to their total evidence. But their high credence that the Earth was flat did not constitute knowledge. For my purposes, what matters is that there is some reading on which (4) expresses a thoroughly probabilistic belief, and some reading on which (5) ascribes that same belief to the Babylonians. The relevant reading of (4) passes the test battery for thoroughly probabilistic content described in §2.5. The corresponding reading of (5) is inconsistent with the claim that the Earth is round. As we investigate probabilistic knowledge, we may stipulate that we are interested in ascriptions of thoroughly probabilistic knowledge, and we may set aside other readings of knowledge ascriptions embedding epistemic vocabulary.

The factivity of probabilistic knowledge has some surprising consequences for our discussion of thought experiments. For example, the experimenters know that Alice probably finds Bert attractive only if Alice does indeed probably find Bert attractive. Does Alice probably find Bert attractive? This question may seem strange. We do not often assess thoroughly probabilistic contents about thought experiments, much less believe them. In real life, we have moderate credences when our limited evidence fails to settle some question, whereas in the construction of thought experiments, such questions are commonly settled by stipulation.

"How am I supposed to know whether Alice probably finds Bert attractive? It's *your* thought experiment." There are two ways that you can know whether Alice probably finds Bert attractive. First, in the construction of thought experiments, probabilistic contents may be stipulated along with propositional ones. The description of Alice in §5.6 includes the stipulation that "she probably does find Bert attractive." Hence you can know that Alice probably finds Bert attractive in just the same way that you know other stipulated contents, such as the fact that Alice is friends with Bert, or that she has entered a psychology study. Although it is not common to use epistemic vocabulary in constructing thought experiments, there is nothing wrong with using it in this way.

Second, you can know some content about a thought experiment even when the content is not explicitly stipulated, namely by inferring that content from what is stipulated. Hence you can know probabilistic contents about Alice in just the same way that you know other contents that you infer about her, such as the fact that she has at least one friend, or that it is nomologically possible for her to enter psychology studies. LYCAN 2001 proposes another interesting example of this second way of getting probabilistic knowledge about a thought experiment. There are several facts stipulated about the Sly Pete case in GIBBARD 1981. Zack is helping Sly Pete cheat, and asserts that if Pete called, he won. Jack sees that Sly Pete has a losing hand, and asserts that if Pete called, he lost. Lycan argues that on the basis of these stipulated facts, we can know that if Pete called, he lost:

> Given that Pete's hand was in fact worse than Stone's, I think we have to conclude with Jack that if Pete called, he lost . . . That is the Hard Line. Everyone I have consulted finds it attractive; at least, everyone finds Jack's conditional easier to fall in with than Zack's. There seems to be a sense in which Jack's conditional is *objectively true* and Zack's is not. (168–9)

In constructing the Sly Pete case, Gibbard does not stipulate that if Pete called, he lost. Lycan proposes that we can nevertheless know this probabilistic content. In particular, we can infer this content from the stipulated fact that Pete had a losing hand.

In addition to the questions I have answered so far, there are some questions that remain open for future research. The content that Jones probably smokes is thoroughly probabilistic, and the same goes for the content that Jones probably smokes *and it is raining*. The former fact is entirely responsible for the latter. The content of the conjunction is thoroughly probabilistic only because the content of its first conjunct is thoroughly probabilistic. This sort of observation raises important questions about knowledge. The content that Jones probably smokes is thoroughly probabilistic, and the same goes for the content that *Smith knows that* Jones probably smokes. Is the former fact entirely responsible for the latter? Alice has a justified true belief that she probably likes Bert. Her belief falls short of knowledge. What is the nature of the content that her justified true belief falls short of knowledge? Is this content thoroughly or nominally probabilistic? It is not clear that these questions can be answered in the abstract. Their answers may ultimately depend on substantive theories about what distinguishes knowledge from mere justified true belief. For instance, as explained in §5.7, the condition that a certain belief is produced by a reliable method might be interpreted as having a nominally probabilistic content or a thoroughly probabilistic content. In stating my case for probabilistic knowledge, I have remained neutral on the nature of the distinction between knowledge and mere justified true belief, and so I will also remain neutral on whether this distinction is thoroughly probabilistic in nature.

A final frequently asked question concerns classification, namely, "Is this an *expressivist* theory of knowledge ascriptions?" The answer will be just the same for my theory of knowledge ascriptions as for my theory of epistemic vocabulary. In short, the answer depends on what notion of expressivism you have in mind. A lot of sentences containing epistemic vocabulary have thoroughly probabilistic contents. The same goes for knowledge ascriptions embedding epistemic vocabulary. Speakers use these sentences to express thoroughly probabilistic beliefs, rather than full beliefs about probabilities. I have explained the meaning of sentences containing epistemic vocabulary by explaining that these sentences can be used to express thoroughly probabilistic beliefs. As a result, my theory is expressivist in the sense of GIBBARD 2003, who uses 'expressivism' for "any account of meanings that follows this indirect path: to explain the meaning of a term, explain what states of mind the term is used to express" (7).[4]

However, this definition of 'expressivism' does not obviously demarcate some useful or interesting feature of theories of meaning. There is one mundane sense of *expressing* such that speakers can use almost any declarative sentence to express some sort of belief. According to my theory, we use epistemic vocabulary to express probabilistic beliefs in exactly this mundane sense. According to tradition, 'Jones smokes' can be used to express a belief with a propositional content. According to my theory, 'Jones probably smokes' can be used to express a belief with a probabilistic content. There is no deep sense in which my theory is forced to explain the meaning of 'Jones probably smokes' by reference to mental states, any more than traditional theories are forced to explain the meaning of 'Jones smokes' by reference to mental states. The same goes for the claim that indicative conditionals can be used to express conditional beliefs. As EDGINGTON 2000 put it, "I don't see anything more 'expressivist' in my account than in a truth-conditional semantics for conditionals" (115). Insofar as probabilistic beliefs play

---

[4] Similar definitions of 'expressivism' are endorsed by ROSEN 1998, WEDGWOOD 2007, and SCHROEDER 2008a, among others.

an especially prominent role in my theory of epistemic vocabulary, whereas full beliefs play a less prominent role in traditional theories of simple sentences, this difference does not reflect any deep philosophical distinction. Perhaps it is especially handy to talk about probabilistic beliefs when explaining what it means to say that sentences containing epistemic vocabulary have probabilistic contents, whereas it is not especially necessary to talk about full beliefs in order to explain what it means to say that simple sentences have propositional contents.

A number of theorists split the difference between Gibbard and Edgington, using 'expressivist' for theories according to which sentences express some special sort of mental state. According to YALCIN 2012a, expressivist theories say that sentences express "states of mind not equivalent to full belief in propositions" (125). In this sense, my theory of epistemic vocabulary is expressivist, since probabilistic beliefs are not equivalent to full beliefs in propositions. According to MACFARLANE 2014, expressivist theories say that sentences express "mental state[s] with what Searle (1979: 3–4) calls . . . *world-to-mind* direction of fit" (167). In this sense, my theory of epistemic vocabulary is *not* expressivist, since probabilistic beliefs have a mind-to-world direction of fit. Remember, probabilistic beliefs include certainties in propositions as a special case. In fact, as argued in §3.6, probabilistic beliefs include the full beliefs expressed by simple sentences. The functional role played by probabilistic beliefs in standard decision theory is like the role played by full beliefs in traditional models of practical reasoning, as opposed to the roles played by desires, intentions, or other mental states with a world-to-mind direction of fit.

Definitions that identify expressivism with special mental states are not concerned with the fact that sentences *express* mental states, so much as with the *character of the mental states* that sentences express. For any definition of expressivism in this spirit, whether my account of 'Jones probably smokes' counts as expressivist will depend on the nature of the thoroughly probabilistic belief that Jones probably smokes. Whether my account of 'Jones smokes' counts as expressivist will depend on the nature of the full belief that Jones smokes. Again, this definition of 'expressivism' does not obviously demarcate some useful or interesting feature of theories of meaning. The classification of either account as expressivist will say at least as much about the nature of our beliefs as it says about the language that we use to express them.

6.4 Relativism

In addition to discussing expressivist theories, it is useful to discuss the relation between my probabilistic theory and relativist theories of epistemic vocabulary.

There are many precise definitions and varieties of relativism. It is especially helpful to compare and contrast my theory with an extremely simple version of the *de se* relativism defended by STEPHENSON 2007 and EGAN 2007, as this comparison best illuminates two significant differences between relativist theories of epistemic vocabulary and my own.

According to *de se* relativism, contents of belief are sets of *centered possible worlds* in roughly the sense of LEWIS 1979a. A centered world is an ordered triple $\langle w, t, x \rangle$ consisting of a possible world, a time, and an individual. Suppose you believe that it is 12:00. According to the *de se* relativist theory of temporal beliefs, the content of your belief is the set that contains some centered world just in case 12:00 is the value of its time coordinate. Accordingly, the content of your belief is not true relative to a world, but relative to a richer circumstance of evaluation. The content of your belief that it is 12:00 is the sort of object that may be true for you now and false for you later. Similarly, suppose you believe that James Bond is probably in London. According to the *de se* relativist theory of beliefs expressed using epistemic vocabulary, the content of your belief is a set of centered worlds. Assume that for any individual and time, there is a unique body of evidence corresponding to the epistemic reach of that individual at that time. Assume that this body of evidence uniquely determines a probability space representing the rational probabilistic beliefs to have about every proposition. Then each centered world determines a probability space, namely the probability space corresponding to the epistemic reach of the individual at the center of that world. When you believe that James Bond is probably in London, the content of your belief is the set that contains some centered world $\langle w, t, x \rangle$ just in case Bond is probably in London according to the probability space corresponding to the epistemic reach of individual x at time t in world w.

To be more precise, the *de se* relativist can borrow some of my formal semantics to specify the content of any sentence containing epistemic vocabulary. The content of a sentence S will be true at $\langle w, t, x \rangle$ just in case my semantic value for S contains the probability space corresponding to the epistemic reach of the individual x at time t in world w. Just like your belief that it is 12:00, the content of your belief that Bond is probably in London is not true relative to a world, but relative to a richer circumstance of evaluation. The content of your belief may be true for a criminal in virtue of her limited evidence, and false for an eavesdropping spy in virtue of her substantial evidence that James Bond is not in London. The same goes not just for the contents of belief, but also for the contents of assertion and the contents of sentences containing epistemic vocabulary as uttered at particular contexts.

As this simple theory demonstrates, relativist theories of epistemic vocabulary may resemble my probabilistic theory in several respects. According to the relativist, sentences do not have probabilistic contents, but their contents may still closely correspond to the contents assigned by my semantics. In addition, the relativist and I agree that the contents of sentences containing epistemic vocabulary do not determine truth conditions of an ordinary sort. The same goes not just for contents of sentences, but also for contents of belief and assertion. Finally, the relativist agrees that knowledge ascriptions embedding epistemic vocabulary also fail to determine truth conditions of an ordinary sort. Just as I have argued that 'Smith knows that it is .6 likely that Jones smokes' has a thoroughly probabilistic content, the relativist may say that the content of this sentence does not determine any set of uncentered possible worlds.

For all our theories have in common, there are still two substantial differences between the relativist theory and mine. First, only my probabilistic theory of epistemic vocabulary is supported by the foundational arguments for probabilistic contents of assertion in §2.2. According to the relativist, probabilistic beliefs are only ever communicated indirectly, namely through the communication of some full belief in a corresponding *de se* proposition. In this respect, relativism fares just as badly as contextualist theories that say that we only use epistemic vocabulary to express full beliefs about our evidence. The relativist fails to provide a unified account of our communication of probabilistic beliefs and full beliefs, fails to provide a unified account of the contents of belief and assertion, and fails to provide a satisfying account of how probabilistic beliefs figure in joint reasoning and guide our collective actions.

Another substantial difference is that according to the relativist, false contents can be true for other people. Suppose that Bond is not in London. Then the content that Bond is probably in London is false. But according to the relativist, the content may nevertheless be true for a criminal in virtue of her limited epistemic reach. By contrast, my probabilistic theory of epistemic vocabulary does not make use of any relation of relative truth. The criminal may be justified in believing the content that Bond is probably in London. But the content of her belief is not true for her, or indeed true in any sense. The content is inconsistent with the true content that Bond is not in London, and that alone is enough to guarantee that the content is false. According to my theory, there are no interesting facts about the relative truth of probabilistic contents in thought experiments. As a result, theorists discussing thought experiments must often simply assert probabilistic contents about imaginary situations, as explained in §6.3. Any theorist considering an imaginary situation has probabilistic beliefs about that situation. These beliefs often have just the same probabilistic contents as beliefs held by the imaginary subjects themselves.

6.5 Objective chance

Suppose that Smith knows that Jones probably smokes. Because knowledge is factive, it follows that it is true that Jones probably smokes. I have argued that this simply means that Jones probably smokes. At first glance, it may be tempting to add that the true content that Jones probably smokes must have some further property. Here is one hypothesis that often naturally occurs to people as they start thinking about probabilistic knowledge: probabilistic beliefs are knowledge only if they have the probabilistic analog of truth, where the probabilistic analog of truth is the property of containing the objective chance function.[5] As HÁJEK 2015 puts it, "Truth is to belief, as agreement with objective chance is to degree of belief" (12). For example, Smith knows that Jones probably smokes only if there is a high objective chance that Smith smokes. Smith knows that Jones is more likely to smoke than Brown only if the objective chance that Jones smokes is higher than the chance that Brown smokes. And so on for knowledge of any probabilistic content.

There may be a sense in which probabilistic beliefs are valuable insofar as they match objective chances. However, as a proposed necessary condition for knowledge, the objective chance hypothesis misses its target. For starters, the hypothesis fails for cases where you have evidence about the future that is *inadmissible* in the sense of LEWIS 1980b.[6] Say you are about to toss a fair coin. If a time traveler informs you that it will land heads, then you may know that it is very likely that the coin will land heads, even if the present objective chance that it will land heads is only .5. Furthermore, according to most theories of objective chance, past events have extreme objective chances. Hence many ordinary probabilistic contents about past events cannot contain the objective chance function. For instance, according to the objective chance hypothesis, the following contents cannot be knowledge:

(6) It's .6 likely that Jones smoked yesterday.

(7) It's almost but not quite certain that Jones smoked yesterday.

(8) It's unlikely that Jones smoked, and it's even less likely that Brown smoked.

---

[5] To be more precise, one could say that a probabilistic content is true just in case it contains the probability space that assigns probabilities to all and only those propositions that are objectively possible, and which assigns each proposition its objective chance.

[6] Thanks to Daniel Drucker for this observation.

This is an unwelcome result. Probabilistic beliefs about the past can intuitively exhibit all the epistemic virtues discussed in chapter 5, just as much as probabilistic beliefs about the future can exhibit them. The intended target of my theory is the sort of belief expressed by sentences containing epistemic vocabulary. These beliefs include many of our beliefs about the future, but they also include probabilistic beliefs about the past. In short, the objective chance hypothesis misses its target because it hits another target. There are indeed beliefs whose truth is determined by facts about objective chances. They are our full beliefs about the objective chances. By contrast, a theory of probabilistic knowledge must apply to all probabilistic beliefs. Thoroughly probabilistic beliefs are not full beliefs about anything. *A fortiori*, they are not full beliefs about objective chances.

It is correct to say that a belief constitutes probabilistic knowledge only if it has the probabilistic analog of truth. The probabilistic analog of truth is not agreement with objective chance, however, but truth itself. Belief is to truth as degree of belief is to *truth*. This deflationary account of factivity is more promising than the objective chance hypothesis. According to the deflationary account, the factivity of knowledge does not essentially depend on principles in the spirit of the Principal Principle. The fact that knowledge entails truth is simply a fact about knowledge itself.

7

Skepticism

7.1 A skeptical puzzle

Suppose that Smith has .6 credence that Jones smokes—or in other words, that Smith believes that it is .6 likely that Jones smokes. According to the third central thesis of this book, Smith's probabilistic belief can be knowledge. But this conclusion raises a skeptical puzzle. Smith is happy to admit that Jones might not smoke. In fact, according to Smith, there is a significant chance that Jones doesn't smoke. And if she doesn't smoke, then it's not *more likely than not* that she smokes. In particular, it is not exactly .6 likely that she smokes, and the belief that Smith has about Jones is wrong. If Smith finds out that Jones doesn't smoke, he should change his mind and accept that his earlier belief was wrong. But if Smith is happy to admit that his belief might turn out to be wrong—and indeed, that there is even a significant chance that it is wrong—then how can his belief constitute knowledge?

This puzzle may appear simple. In fact, there are several skeptical arguments mixed up in it. In this chapter, I spell out four arguments against the claim that probabilistic beliefs can constitute knowledge. These different arguments each call for different answers. Together, their answers support a bright conclusion. As long as some probabilistic beliefs can be true, and some true beliefs can be knowledge, some probabilistic beliefs can be knowledge.

7.2 The argument from inconsistency

An initial skeptical objection to Smith's .6 credence is that this probabilistic belief is not even consistent. According to the skeptic, this belief entails the possibility that it itself is wrong, and thereby entails a contradiction. Call this the *argument from inconsistency*. In more detail, the skeptic points out that the following inference is valid:

(1) a. It is .6 likely that Jones smokes.
    b. Hence it is .4 likely that Jones doesn't smoke.

    c. Hence it might be that Jones doesn't smoke.

    d. Hence it might not be .6 likely that Jones smokes.

    e. From (a) and (d): it *is* .6 likely *and might not be* .6 likely that Jones smokes.

This inference has multiple readings. For sake of argument, let us follow the skeptic in interpreting (1-a) and (1-e) so that the former entails the latter.[1] The skeptic continues by observing that (1-e) is a sentence of the form '*p* and it might not be that *p*'. Sentences of this form often sound bad. According to YALCIN 2007, they sound bad because their contents are semantic contradictions. The skeptic embraces this result and concludes that (1-e) is a contradiction. Since (1-a) entails a contradiction, (1-a) cannot be true. Hence the content of (1-a) cannot be knowledge for Smith. The same goes for many other sentences containing epistemic vocabulary, including any sentence expressing moderate credence in a proposition. According to the skeptic, the argument from inconsistency demonstrates that we have much less probabilistic knowledge than we thought.

How should we respond to the argument from inconsistency? In short, the skeptic misdiagnoses (1-e). This sentence does sound bad, but not because it is a semantic contradiction. The arguments in YALCIN 2007 apply to some but not all readings of sentences containing nested epistemic vocabulary. The sentence (1-e) is not a contradiction on its intended reading in the context of the above inference, in which it is validly derived from a consistent sentence. According to the semantics for probability operators defended in chapter 3, Smith may believe the content of 'It is .6 likely that Jones smokes' in virtue of having .6 credence that Jones smokes. At the same time, Smith may believe the content of 'it might not be .6 likely that Jones smokes' by having some other conditional credence that Jones smokes, conditional on some proposition that is determined by the context in which this sentence is uttered. For instance, Smith may believe that it might not be .6 likely that Jones smokes in virtue of having .9 conditional credence that Jones smokes, given that Brown smokes. The upshot is that Smith can consistently believe that it is .6 likely that Jones smokes, while also believing that it might be more than .6 likely.

The argument from inconsistency is one interpretation of the skeptical argument outlined in §7.1. Against this argument, one should imagine Smith defending his moderate credence that Jones smokes, precisely on the grounds that it

---

[1] Assume that context contributes the same partition to the interpretation of '.6 likely' in (1-a) and (1-e), that this partition is decisive with respect to the proposition that Jones smokes, and that the logical operators in (1-e) are interpreted relative to the partition containing just the trivial proposition. Then the desired entailment holds.

is moderate. "The claim that it is merely .6 likely that Jones smokes is *perfectly compatible* with the possibility that Jones does not smoke!" Addressed to the argument from inconsistency, this response is exactly right. Any moderate credence that Jones smokes is consistent with the belief that Jones might not smoke. The skeptic about probabilistic knowledge cannot fault the former probabilistic belief merely for being inconsistent with the latter.

7.3 The argument from closure

Smith believes that it might not be .6 likely that Jones smokes. This does not prevent his .6 credence that Jones smokes from being *consistent*, but could it nevertheless prevent his .6 credence from being *knowledge*? Consider the probabilistic content that it is certain that Jones doesn't smoke. This content is possible according to Smith. The skeptic may use this possibility to spell out a second challenge for the claim that Smith's .6 credence is knowledge, namely the *argument from closure*:

(2)   a. If Smith knows that it is .6 likely that Jones smokes, then Smith knows that it is not the case that Jones certainly doesn't smoke.
       b. Smith doesn't know that it is not the case that Jones certainly doesn't smoke.
       c. Therefore, Smith doesn't know that it is .6 likely that Jones smokes.

The second premise of the argument from closure seems compelling. After all, Smith himself believes that it might well turn out to be the case that Jones certainly doesn't smoke, and so it is hard to see how his knowledge could rule out that same possibility. The first premise of the argument also seems compelling. According to this premise, if Smith knows (3), then he also knows (4):

(3)   It is .6 likely that Jones smokes.

(4)   It is not the case that Jones certainly doesn't smoke.

There is a reading of these sentences such that (3) entails (4).[2] For sake of argument, we may spot the skeptic the further assumption that Smith knows that this entailment holds. Given this assumption, the closure of knowledge under known entailment entails the first premise of the argument from closure. Finally,

---

[2] Assume that the epistemic expressions in both sentences are interpreted relative to the same partition, that this partition is decisive with respect to the proposition that Jones smokes, and that the initial 'not' in (4) is interpreted relative to the partition containing just the trivial proposition. Then the desired entailment holds.

the first and second premise together seem to entail that Smith doesn't know that it is .6 likely that Jones smokes.

The argument from closure presents a harder challenge than the argument from inconsistency. To compare the arguments, it is helpful to introduce some vocabulary. Let us say that a probability space is *divine* just in case exactly one world is in its domain. A set of probability spaces is *pious* just in case it contains some divine probability space. A set of probability spaces is *heretical* just in case it is not pious. Examples of pious contents include the content that Jones might smoke, that Jones probably smokes, that Jones probably doesn't smoke, and that it is less than .3 likely that Jones smokes. Examples of heretical contents include the content that it is .6 likely that Jones smokes, that it is likely but not certain that Jones smokes, that Jones might smoke but it is more likely that Brown smokes, and that Jones might smoke and might not smoke. These heretical contents are each perfectly consistent. That is, they each contain some probability spaces. But they do not contain any divine probability spaces. Intuitively, heretical contents are exactly those contents that cannot be believed by a subject who is certain about exactly which world is actual. For example, let God be a subject who is certain of every true proposition. God does not have .6 credence that Jones smokes, or indeed any moderate credences, since God believes only pious contents.

Having introduced this vocabulary, we can distinguish two complaints about the belief that it is .6 likely that Jones smokes. The argument from inconsistency is based on the false claim that this belief is inconsistent. The argument from closure is based on the true claim that the belief is heretical. Even though it is perfectly consistent to say that it is .6 likely that Jones smokes, Smith cannot rule out that this content is something that God does not believe. According to the skeptic, it follows that this content cannot be knowledge for Smith. More generally, since God does not believe any heretical contents, one can never rule out that a heretical content is something that God does not believe. Hence the argument from closure can be extended to challenge knowledge of any heretical content.

The argument from closure can be further extended to support a skeptical conclusion about pious probabilistic beliefs. In its most general form, the argument from closure does not support the conclusion that pious beliefs are automatically incapable of being knowledge. But it does impose stringent conditions on what it takes for a pious belief to be knowledge. Let us say that a content p is a *propositional closure* of the content q just in case p is a nominally probabilistic content that entails q, and q is not entailed by any weaker nominally probabilistic content. For example, the content that Jones is at least .6 likely to smoke has a unique propositional closure, namely the set of probability spaces according to which it is certain that Jones smokes. The most general form of the argument from closure makes use of the fact that any probabilistic content entails the complement of the union of the propositional closures of its complement.[3] The first premise of the argument says that you know the former content only if you also know the latter. For example, you know that Jones is at least .6 likely to smoke only if you also know that it is not the case that Jones certainly doesn't smoke. To put it more intuitively, the first premise of the general argument from closure says that you know some content only if you also know that God does not disbelieve it. The second premise says that you do not know that God does not disbelieve the content in question. The argument concludes that you do not know that content itself.[4]

The general argument from closure presents a serious challenge for much of our ordinary probabilistic knowledge. In many cases, someone who believes a probabilistic content will also believe that the union of the propositional closures of its complement might well be the case, or to put it more intuitively, that it might well turn out that God believes otherwise. In such cases, it is hard to see how the subject could know the *complement* of the union of the closures of the complement of the belief in question. Again, we appear to have much less probabilistic knowledge than we thought.

How should we answer the argument from closure? We should start by recognizing that this argument closely resembles a familiar sort of skeptical argument. For example, consider the following argument adapted from DRETSKE 1970:

(5) a. If Smith knows that the caged animal in front of him is a zebra, then Smith knows that it is not the case that the animal is a cleverly disguised mule.

  b. Smith doesn't know that it is not the case that the animal is a cleverly disguised mule.

  c. Therefore, Smith doesn't know that the caged animal in front of him is a zebra.

Both this argument and the probabilistic argument from closure depend on the claim that knowledge is closed under known entailment. According to traditional closure principles, the relevant entailment relations hold between propositions,

---

[3] Any content is entailed by each of its propositional closures, and hence entailed by the union of its closures. Hence the complement of an arbitrary content p is entailed by the union of its closures. Hence the contrapositive entailment relation also holds: the complement of the union of the closures of the complement of p must be entailed by p itself.

[4] The argument (2) is not exactly an instance of the general argument from closure, since the union of the propositional closures of the complement of the content that it is .6 likely that Jones smokes is actually that Jones certainly doesn't smoke or *certainly smokes*. The second disjunct is omitted from (2) for ease of exposition.

such as the claim that the caged animal is a zebra and the claim that it is not a cleverly disguised mule. In the probabilistic argument from closure, the relevant entailment relations hold between probabilistic contents, such as the claim that it is .6 likely that Jones smokes and the claim that it is not certain that she doesn't. But traditional arguments from closure and the probabilistic argument from closure are otherwise the same. Hence we have a robust source of answers to our argument from closure: answers to traditional closure arguments against propositional knowledge.

For instance, one might simply deny the premise that knowledge is closed under known entailment. Alternatively, in the spirit of MOORE 1939, Smith himself might respond to either argument from closure by denying the second premise of the argument, claiming that he knows that certain skeptical possibilities do not obtain. Some dogmatists about perceptual knowledge might add that when it perceptually seems to Smith as if the caged animal in front of him is a zebra, he may be directly justified in believing this proposition, where that justification is sufficient for knowledge. If this claim is correct, then Smith could have similar knowledge of the content that it is .6 likely that Jones smokes, namely in some cases where he is directly justified in believing this probabilistic content on the basis of his perceptual experiences.[5]

Additional anti-skeptical strategies resist the alleged ramifications of the argument from closure. For instance, the epistemic contextualist denies that closure arguments undermine ordinary knowledge ascriptions. According to a traditional contextualist about propositional knowledge ascriptions, the sentence (6) has different contents as uttered in different contexts:

(6)   Smith knows that the caged animal is a zebra.

As uttered in skeptical contexts, (6) is false. But as uttered in ordinary contexts, (6) may well be true. According to a contextualist about probabilistic knowledge ascriptions, the same goes for sentences like (7):

(7)   Smith knows that it is .6 likely that Jones smokes.

The sentence 'it is .6 likely that Jones smokes' may well be true as uttered in skeptical contexts, just as 'the caged animal is a zebra' may be true as uttered in skeptical contexts. But the knowledge ascription (7) is false as uttered in some skeptical contexts, including the context of the argument from closure itself.

---

[5] For a classic argument for denying closure, see DRETSKE 1970. For a classic defense of perceptual dogmatism, see PRYOR 2000.

To give a more specific example, suppose that you are in the extension of 'knows' as uttered in a context with respect to some content only if you can eliminate all the alternatives inconsistent with that content that are relevant by the standards of that context.[6] When the content in question is probabilistic, these relevant alternatives are also probabilistic. Suppose that Jones flipped a coin in order to decide whether to quit smoking. The coin was biased in favor of smoking, with objective chance .4 that it would land heads and cause her to quit. Suppose that Smith knows these objective chance facts, and thereby comes to know by inference that it is .6 likely that Jones still smokes. According to the relevant alternatives contextualist, 'Smith knows that it is .6 likely that Jones smokes' may be true as uttered in ordinary contexts, namely because Smith can eliminate ordinary alternatives to the content that it is .6 likely that Jones smokes. Smith can eliminate the possibility that Jones flipped a fair coin in order to decide whether to quit smoking, for instance, as well as the possibility that Jones decided to ignore the coin flip altogether and keep smoking regardless of its outcome. However, in addition to these ordinary alternatives to the content that it is .6 likely that Jones smokes, there are some alternatives that Smith cannot eliminate. For instance, Smith cannot eliminate the possibility that an evil demon replaced the biased coin with a fair one just before Jones flipped it. As uttered in a context where this possibility is relevant, 'Smith knows that it is .6 likely that Jones smokes' is false.

In addition to far-fetched contents about evil demons, the contextualist may identify a simpler probabilistic content that Smith cannot eliminate, namely the content *that Jones certainly doesn't smoke*. This content is an alternative that is inconsistent with the content that it is .6 likely that Jones smokes. Furthermore, it is an alternative that is relevant in the context of the argument from closure. Hence in the context of that argument, 'Smith knows that it is .6 likely that Jones smokes' is false. The upshot of contextualism about probabilistic knowledge ascriptions is just the same as with traditional contextualism. Ascriptions of probabilistic knowledge may be false as uttered in skeptical contexts. But many ordinary knowledge ascriptions are nevertheless perfectly true.

There are many different senses in which a content can be *relevant* in a context. A content can be relevant in some sense without being relevant *as a challenging alternative*, or in other words, without being relevant in the sense relevant for epistemic contextualism. If we are debating whether the external world exists as

---

[6] The relation of *eliminating* a probabilistic content may be understood in any number of ways, each corresponding to a more detailed contextualist theory. For example, LEWIS 1996 proposes that "the uneliminated possibilities are those in which the subject's entire perceptual experience and memory are just as they actually are" (553). For alternative proposals, see DRETSKE 1970, GOLDMAN 1976, and COHEN 1988.

we are walking along in the woods, we may step over a tree branch together. The claim that there is a tree branch in front of us might be relevant in some sense in our context, but not relevant as a challenge for your claim that the external world does not exist. The content that Jones certainly doesn't smoke might often be relevant in some sense when ordinary speakers are talking about whether it is .6 likely that Jones smokes, but not relevant as a challenging alternative to the claim that it is .6 likely that Jones smokes.

Any epistemic contextualist who appeals to relevant alternatives should say something about which possibilities are relevant as challenging alternatives in a given context. LEWIS 1996 offers several rules for what possibilities count as relevant in this sense, and these rules can easily be extended to probabilistic contents. For instance, the Rule of Actuality says that if it is indeed .5 likely that Jones smokes, then it is a relevant possibility in your context that it is .5 likely that Jones smokes. The Rule of Attention adds that if you are paying attention to some probabilistic content, then that content will also be relevant in your context. For example, when you are talking with someone, you often pay attention to probabilistic contents that you think they might believe. If you are talking with an expert who knows whether Jones smokes, then you will often pay attention to the content that Jones certainly smokes, as well as the content that Jones certainly doesn't smoke, since you realize that the expert believes one of these two contents. As a result, you will fail to satisfy 'knows that it is .6 likely that Jones smokes' as uttered in this context. The same goes for contexts where you believe that an expert might be eavesdropping on your conversation, and even for some contexts where you simply imagine that an expert might say that your probabilistic beliefs are false.

In addition to being constrained by traditional rules governing relevance, challenging alternatives to probabilistic knowledge exhibit an additional noteworthy trend. As a general rule, thoroughly probabilistic beliefs are more easily challenged by other thoroughly probabilistic contents, and less easily challenged by nominally probabilistic contents. For example, your .6 credence that Jones smokes is more easily challenged by the content that it is .7 likely that Jones smokes, and less easily challenged by the content that Jones certainly doesn't smoke. What explains this contrast? One potentially relevant asymmetry concerns the contents that you consider possible. When you have .6 credence that Jones smokes, you necessarily believe that it might be that Jones certainly doesn't smoke.[7]

---

[7] To be more precise, you necessarily believe the content of 'it might be that Jones certainly doesn't smoke' on a natural interpretation of this sentence, namely as long as 'might' is interpreted relative to a partition that is decisive with respect to whether Jones smokes.

By contrast, you don't necessarily believe that it might be .7 likely that Jones smokes. The routine presence of the former possibility may help undermine its intuitive skeptical force. Another hypothesis is that nominally probabilistic and thoroughly probabilistic alternatives are typically raised in different sorts of skeptical scenarios. CROSS 2010 argues that some skeptical scenarios are more successful than others, namely scenarios that help explain why you have less knowledge than you think you have, as opposed to scenarios that merely raise the abstract possibility that your beliefs are in error. It might be that nominally probabilistic alternatives are more often raised in scenarios of the latter sort. To sum up, relevant alternatives contextualism does not face any distinctive challenges when it comes to addressing probabilistic versions of the argument from closure.

Another answer to the argument from closure is provided by interest-relative invariantism, according to which what you know depends in part on your practical interests.[8] As summarized by WEATHERSON 2011a, interest-relative invariantism says that there are subjects such that one has knowledge and the other does not, where the only relevant difference between these subjects concerns their interests, and the relevant knowledge is not "about their interests, or something that is supported by propositions about their interests, and so on" (594). For example, suppose that Smith parked his car several hours ago, leaving it in his usual parking spot. According to the interest-relative invariantist, Smith may know that his car is still there if he is merely planning on using it to deliver lunch to some friends, but not if he is planning on using it to deliver an urgent blood transfusion to the local hospital. Probabilistic knowledge could in principle exhibit just the same sort of interest relativity. Consider the following example:

> There are two nearby mine shafts, shaft A and shaft B. In one of the shafts, ten miners have been hard at work. They decided which shaft to enter according to a fair coin flip. Smith wants to deliver some lunch to the miners. He knows that they are in shaft A or shaft B, depending on the outcome of the coin flip. Shaft A is closer to his current location. Smith could call someone to find out the location of the miners, but the phone call would be extremely expensive.

Suppose Smith decides to visit shaft A first, since it is closer to his current location. In this case, Smith may know that he should visit shaft A first, namely because he knows that it is closer than shaft B, and he knows that the miners are equally likely to be in either shaft.

By contrast, suppose that instead of deliberating about the efficient delivery of lunches, Smith had instead been deliberating about a matter of life and death.

---

[8] For representative examples of interest-relative invariantism, see HAWTHORNE 2004, STANLEY 2005, FANTL AND McGRATH 2010, and WEATHERSON 2011a.

For example, imagine Smith facing the decision described in the miners case described in KOLODNY AND MACFARLANE 2010:

> Ten miners are trapped either in shaft A or in shaft B, but we do not know which. Flood waters threaten to flood the shafts. We have enough sandbags to block one shaft, but not both. If we block one shaft, all the water will go into the other shaft, killing any miners inside it. If we block neither shaft, both shafts will fill halfway with water, and just one miner, the lowest in the shaft, will be killed. (115)

Assume that if the miners are equally likely to be in shaft A or shaft B, then Smith should flood neither shaft in order to minimize the expected number of deaths. Also, suppose that just as before, Smith could place an expensive phone call to find out the location of the miners. Smith does not know that he should flood neither shaft, because in this second case, he does not know that the miners are equally likely to be in shaft A or shaft B. The interest-relative invariantist concludes that whether Smith knows that the miners are equally likely to be in shaft A or shaft B depends in part on his practical interests.

According to some interest-relative invariantists, observing that knowledge is interest relative helps resolve skeptical challenges like the argument from closure. HAWTHORNE 2004 argues that the interest relativity of knowledge helps explain why we are reluctant to ascribe knowledge in the context of an epistemology classroom. As epistemologists, we correctly observe that Smith cannot rely on his .5 credence in deciding whether to block or flood each shaft. We incorrectly assume that whether his credence is knowledge does not depend on his practical environment, and we conclude that his .5 credence is never knowledge. According to Hawthorne, appreciating that knowledge is destroyed in certain practical environments should forestall this reasoning and free us to conclude that most ordinary knowledge ascriptions are true. The upshot is the same as the upshot of other responses to skepticism: the argument from closure does not present a distinctive threat to our knowledge of probabilistic contents. The argument is exactly as challenging as traditional skeptical arguments, as it simply transposes them into an argument about probabilistic belief.

7.4 The argument from disjunction

In addition to traditional challenges for knowledge, probabilistic knowledge faces some special challenges of its own. The traditional skeptic argues that subjects lack knowledge, but not by arguing against the contents that they allegedly know. That is, the traditional skeptic does not go around arguing, "That animal is *not* a zebra! It is a cleverly disguised mule!" By contrast, a skeptic about probabilistic knowledge may argue that subjects lack knowledge of some content by arguing against that content itself. For instance, consider the following argument:

(8)   a. Either Jones smokes or Jones doesn't smoke.
      b. If Jones smokes, then it is not .6 likely that Jones smokes.
      c. If Jones doesn't smoke, then it is not .6 likely that Jones smokes.
      d. Therefore, it is not .6 likely that Jones smokes.
      e. Therefore, Smith doesn't know that it is .6 likely that Jones smokes.

Here, the skeptic argues that however things turn out—that is, whether or not Jones smokes—Smith's belief is false. Since knowledge is factive, the skeptic concludes that Smith's belief is not knowledge. This skeptical argument is the *argument from disjunction*. This sort of argument threatens to undermine a lot of our probabilistic knowledge, since the same sort of argument can be used to challenge your knowledge of any heretical content. For any possible world, any heretical content will be inconsistent with the nominally probabilistic content according to which only that world is possible. Hence in order to challenge knowledge of an arbitrary heretical content, one may argue that some such singleton content must be true, and also that this true singleton content entails the complement of the heretical content in question. If this general sort of argument is successful, then we have much less probabilistic knowledge than we thought.

The argument from disjunction can seem especially threatening when the disjuncts are themselves relevant alternatives to the knowledge that the argument challenges, in the sense discussed in §7.3. Remember, God does not have any moderate credences. The skeptic points out that in particular, God does not have .6 credence that Jones smokes. God disagrees with the claim that it is .6 likely that Jones smokes. To make matters worse, it appears that God must know any content that God believes. Hence it appears that God not only *believes* that it is not .6 likely that Jones smokes, but in fact *knows* this content, from which it follows that Smith doesn't know that it is .6 likely that Jones smokes. Again, this line of thought can be used to challenge knowledge of any heretical content. For any heretical content, it appears that God knows that the content is false, from which it follows that no one knows the content.

The argument from disjunction is more severe than the argument from closure, as the former challenges your knowledge of contents by challenging those very contents themselves. Fortunately, appreciating the severity of this challenge leads us to the correct answer to the argument from disjunction. The argument fails before it even mentions knowledge, namely as it targets the content that it is .6 likely that Jones smokes:

(8)   a. Either Jones smokes or Jones doesn't smoke.
      b. If Jones smokes, then it is not .6 likely that Jones smokes.
      c. If Jones doesn't smoke, then it is not .6 likely that Jones smokes.
      d. Therefore, it is not .6 likely that Jones smokes.

This initial segment of the argument from disjunction appears to be an instance of constructive dilemma. But it is not actually an instance of constructive dilemma at all. In fact, this inference is invalid. The semantics for epistemic vocabulary defended in chapters 3 and 4 can help us diagnose this inference. According to my semantics, apparent instances of constructive dilemma sometimes turn out to be invalid when they embed sentences with thoroughly probabilistic contents. For comparison, imagine that a fair die has been rolled, and you have not yet seen how it landed. The die has three low numbers: 1, 2, and 3. The die has three high numbers: 4, 5, and 6. Consider the following inference about the number rolled:

(9)   a. The number is either low or high.
      b. If the number is low, it is not .5 likely that it is even.
      c. If the number is high, it is not .5 likely that it is even.
      d. Therefore, it is not .5 likely that the number is even.

This inference is not actually an instance of constructive dilemma, namely because it equivocates. As explained in §4.4, the premises of inferences like (9) are naturally interpreted as expressing probabilistic beliefs involving your conditional credences, while the conclusion is naturally interpreted as expressing your all-things-considered credences. As a result, the inference is invalid. The same diagnosis applies to the argument from disjunction. The premises of the argument of disjunction are naturally interpreted as expressing probabilistic beliefs involving your credences conditional on the content that Jones smokes and conditional on the content that she doesn't, while the conclusion is naturally interpreted as expressing your all-things-considered credences. In more formal terms, the conditional operators in (8-b) and (8-c) are naturally interpreted relative to the partition of propositions that specify whether Jones smokes, while the negation and probability operators in (8-d) are naturally interpreted relative to the trivial partition. Hence on their most natural interpretation, the former premises of the argument from disjunction do not entail the latter.

   In addition to constructive dilemma, a number of other inference rules appear to have instances that challenge probabilistic knowledge. For example, consider the following apparent instance of *modus tollens*, discussed briefly in YALCIN 2012C:

(10) a. If the marble is not big, then John does not know it is probably big.
      b. John knows the marble is probably big.
      c. Therefore, the marble is big.

According to this argument, the fact that a certain content is knowledge appears to entail that its propositional closure is true. But fortunately, as Yalcin recognizes, inferences like (10) are not valid. The correct assessment of (10) is just the same as for the following closely related argument, which does not mention knowledge:

(11) a. If the marble is not big, then it is not probably big.
      b. The marble is probably big.
      c. Therefore, the marble is big.

The invalidity of (11) is more obvious than the invalidity of (10), but the nature of the invalidity is the same in both cases. Both (10-b) and (11-b) have thoroughly probabilistic contents. When it comes to sentences with thoroughly probabilistic contents, apparent instances of *modus tollens* are sometimes invalid. For comparison, consider the following argument about the outcome of rolling a fair die:

(12) a. If the number rolled is low, it is probably odd.
      b. The number is not probably odd.
      c. Therefore, it is not low.

As discussed at length in §4.4, this inference is invalid. Appearances to the contrary, (12) is not a genuine instance of *modus tollens*. The same goes for the inferences (10) and (11) considered above. These inferences are not actually genuine instances of any classically valid inference rule.

    At first glance, it may appear that a probabilistic content is true if and only if it contains the probability space according to which the actual world is certain. To restate the point more intuitively, it may appear that a probabilistic content is true if and only if God believes it. But on reflection, it is important to distinguish these two properties of probabilistic contents. I argued in §6.5 that probabilistic contents are not true in virtue of containing the objective chance function. The same arguments explain why probabilistic contents are not true in virtue of containing the probability space according to which the actual world is certain. The truth of a thoroughly probabilistic content is distinct from the truth of any nominally probabilistic content. The fact that Jones probably smokes is distinct from the fact that God believes that Jones probably smokes, for instance. The same goes for any heretical content. It is .6 likely that Jones smokes. The miners are equally likely to be in shaft A or shaft B. It is probable but not certain that Alice finds Bert attractive. Just reflect, and you will find that there are plenty of true probabilistic contents that God does not believe. In this respect, probabilistic contents are like *de se* contents. Suppose that Smith expects to be in the hospital until Tuesday, and that this *de se* belief constitutes knowledge for Smith. The content of that *de se* belief is not something that God believes, and so it is not something that God knows, even if God knows every true uncentered proposition.[9]

So far in this section, I have been talking as if we are in an ordinary context. There is an unfortunate but familiar complication for our present discussion: as soon as we start talking about the fact that God does not believe some content, we might be raising some possibility that we cannot rule out, some possibility that challenges the epistemic status of beliefs that we ordinarily take ourselves to know. The argument from disjunction may raise just the same sort of skeptical possibilities as the argument from closure. God is like the ultimate eavesdropper. As you consider the argument from disjunction, you cannot eliminate the possibility that God would disagree with many of your beliefs, including beliefs that you would otherwise have been happy to identify as knowledge in an ordinary context. Just considering the argument from disjunction may thereby prevent your saying that various probabilistic beliefs constitute knowledge for you. If knowledge is the norm of assertion, you may even be reluctant to express those same beliefs. This does not demonstrate that your probabilistic beliefs are false, only that they are challenged by the argument from closure addressed in §7.3.

So far I have argued that the argument from disjunction does not undermine our knowledge of probabilistic contents any more than it undermines probabilistic contents themselves. But what if the argument from disjunction is successful in undermining both? Upon considering the argument from disjunction, some readers might find it tempting to reject the probabilistic contents that it challenges. For instance, one might start using 'false' for any probabilistic content that fails to contain the probability space according to which the actual world is certain. "I still believe that it is .6 likely that Jones smokes, but I know that it is false that it is .6 likely." Alternatively, one might even refuse to use 'believe' for contents that are false in this sense. "I don't actually believe that it is .6 likely that Jones smokes. It's just that I have no choice but to act as if I believe it." This dramatic conclusion suggests that strictly speaking, you ought to assert a content only when you would also assert some propositional closure of it. For instance, you ought to assert that it is at least .6 likely that Jones smokes only when you

---

[9] For many arguments in this chapter, it suffices to stipulate that God is a subject with propositional knowledge that is inconsistent with a given heretical content. But see KRETZMANN 1966 and KVANVIG 1986 for related discussion of the *de se* knowledge of genuinely omniscient subjects.

would also assert that Jones smokes. You should refrain from ever asserting that it is exactly .6 likely that Jones smokes. More generally, since heretical contents have empty propositional closures, you should refrain from ever asserting any heretical probabilistic content.[10]

The problem with this response is that it divorces your probabilistic beliefs from their essential role in your practical reasoning. The heretical content that it is .6 likely that Jones smokes does fail to contain the probability space that represents what God believes, i.e. the probability space according to which every true proposition is certain. But believing this fact about the heretical content is consistent with having .6 credence that Jones smokes. As you reason about questions of practical importance, it is the second attitude that matters, not the first. Suppose that the miners are trapped. They are equally likely to be in shaft A or shaft B. God believes that they are not equally likely to be in shaft A or shaft B. In light of these facts, what should you do? The answer is that you should flood neither shaft. Your decision should be determined by your credences, not your full beliefs about what God believes. Furthermore, it is not just that the latter beliefs *shouldn't* determine your decision—in fact, they *can't* determine it. For sake of argument, suppose you reflect on what God believes and conclude that you should flood shaft A or you should flood shaft B. This conclusion alone does not settle the question of what you should do, since it leaves you to figure out which shaft you should flood. In many situations of ignorance, acting on thoroughly probabilistic contents is not only rationally necessary, but also the only practically available option.

I have stipulated that in the miners case, it is true that the miners are equally likely to be in each shaft. This true content is not merely some proposition about what is likely given the limited evidence that you are stipulated to have. Similarly, the content that you should flood neither shaft is not some proposition about what you subjectively ought to do in light of your limited evidence. Again, your thoroughly probabilistic beliefs are distinct from full beliefs in propositions of any sort. This distinction is reflected in the theoretical roles played by these different sorts of beliefs, namely those theoretical roles described in §1.2. For instance, another person who knows nothing about your evidence may nevertheless have strong opinions about whether you should flood neither shaft. As you gain more evidence, you yourself may change your mind about whether you should flood neither shaft, and retract your earlier assertion that you should flood neither

---

[10] Any non-empty nominally probabilistic content contains some divine probability space. By definition, heretical contents do not contain divine probability spaces. Hence heretical contents cannot be entailed by non-empty nominally probabilistic contents, from which it follows that no heretical content has a non-empty propositional closure.

shaft, without changing your mind or retracting any assertion about what you subjectively ought to have done in light of your evidence. The same goes for your belief that the miners are equally likely in either shaft. As you gain evidence about the miners, you may change your mind about whether the miners are probably in shaft A, without changing your mind about what you subjectively ought to have believed in light of your earlier evidence. The probabilistic contents of your credences about the miners play several distinctive theoretical roles, and these roles cannot be played by propositions about your evidence.

Let us take stock of our position with respect to the skeptic. The skeptical arguments considered so far have limited force. The argument from closure undermines probabilistic knowledge only insofar as familiar skeptical arguments undermine propositional knowledge. If we can answer the latter arguments, we can answer the former. The argument from disjunction undermines probabilistic knowledge only insofar as it undermines probabilistic beliefs themselves. As mentioned in §7.1, the conclusion of our investigation is bright: as long as some probabilistic beliefs can be true, and some true beliefs can be knowledge, some probabilistic beliefs can be knowledge.

7.5 The argument from safety

Suppose again that Jones flipped a coin in order to decide whether to quit smoking. Smith knows that the coin was biased in favor of smoking, with objective chance .1 that it would land heads and cause Jones to quit. Suppose that Smith infers that it is .6 likely that Jones smokes. It is natural to conclude that Smith's .6 credence could turn out be knowledge. Against this conclusion, though, the skeptic may object that the coin could easily have come up heads. There is a close world where the coin came up heads and Jones quit smoking. At this world, it is not .6 likely that Jones smokes. The possibility that Smith is wrong is not just some abstract epistemic possibility for Smith. It is a possibility that is true at some close world. Furthermore, in the close worlds where Jones quit smoking, Smith nevertheless still believes that it is .6 likely that she smokes. Taken together, these facts raise a final skeptical challenge for the claim that Smith knows that it is .6 likely that Jones smokes, namely the *argument from safety*:

(13)   a. If Smith knows that it is .6 likely that Jones smokes, then there is no close world where he falsely believes that it is .6 likely that she smokes.

  b. There is a close world where Smith falsely believes that it is .6 likely that Jones smokes.

  c. Therefore, Smith does not know that it is .6 likely that Jones smokes.

For sake of argument, let us assume that (13) has a valid reading. As with the three skeptical arguments already considered, this argument can be extended to challenge a wide variety of probabilistic beliefs. According to the skeptic, many probabilistic beliefs based on information about objective chance facts could easily have been false. Assuming that knowledge is safe, it follows that these beliefs cannot be knowledge.

The assumption that knowledge is safe is controversial. Those who reject this assumption may reject the first premise of the above argument. In the remainder of this chapter, I explore another response. I challenge the second premise of the argument, thereby developing a response that can be accepted even by advocates of the safety condition for knowledge. This response requires a substantial detour through several intriguing issues in the philosophy of language. In order to simplify our discussion, it will be helpful to temporarily shift our attention to another example of probabilistic knowledge derived from knowledge of objective chance facts. Consider the following case:

> Lottery: Smith has entered a lottery with exactly one hundred tickets, purchasing ticket number 35. As Smith watches, all one hundred lottery tickets are put into a hat. A lottery official pulls out the winning ticket and waves it in the air. Smith knows that each ticket is equally likely to be the winning ticket, and so he knows that his ticket probably lost the lottery.

Here is a troubling skeptical argument: Smith could easily have won the lottery, since any number could easily have been selected as the winner. There is a close world where Smith won the lottery. This close world is not a world where Smith probably lost, but it is a world where Smith believes he probably lost. It appears that Smith's belief is not safe. How, then, can Smith's belief be knowledge?

An important initial observation is that according to our description of the Lottery case, it is true that Smith probably lost the lottery. In fact, each of the following probabilistic contents is true:

(14)   Ticket number 1 probably lost the lottery.
       Ticket number 2 probably lost the lottery.
       Ticket number 3 probably lost the lottery.
       . . .
       Ticket number 100 probably lost the lottery.

At first glance, one might be tempted to object that these contents cannot all be true. After all, some ticket won the lottery, and that ticket did not probably lose. To put it another way, one might worry that one of these probabilistic contents must be false, namely because it fails to contain the probability space according to which the actual world is certain. In other words, one might worry that one of these probabilistic contents is something that God does not believe. In response to this worry, it should be conceded that God does not believe each content in (14). The conjunction of these contents is heretical. In this respect, the conjunction is just like the content that it is .6 likely that Jones smokes, or the content that the miners are equally likely to be in shaft A or shaft B. The problem with the worry is that for probabilistic contents, truth does not consist in containing the probability space according to which the actual world is certain. As argued in §7.4, there are contents that are both heretical and true. The conjunction of the true contents in (14) is just another example of this sort.

In addition to supposing the contents in (14) are true in the *Lottery* case, let us also suppose that as the winning ticket is pulled from the hat, the lottery official introduces a name for the ticket. As Smith watches, the lottery official announces: "I hereby dub this ticket *Winner!*" Having stipulated these facts, we may conclude that the following probabilistic content is false in the *Lottery* case:

(15)   Winner probably lost the lottery.

Taken together, the sentences in (14) and (15) illustrate a remarkable fact about epistemic vocabulary, a fact that will eventually assist us in responding to the argument from safety. There are one hundred sentences identified in (14). Exactly one of these sentences contains a name that refers to the same ticket as 'Winner' in (15). This sentence differs from (15) only by swapping out 'Winner' for some other name that refers to the very same ticket. The probabilistic content of the belief expressed by (15) is distinct from the content of the belief expressed by its counterpart in (14). This difference in content makes for a difference in truth value: (15) is false, whereas every sentence in (14) is true. This conclusion brings us to our remarkable fact, namely that the expression 'probably' creates a *hyperintensional context*—that is, the substitution of necessarily coreferring expressions in the scope of 'probably' can change the truth value of the sentence that contains it. The same goes for many sentences containing probability operators and other epistemic vocabulary.

Although much has been said about hyperintensional contexts and much has been said about epistemic modals, very little has been said about both at once. Discussions of hyperintensionality often focus on hyperintensional contexts that arise in the scope of attitude verbs. For example, consider the following belief ascriptions:

(16)   Smith believes that ticket number 1 probably lost the lottery.
Smith believes that ticket number 2 probably lost the lottery.
Smith believes that ticket number 3 probably lost the lottery.

. . .

Smith believes that ticket number 100 probably lost the lottery.

Each of these sentences is true. Among them, there is a sentence that ascribes a belief about the winning ticket to Smith. Replacing the name of that ticket with 'Winner' changes this true sentence into a false sentence, just like replacing 'Hesperus' with 'Phosphorus' can change the truth value of a belief ascription. This is just another illustration of the familiar fact that attitude ascriptions contain hyperintensional contexts.[11]

By stipulation, in the *Lottery* case, the contents of the beliefs ascribed by the sentences in (16) are not merely believed by Smith; they are also true in the *Lottery* case itself. It is indeed true that ticket number 1 probably lost the lottery, that ticket number 2 probably lost the lottery, and so on for every numbered ticket. It is indeed false that Winner probably lost the lottery. Hence 'Winner probably lost the lottery' contains a hyperintensional context, even though it does not contain any attitude verbs. To sum up: just like sentences that ascribe probabilistic beliefs, sentences that *express* probabilistic beliefs can contain hyper-intensional contexts. Hence by reflecting on features of familiar hyperintensional contexts, namely those that appear in belief ascriptions, we can gather useful information about the hyperintensional contexts that are created by epistemic vocabulary.

For the purpose of answering the argument from safety, one especially significant observation concerns the interpretation of bound pronouns in hyperintensional contexts. Let us start by observing some facts about bound pronouns in the scope of attitude verbs. For example, consider the following belief ascription:

(17)   Smith believes that every ticket probably lost the lottery.

---

[11] 'Smith believes that Winner probably lost the lottery' may have multiple readings, including a *de re* reading on which it is true in virtue of Smith believing that Winner probably lost when thinking of it as the ticket with a certain number on it. For simplicity, I shall set aside potential *de re* readings of this ascription and its complement.

In the context of the following dialogue, (17) says something true:

(18) a. Which ticket won? Was it ticket number 1? Ticket number 2?
b. Smith believes that every ticket probably lost the lottery.

But in the context of the following dialogue, (17) says something false:

(19) a. Which ticket won? Was it the ticket that was just pulled from the hat?
b. #Smith believes that every ticket probably lost the lottery.

The belief ascription (17) is context sensitive. In particular, the content of this belief ascription as uttered in a context depends on which way of thinking of the lottery tickets is relevant in that context. Depending on what way of thinking of the tickets is relevant, (17) can be used to ascribe different collections of beliefs to Smith. In some contexts, (17) merely entails that Smith believes that ticket number 1 probably lost the lottery, that Smith believes that ticket number 2 probably lost the lottery, and so on. In other contexts, it entails the false content that Smith believes that the ticket that was just pulled from the hat probably lost the lottery.[12]

Familiar discussions of hyperintensionality often focus on pairs of names like 'Hesperus' and 'Phosphorus' that are associated with different ways of thinking of an object. Adding to these examples, KRIPKE 1979 observes that even the single name 'Paderewski' can be associated with different ways of thinking of an object, namely as that name is uttered in different contexts. Kripke observes that as a result, 'Peter believes Paderewski is a good musician' is context sensitive. By fixing some way of thinking of Paderewski, context may affect the truth value of this belief ascription. The sentence 'Smith believes that every ticket probably lost the lottery' illustrates that quantifier phrases like 'every ticket' can induce just the same sort of context sensitivity as names like 'Paderewski'. Of course, it is a familiar fact that sentences containing quantifier phrases like 'every ticket' are context sensitive, namely because context can help determine what objects are in the domain of the quantifier. It is a less familiar fact that such sentences can be context sensitive because context helps determine the relevant ways of thinking of objects in the domain of a quantifier. According to one classic semantic treatment of pronouns, inspired by the treatment of variables in TARSKI 1936, bound

---

[12] According to the *Epistemic Containment Principle* defended by VON FINTEL AND IATRIDOU 2003, "a quantifier cannot have scope over an epistemic modal" (174). For critical discussion of this principle, see SWANSON 2010. Also, note that von Fintel and Iatridou concede that quantifier phrases can bind pronouns across epistemic modals, observing that 'every student is such that he may be standing at the front of the classroom' has an epistemic reading. The reader may sidestep controversy about the Epistemic Containment Principle by rephrasing my lottery sentences using relative clauses from which 'probably' cannot be extracted.

pronouns have denotations relative to an assignment function. The upshot of our present discussion is that bound pronouns not only have assignment-relative denotations; as Frege might have put it, they also have assignment-relative *senses*. These senses are determined by context, and they can affect the truth value of belief ascriptions embedding quantified sentences.[13]

Having described these facts about belief ascriptions, we can now identify similar facts about sentences containing epistemic vocabulary. Consider the following sentence:

(20)   Every ticket probably lost the lottery.

This sentence is not a belief ascription. But it exhibits just the same sort of context sensitivity as the belief ascription (17) that embeds it. Just like (17), the content of (20) as uttered in a context depends on which way of thinking of the lottery tickets is relevant in that context. This difference in content makes for a difference in truth value. In the context of the following dialogue, (20) says something true:

(21)   a. Which ticket won? Was it an odd numbered ticket? Was it ticket number 35?
       b. Every ticket probably lost the lottery.

But in the context of the following dialogue, (20) says something false:

(22)   a. Which ticket won? Was it the ticket that was just pulled from the hat?
       b. #Every ticket probably lost the lottery.

In the context of the first dialogue, (20) entails that ticket number 1 probably lost the lottery, that ticket number 2 probably lost the lottery, and so on. In many contexts, (20) is naturally read as entailing these true probabilistic contents. But in the context of the second dialogue, the same sentence entails that the ticket that was just pulled from the hat probably lost the lottery. In this second context, (20) says something false.[14]

How are these facts about hyperintensional contexts relevant to our answer to the argument from safety? Answering the skeptical argument requires one more observation. Having argued that the sentence (20) is context sensitive, we can now turn our attention to the following sentence:

(23)   Every close world is probably such that Smith lost in it.

---

[13] For further discussion, including other considerations in favor of associating bound pronouns with senses or guises, see §3.5 of ALONI 2000, §1 of Moss 2012b, and CHARLOW AND SHARVIT 2014.

[14] For an alternative account of quantifiers binding into the scope of epistemic vocabulary, see YALCIN 2015. By contrast with my account, Yalcin's account fails to predict that (20) exhibits the context sensitivity described here. I leave further comparison of our accounts for future research.

This sentence is not a sentence of ordinary language, since the quantifier in (23) ranges over possible worlds, as opposed to lottery tickets. But in other respects, this sentence is just like (20). In particular, observe that (23) is context sensitive. In the context of the following dialogue, (23) says something true:

(24) a. How many close worlds are probably such that Smith lost the lottery in them? Could Smith have easily cheated to make sure that he would win?
  b. Smith did not cheat, and there is no close world in which he cheated. At every close world, the winning ticket was drawn at random.
  c. Ah—in that case, every close world is probably such that Smith lost in it.

But in the context of the following dialogue, (23) says something false:

(25) a. How many close worlds are probably such that Smith lost the lottery in them? Are there any close worlds where Smith won the lottery?
  b. Yes, there are some close worlds where Smith won. In those worlds, he did not lose the lottery.
  c. #Every close world is probably such that Smith lost in it.

Just like (20), the sentence (23) contains a hyperintensional context and a quantifier binding into that context. Just like (20), the sentence (23) is context sensitive. The truth value of (23) as uttered in a context depends on which ways of thinking of objects are relevant in that context. In this case, the relevant objects are not lottery tickets, however, but possible worlds. The sentence (23) is false as uttered in context of (25). But in the context of (24), the sentence (23) says roughly that in all close worlds, considered as such, it is probable that Smith lost the lottery. In this context, we are not thinking of each close world as a world where Smith wins or loses the lottery, but rather as an arbitrary close world where Smith plays the lottery. As uttered in this sort of context, (23) may well be true. The content of (23) is a thoroughly probabilistic content. It is a conjunction of contents that you believe in virtue of having certain credences, where these credences are probabilistic beliefs about possible worlds.

In light of these observations, let us again consider the lottery example described at the start of this section. Smith believes that he probably lost the lottery. Is his belief safe? Consider the following sentence:

(26) There is no close world where Smith falsely believes that he probably lost the lottery.

This sentence is context sensitive. As uttered in some contexts, (26) says something false. But this is only a limited victory for the skeptic. As uttered in other contexts, (26) says something true. In these contexts, you may explain: "Smith has a safe probabilistic belief that he probably lost the lottery, since every close world is probably such that Smith lost the lottery at that world." The context sensitivity of sentences like (26) means that one can answer the argument from safety just as an epistemic contextualist answers the argument from closure. Although safety conditions and knowledge ascriptions may both be false as uttered in some contexts, many ordinary safety conditions and knowledge ascriptions may nevertheless be perfectly true.

With this in mind, we may finally return to our original example of Smith and Jones. Smith believes that it is .6 likely that Jones smokes. According to the argument from safety, his belief is not safe, and hence it cannot be knowledge. But the argument from safety fails, because Smith's belief is indeed safe. Assume that there are no close worlds where Jones flips a fair coin in order to decide whether to quit smoking. There are no close worlds where an evil demon replaced the biased coin with a fair one just before Jones flipped it. There are no close worlds where Jones decided to ignore the coin flip altogether and keep smoking regardless of its outcome. And so on. At all close worlds, Jones flipped a biased coin, and there was .4 objective chance that the coin would land heads and cause her to quit. In light of these background assumptions, every close world is such that we may correctly assign .6 credence to the claim that Jones smokes at that world. Hence the probabilistic belief that it is .6 likely that Jones smokes is safe. As far as the safety condition is concerned, this .6 credence can indeed be knowledge.

Having responded to the argument from safety, I will end by addressing several questions raised by my response. I have compared the following sentences:

(17)   Smith believes that every ticket probably lost the lottery.

(20)   Every ticket probably lost the lottery.

(23)   Every close world is probably such that Smith lost in it.

As uttered at a certain context, (17) may be true in virtue of Smith believing certain thoroughly probabilistic contents, such as the content that ticket number 35 probably lost the lottery. The sentence (20) may be true in virtue of the fact that certain probabilistic contents are indeed true, such as the claim that ticket number 35 probably lost the lottery. Analogously, (23) should be true in virtue of the fact that certain probabilistic contents are true, namely the contents of our credences about close possible worlds. This analogy raises foundational questions about how to model our beliefs about other possible worlds, such as the thoroughly probabilistic belief that a given close world is probably such that Smith lost in it. Consider the claim that *Smith lost the lottery*. This claim corresponds to a way that the world might be. According to some theorists, it is represented by a set of possible worlds, namely the worlds where Smith lost the lottery. What about the claim that *a certain close world is such that Smith lost the lottery in it*? Does this claim correspond to a way that the pluriverse of all possible worlds might be? Can this claim ultimately be represented by a set of possible worlds? And most importantly for our purposes, what does it mean to believe that this claim is probable, or to have a high credence in this claim?

These foundational questions are not questions for me alone. In discussing quantifiers that range over possible worlds, we have come across a fact that everyone must explain, namely that we can think about possible worlds, just like we think about any other sort of object. This fact is relevant when we explicitly talk about possible worlds in the metaphysics classroom. The same fact is relevant when we talk about the safety condition for knowledge in the epistemology classroom. The question of how to represent credences about possible worlds depends on the question of how to represent any sort of belief about possible worlds, which in turn may ultimately depend on difficult questions about the nature of possible worlds themselves. I will not address these questions here. For the purpose of answering the argument from safety, what matters is that we have ways of thinking about possible worlds, just like we have ways of thinking of ordinary objects. As some might put it, we can think about possible worlds under different guises, or modes of presentation. Just as you believe that every ticket probably lost the lottery, provided that you are thinking of the tickets in a certain way, you can believe that every close world is probably such that Smith lost in it. Just as the content of your probabilistic beliefs about ordinary objects can be true, the same goes for the contents of your probabilistic beliefs about close worlds. Just as it may be true that every ticket probably lost the lottery, it may be true that every close world is probably such that Smith lost in it. Furthermore, the same goes for the probabilistic contents of safety conditions for particular instances of probabilistic knowledge. It may be true that at every close world where Smith has .6 credence that Jones smokes, it is .6 likely that Jones smokes at that world.

As the safety condition is spelled out in this section, it is a modal condition on probabilistic knowledge. It is worth noting that in addition to safety, other proposed necessary conditions for knowledge may also be interpreted as modal conditions. Consider factivity, for instance. What does it mean to say that knowledge entails truth? According to the interpretation explored in §6.2, it simply means that the probabilistic content of a knowledge ascription is a subset of the content of the knowledge that it ascribes. But one might also interpret factivity as a modal condition, requiring that every possible world is such that if it is true at that world that Smith knows that it is .6 likely that Jones smokes, then the probabilistic content that it is .6 likely that Jones smokes is also true at that same world.

At this point, one might worry that all this talk of truth has gone too far. Consider the probabilistic content that it is .6 likely that Jones smokes. What exactly does it mean to say that this content is probabilistic? In the first chapter of this book, I said that probabilistic contents are sets of probability spaces, where probability spaces are objects that determine assignments of probability to propositions. According to many theories of propositions, propositions are the sorts of objects that can be true or false at possible worlds. Given my claims in this chapter about probabilistic truth, this definition raises a worry. As it turns out, there is a sense in which *probabilistic contents* can be true or false at possible worlds. For instance, the content that it is .6 likely that Jones smokes can be true at a world—namely, just in case that world is .6 likely to be a world where Jones smokes. This particular truth condition is just another probabilistic content, namely the content that you believe when you have .6 credence that Jones smokes at the world in question. But absent some independent grasp of the distinction between propositions and probabilistic contents, one might wonder whether my definition of the latter is even consistent. Call this the problem of *creeping propositionalism*: if probabilistic contents are themselves true or false at worlds, then what distinguishes them from the propositions to which their members are assigning probabilities?[15]

The problem of creeping propositionalism is best answered not in the abstract, but in the context of a more substantive theory of the nature of propositions. To give one simple example, suppose that propositions are sets of worlds. Then probabilistic contents are sets of probability spaces whose measures are defined on sets of worlds. From these two claims, it follows that propositions and probabilistic contents are not the same sort of object. For propositions, relations of truth coincide with relations of set membership. Propositions are true at a world just in case they contain that world as a member. Propositions are true *simpliciter* just in case they contain the actual world as a member. For probabilistic contents, by contrast, truth at a world does not coincide with set membership. Hence there is no danger that probabilistic contents might turn out to be propositions after all.

A close variant of the problem of creeping propositionalism concerns the distinction between nominally and thoroughly probabilistic contents. At a first

[15] I am grateful to Josh Dever and Jeff Russell for raising versions of this objection.

pass, one might say that nominally probabilistic contents are distinctive in virtue of the fact that they are true or false at worlds. But more carefully, one should identify nominally probabilistic contents as those contents according to which some proposition is certain. In addition, there is another general property that distinguishes nominally probabilistic contents from thoroughly probabilistic contents: thoroughly probabilistic contents are distinct from their propositional closures, whereas nominally probabilistic contents are not. As a result, nominally probabilistic contents share several features that not all thoroughly probabilistic contents share. For instance, every nominally probabilistic content that is true is believed by anyone who knows which world is actual. By contrast, consider the thoroughly probabilistic content that it is .6 likely that Jones smokes. This content is true, but it is not believed by everyone who knows which world is actual. Here is another feature shared by nominally probabilistic contents: every nominally probabilistic content is such that if it is believed by someone who knows which world is actual, then it is true. By contrast, consider the thoroughly probabilistic content that it is not .6 likely that Jones smokes. This content is believed by anyone who knows which world is actual. But it may nevertheless be .6 likely that Jones smokes, and hence not true that it is not .6 likely that she smokes.

At first glance, either of the problems of creeping propositionalism described above might appear to resemble the problem of *creeping minimalism* often raised against expressivist theories in metaethics. According to many ethical expressivists, sentences containing ethical vocabulary express different sorts of attitudes from the beliefs expressed by ordinary descriptive sentences. An expressivist may say that ethical sentences express attitudes of tolerance or disapproval, for instance. The *quasi-realist* develops this expressivist theory by endorsing a deflationary theory of truth. According to the quasi-realist, ethical sentences may be true or false, and even true or false at particular possible worlds. Against this view, many have objected that there is ultimately nothing to distinguish quasi-realism from the realist view that ethical sentences express just the sort of beliefs that the expressivist initially said they do not express.

In light of the similarities between creeping minimalism and creeping propositionalism, it is useful to note that the problem of creeping propositionalism is easier to solve. Propositions and probabilistic contents are by definition different sorts of objects. And thoroughly probabilistic contents can be distinguished from nominally probabilistic contents, where ethical beliefs cannot be similarly distinguished from descriptive beliefs. If the content that murder is wrong is true at every world, then it follows that this content is true. But the same cannot be said for all thoroughly probabilistic contents, as demonstrated by the argument from disjunction in §7.4. There is no danger that the thoroughly probabilistic content that it is not .6 likely that Jones smokes might turn out to correspond to a proposition after all.

Even granting that one can distinguish thoroughly and nominally probabilistic contents, there is a final objection to consider. A diehard opponent of probabilistic knowledge might insist that certain special features of propositions must be features of any content that can be true or false at all. For instance, my opponent might insist that a content is true only if it corresponds to a proposition that contains the actual world. If that is correct, then thoroughly probabilistic contents can at best have some truth-like property, perhaps identified as the property of *quasi-truth*. Accordingly, my opponent might conclude that thoroughly probabilistic contents can at best have some knowledge-like property, perhaps identified as the property of *quasi-knowledge*. This final objection raises the same sort of concern as the objection addressed at the end of §5.8. The position of my diehard opponent is not inconsistent, but it is insufficiently motivated. At a certain point, we should compare our opposing theories by examining their consequences, exploring the benefits of accepting or rejecting probabilistic truth and knowledge. That is my project for the remainder of this book. In the final three chapters, I argue that probabilistic knowledge has fruitful applications in the context of many debates in epistemology, ethics, and the philosophy of law. I hope that these applications might motivate even my most skeptical opponents to accept that probabilistic beliefs can indeed be knowledge.

8

Knowledge and belief

8.1 The knowledge norm of belief

Probabilistic knowledge has significant applications both in and outside of epistemology. At the end of chapter 5, I described several applications of probabilistic knowledge for debates in the philosophy of language. In this chapter and the next, I explore its applications for epistemological debates. I start by discussing a knowledge norm governing probabilistic belief. I describe the consequences of this norm for debates about what you should believe when you find out that you disagree with an epistemic peer. In §8.2, I develop a novel position in these debates—namely, that you should sometimes respond to peer disagreement by adopting imprecise credences, thereby suspending judgment about probabilistic contents that you and your peer disagree about. In §8.3, I argue that even though the knowledge norm sometimes recommends that disagreeing subjects adopt imprecise credences, it could also recommend that disagreeing subjects remain steadfast in their credences, or even recommend that they adopt a precise compromise of their respective credences. In §8.4, I discuss another question of interest to epistemologists, namely what subjects can know on the basis of statistical inference. In §8.5, I discuss recent debates about how we gain knowledge by perception. I use probabilistic knowledge to defend theories of perceptual knowledge against several recent objections. The arguments in this chapter bear on a wide range of topics in epistemology, but they serve a common goal. Each argument supports my central thesis that probabilistic beliefs can be knowledge, namely by showing that this thesis can be used to defend compelling positions in significant debates.

The main focus of this chapter is the relationship between what you know and what you should believe. The knowledge norm of belief is an especially simple account of this relationship. Belief *aims at* knowledge. Knowledge *sets the standard for* belief. These proverbial claims are elucidated by the thesis that knowledge is both necessary and sufficient for permissible belief. As WILLIAMSON 2005a puts it, "if one knows that *P*, then one can hardly be wrong to believe that P; conversely, given that one does not know that P, it arguably is wrong to believe that P" (108). The knowledge norm of belief is commonly understood as governing full beliefs. But the proverbial claims mentioned above hold equally for probabilistic beliefs, and arguments for the knowledge norm of full belief often equally support the thesis that you should believe a probabilistic content if and only if you know it.[1]

At first glance, the knowledge norm of belief may appear unreasonably demanding, whether it is applied to probabilistic or propositional beliefs. Suppose that Smith reads the clock in the village square and concludes that it is 2:00. As in the case described by RUSSELL 1948, the village clock is stopped and only coincidentally reads the correct time. Smith does not know that it is 2:00. There seems to be a sense in which Smith nevertheless should believe that it is 2:00. After all, that is just what the village clock told him to believe, and he has no reason to distrust the clock. Does this simple example prove that the knowledge norm is false? For the purposes of this chapter, it does not matter whether there is some sense in which Smith should believe that it is 2:00 when he looks at the clock. What matters is that there is *at least one sense* in which subjects stuck in Gettier cases could be doing better, some sense in which their beliefs are epistemically deficient. This sense is captured by a demanding norm that their beliefs fail to meet. The knowledge norm of belief is valuable insofar as it accounts for our negative judgments about subjects in Gettier cases. In this chapter, I argue that the same norm can account for many other intuitive judgments along with it.

Is there one fundamental sense in which Smith should believe it is 2:00, and another fundamental sense in which he should not? Throughout this chapter, I remain neutral on this question. The knowledge norm may turn out to be the only fundamental norm of belief, in which case we might explain our initial sympathy for Smith by saying that he forms his beliefs in the right way, namely according to dispositions that would normally lead to knowledge.[2] Alternatively, it may turn out that the knowledge norm is merely one among many fundamental epistemic norms.[3] Finally, it may turn out that the knowledge norm is grounded in some more fundamental norm of belief, in which case Smith may fail to satisfy the knowledge norm while satisfying the norm that grounds it.[4] At the end of the day, the arguments of this chapter are incompatible only with the claim that there is no sense at all in which you should believe something if and only if you know it.

---

[1] For recent arguments in defense of knowledge norms of belief, see WILLIAMSON 2000, SUTTON 2007, and BLOME-TILLMANN 2013.

[2] This response is defended in LASONEN-AARNIO 2010 and WILLIAMSON 2015.

[3] For arguments in defense of epistemic value pluralism, see RIGGS 2002 and KVANVIG 2005.

[4] This response is defended in WILLIAMS 1978 and WEDGWOOD 2002.

When it comes to norms governing probabilistic beliefs, there is one especially notable alternative to the knowledge norm of belief. Rather than saying that you should believe a probabilistic content if and only if you know it, one might say that you should believe a probabilistic content if and only if that content contains your *evidential probabilities* in the sense of WILLIAMSON 2000. According to this norm, your credence in a proposition should match its probability given all the propositions that you know—that is, the probability that results from feeding your propositional knowledge to an initial measurement of "the intrinsic plausibility of hypotheses prior to investigation" (WILLIAMSON 2000, 211). This evidential probability norm is one way of spelling out the intuitive thought that what you should believe depends on what you know. But it fails to illuminate the normative notion that we are targeting in this chapter. The evidential probability norm says that Smith should have an extremely high credence that it is 2:00 in the case described above. By contrast, the knowledge norm of probabilistic belief captures the sense in which that high credence is epistemically deficient. It is not enough to say that your credences should be *based on* your propositional knowledge. There is an important sense in which your credences should *constitute* knowledge, just like your full beliefs.[5]

8.2 Peer disagreement

Suppose you find yourself disagreeing with an epistemic peer—namely, someone whom you antecedently trust just as much as yourself to form true beliefs about the question under dispute. How should you update your own beliefs upon learning what your peer believes? For instance, consider the following example:

> *Copilot Beliefs*: You and a trusted copilot are flying to Hawaii, when an unexpected storm hits and you suddenly realize that you might not have enough fuel to get to your destination. If you don't have enough fuel, you should land immediately. You express your concern to your copilot, and you each do some calculations. You breathe a sigh of relief when your calculations say that you have enough fuel to make it to your destination. But then your copilot tells you that according to her calculations, you do not have enough fuel.

Assume that your copilot is your epistemic peer with respect to the question of whether you have enough fuel. After learning that your copilot believes you do not have enough fuel, what should you believe? At first glance, it is intuitive to say that you should take her opinion seriously, that you should not simply go

---

[5] See §6.1 for further discussion of the relation between probabilistic knowledge and evidential probability.

on believing that you have enough fuel. Here is one compelling explanation of this intuitive verdict: given the facts of the case described above, it is natural to conclude that you don't know whether you or your copilot got your calculations right. And in light of your ignorance, you should suspend judgment about the question under dispute.

The verdict that you should suspend judgment in cases of peer disagreement is endorsed by a number of authors. FOLEY 2001 argues that when we disagree about an issue, "[i]nsofar as it is reasonable for me to regard us as exact epistemic peers with respect to the issue, it is reasonable for me to withhold judgment until I better understand how one or both of us has gone wrong" (110–11). FELDMAN 2003 agrees: "In the situations most plausibly thought to be cases of reasonable disagreement, suspension of judgment is the reasonable attitude to take toward the disputed proposition" (189). HAWTHORNE AND SRINIVASAN 2013 account for these intuitive claims by introducing a knowledge norm of disagreement. According to Hawthorne and Srinivasan, what you should believe in cases like *Copilot Beliefs* depends on what you know. Insofar as it is natural to imagine that you do not know that you have enough fuel, it follows from the knowledge norm that you should not simply go on believing it. According to the knowledge norm of belief, you should always suspend judgment about questions to which you do not know the answer, and questions under dispute among epistemic peers are no different from any others.

Hawthorne and Srinivasan mount a strong defense of the knowledge norm of disagreement. In particular, they respond to several natural objections, including the objection that the knowledge norm is not sufficiently action-guiding. However, there is one respect in which their arguments are severely limited. According to Hawthorne and Srinivasan, their norm "says nothing about how [subjects] should respond in cases where their disagreement is a matter of divergent credences as opposed to conflicts of all-or-nothing belief. Despite the prevailing trend in the disagreement debate, our discussion will for the most part proceed without mention of credences" (13). Hawthorne and Srinivasan do not discuss examples like the following:

> *Copilot Credences*: You and a trusted copilot are flying to Hawaii, when an unexpected storm hits and you suddenly realize that you might not have enough fuel to get to your destination. If you don't have enough fuel, you should land immediately. You express your concern to your copilot, and you each do some calculations. On the basis of your calculations, you have .99 credence that you have enough fuel. But then your copilot tells you that on the basis of her calculations, she has .51 credence that you have enough fuel.

Suppose that before you find out that your copilot disagrees with you, you trust her just as much as you trust yourself to form true probabilistic beliefs about whether you have enough fuel. Given the facts of the case described above, it is natural to conclude that you should not simply remain steadfast in your credences after learning what your copilot believes. This example closely resembles *Copilot Beliefs*. In both cases, it is natural to conclude that you should suspend judgment about the contents that you and your copilot disagree about, on the grounds that this suspension of judgment is what an appropriate sense of epistemic humility demands. The difference is that in *Copilot Credences*, you and your peer disagree about probabilistic contents, such as the set of probability spaces according to which it is .99 likely that you have enough fuel. And indeed, in many standard cases of peer disagreement, epistemic peers disagree in their probabilistic beliefs.

Although Hawthorne and Srinivasan explain our intuitions about *Copilot Beliefs*, they refrain from giving any explanation of our very similar intuitions about *Copilot Credences*. Absent any such explanation, one might worry that their account of *Copilot Beliefs* is insufficiently general. Accepting probabilistic knowledge solves this problem. As long as probabilistic beliefs can be knowledge, the knowledge norm applies equally to cases of peer disagreement about probabilistic contents. Insofar as it is natural to imagine that you do not know whether it is .51 or .99 likely that you have enough fuel, it follows from the knowledge norm that you should not believe either of these contents.

If you should not believe these probabilistic contents, then what should you believe? Recall that in *Copilot Beliefs*, you should suspend judgment on propositions that are consistent with but not entailed by your knowledge, such as the proposition that you have enough fuel to get to Hawaii. The corresponding verdict about *Copilot Credences* is that you should suspend judgment on the *probabilistic contents* that are consistent with but not entailed by your knowledge. Absent sufficient evidence, you should suspend judgment about whether it is .51 likely that you have enough fuel to get to Hawaii, and also about whether it is .99 likely that you have enough fuel.

What does it mean to suspend judgment about a probabilistic content? To a first approximation, you suspend judgment about a proposition when you neither believe the proposition nor believe its complement.[6] In the probabilistic case, suspending judgment about a probabilistic content should similarly require that you neither believe that set of probability spaces nor believe its complement. In order to represent this state of suspending judgment, we must revise an idealizing assumption introduced in §2.3, namely that your total belief state is represented by a single probability space. For any set of probability spaces, a single

---

[6] FRIEDMAN 2013 argues that strictly speaking, suspending judgment involves adopting an agnostic attitude. This conclusion supports my claim that suspending judgment about probabilistic contents involves adopting imprecise credences.

probability space will be contained either in that set or in its complement. Hence a single probability space represents the belief state of a maximally opinionated subject, someone who does not suspend judgment on any probabilistic content. By contrast, suspending judgment on a probabilistic content requires having *imprecise* credences. An imprecise credal state is not represented by a single probability space, but by a set of probability spaces. Following VAN FRAASSEN 1990, we may call this set your *representor*. The members of this set are like the members of an imaginary mental committee, where your beliefs are just those contents that your mental committee members unanimously believe. That is, you believe a probabilistic content just in case it contains every probability space in your representor, and you suspend judgment with respect to a content just in case it contains some but not all of those probability spaces. When you suspend judgment about whether it is .99 likely that you have enough fuel, for instance, your representor contains at least one probability space according to which it is .99 likely that you have enough fuel, and another according to which it is not .99 likely.

The knowledge norm of disagreement can tell you to suspend judgment when you disagree with your copilot about how likely it is that you have enough fuel. Standard views of peer disagreement are incapable of delivering this verdict. Roughly speaking, these standard views fall into two categories. *Steadfast* views say that you may stand by your credences when you find out that you disagree with an epistemic peer. For instance, according to many steadfast views, you should stand by your .99 credence that you have enough fuel in *Copilot Credences*, if your original calculations were indeed correct. By contrast, *conciliatory* views say that you should respond to peer disagreement by adopting some compromise of what you and your peer believe. When you find out that you disagree with your copilot, your credence that you have enough fuel should be strictly between .51 and .99. For instance, according to COHEN 2013, among others, you should end up with exactly .75 credence that you have enough fuel, since "when peers discover they disagree, each should adopt the simple average of their credences, that is, they should split the difference between their credences" (100). To sum up, whether you remain steadfast or compromise, you will end up with precise credences. Hence neither standard view of disagreement can recommend that you genuinely suspend judgment about the probabilistic questions that you and your peer disagree about, such as whether it is .99 likely that you have enough fuel.[7]

---

[7] There are other reasons to reject the claim that epistemic peers should always split the difference between their credences, in addition to the reasons mentioned in this chapter. For further discussion, see MOSS 2011.

The foregoing discussion provides us with a modest argument for probabilistic knowledge. Assume that there is some intuitive sense in which you should suspend judgment in response to peer disagreement when you are ignorant about the question under dispute. Hawthorne and Srinivasan spell out the consequences of this norm for disagreements about propositional contents, explaining why agents in cases like *Copilot Beliefs* should not remain steadfast in their full beliefs. As long as credences can be knowledge, this same norm can help explain why agents in very similar cases should not remain steadfast in their credences. Accepting probabilistic knowledge allows us to extend a natural motivation for the knowledge norm of disagreement to its appropriate conclusion.[8]

8.3 Applying the knowledge norm of belief

I have suggested that in some cases of peer disagreement, it is natural to say that you should suspend judgment about a probabilistic content. Steadfast and conciliatory views cannot deliver this verdict. But this is not yet a reason to reject steadfast or conciliatory views. As mentioned in §8.1, it may turn out that belief is governed by multiple epistemic norms. Suppose that in addition to the knowledge norm, belief is governed by some justification norm, such as the norm that your credences ought to match your evidential probabilities. Steadfast or conciliatory credences might be recommended by this norm, even if they are not knowledge. Hence there might be some sense in which you should have steadfast or conciliatory credences about whether you have enough fuel in *Copilot Credences*, even if there is another sense in which your credences should be imprecise.

For sake of argument, suppose that there is one sense in which you should suspend judgment in light of your ignorance in peer disagreement cases, and another sense in which you ought to have precise credences, either steadfast or conciliatory in nature. The knowledge norm still has an important consequence for the debate between steadfast and conciliatory views. Given that beliefs may be judged according to multiple intuitive standards, it may not be clear what normative standard is being tracked by ordinary judgments about what particular subjects should believe. Advocates of steadfast and conciliatory views cannot safely assume that our intuitions about particular examples are relevant to the debate between them.

This upshot of my discussion is similar in spirit to a conclusion defended by VAN WIETMARSCHEN 2013. According to van Wietmarschen, steadfast and conciliatory views themselves concern different sorts of epistemic assessment.

---

[8] Although I focus on cases of peer disagreement for simplicity, other cases from the literature on higher-order evidence provide a similar motivation for accepting probabilistic knowledge.

Steadfast views are supported by intuitions about whether subjects have propositional justification for their beliefs, whereas conciliatory views are supported by intuitions about whether subjects have doxastic justification for their beliefs. As a result, intuitions cannot settle the debate between these views. As van Wietmarschen explains:

> One of the most prominent argumentative strategies in the peer disagreement debate is as follows. One constructs a particular example of a peer disagreement. One generates an intuition about what the parties should believe ... One uses this intuition to defend or attack a certain view about the epistemic significance of peer disagreement. This strategy is flawed. My discussion shows that the central questions raised about these cases are ambiguous between different standards of epistemic justification. (422)

According to van Wietmarschen, advocates of steadfast and conciliatory views cannot make their case by appealing to intuitions about peer disagreement cases. Let us set aside the question of whether van Wietmarschen correctly identifies a source of ambiguity in our intuitions about these cases. I have suggested that whether or not his objection stands, steadfast and conciliatory views do face another problem of this same sort. As we evaluate subjects in peer disagreement cases, sometimes our intuition that certain credences are impermissible may be grounded in our recognition that those credences do not amount to knowledge. But if steadfast and conciliatory views concern the application of another normative standard altogether, then intuitions guided by the knowledge norm of disagreement do not provide evidence for or against these views. The intuition that steadfast credences are impermissible in *Copilot Credences*, for instance, does not necessarily tell against steadfast views of disagreement. When you imagine your copilot denying that it is .99 likely that you have enough fuel, it is natural to imagine that you cannot rule out the possibility that she is correct, and that your .99 credence therefore fails to be knowledge. But even if your steadfast credence fails to satisfy the knowledge norm, it might still satisfy other norms of belief, including whatever norm is under discussion in the debate between steadfast and conciliatory views.

Conversely, intuitions to the effect that you should remain steadfast in your credences may be grounded in our recognition that some steadfast credences amount to knowledge. For example, consider a variation on the following case from CHRISTENSEN 2007:

> *Mental Math*: Suppose that five of us go out to dinner. It's time to pay the check, so the question we're interested in is how much we each owe ... I do the math in my head and become highly confident that our shares are $43 each. Meanwhile, my friend does the math in her head and becomes highly confident that our shares are $45 each. (193)

SOSA 2010 argues that remaining steadfast is intuitively required in a variant of *Mental Math* in which my friend and I decide to double-check our results:

> *Calculator*: My friend and I are now out of each other's sight, neither of us privy to what the other does in double-checking our results. I take out pencil and paper, and perform the calculation that way; then I remember the calculator in my pocket, and I perform the calculation that way too. And all of these procedures repeatedly converge on one result: [$43]. At the end of the period of rechecking I again compare notes with my friend, who insists that his rechecking has confirmed his initial result: $45. (292–3)

According to Sosa, the intuitive verdict in *Calculator* is that I should stand by my results after I have carefully checked them. LACKEY 2010 defends steadfast intuitions about a similar example, explaining that "if the case is modified to include more and more rounds of calculation done by me on paper, on perhaps even on a calculator, we may ultimately end up altogether eliciting nonconformist intuitions, even if [my friend] is busy doing the same number of calculations" (317). This intuition might be best explained by traditional steadfast views, such as the view that you are justified in standing by your credences just in case they are supported by correct calculations. But on the other hand, the intuition might be best explained by the knowledge norm of disagreement, according to which you are justified in standing by your credences just in case they constitute knowledge. Suppose that when I double-check my calculations, I come to know that it is extremely likely that our shares of the check are $43 each—and furthermore, suppose that I continue to know this probabilistic content even after learning that my friend disagrees with it. Then according to the knowledge norm, I should remain steadfast in my extremely high credence.

In addition to accounting for intuitions about steadfast credences, the knowledge norm could also account for intuitions that support your adopting conciliatory credences. For instance, Christensen argues that in the original *Mental Math* case, it is intuitively obvious that I should compromise with my friend. As long as my friend and I are on equal footing in relevant respects, "it seems quite clear that I should lower my confidence that my share is $43 and raise my confidence that it's $45. In fact, I think (though this is perhaps less obvious) that I should now accord these two hypotheses roughly equal credence" (193). Just as the knowledge norm can tell me to suspend judgment or remain steadfast, the knowledge norm could in principle deliver this conciliatory verdict. As I learn what my peer believes, I could come to know some probabilistic content that I did not know before. Suppose that my friend has .05 credence that our shares are $43 each, and say I have .5 credence that she is right. As a result, I believe that it is .5 likely that it is .05 likely that our shares are $43 each. In addition, suppose I believe that it is .5 likely that it is .95 likely that our shares are $43 each. These probabilistic beliefs together entail the thoroughly probabilistic conclusion that it is .5 likely that our shares are $43 each.[9] If both of the former probabilistic beliefs are knowledge, then I can come to have inferential knowledge of my conciliatory conclusion. According to the knowledge norm of probabilistic belief, it follows that I should have .5 credence that our shares are $43 each.

To sum up our discussion so far, the knowledge norm yields different verdicts in three potential sorts of peer disagreement cases. There are bad cases in which disagreements undermine your knowledge and you should suspend judgment about questions under dispute. In *Copilot Credences*, for instance, one might say that you should suspend judgment about whether it is .99 likely that you have enough fuel to get to Hawaii. In addition, there are two sorts of good cases. First, your original credences could constitute knowledge even after you learn what your peer believes, in which case you should remain steadfast in your credences. In *Calculator*, for instance, one might say that you know that your share of the check is probably $43. Alternatively, you could come to know some other credences on the basis of facts about your disagreement, in which case you should adopt conciliatory credences. In *Mental Math*, one might say that you know that you and your peer are about equally likely to be correct in your calculations, and that you should update your credences accordingly.

In the cases mentioned above, how do we know when the knowledge norm of probabilistic belief recommends suspending judgment, when it recommends remaining steadfast, and when it recommends compromising? The knowledge norm of belief does not itself answer these questions. The knowledge norm says that what you should believe depends on your knowledge, but it does not say anything about what probabilistic knowledge you have. This is intuitively as it should be, since one should not expect norms stating conditions on rational attitudes to have further substantial consequences about when their conditions are satisfied. In this respect, the knowledge norm is less ambitious than views that deliver steadfast or conciliatory verdicts on the basis of non-epistemic features of your situation. The knowledge norm of belief delivers verdicts only once we have independently determined what you know when you find out what your peer believes. As discussed in §6.1, it may be impossible to state necessary and sufficient conditions for whether you know some probabilistic content, either by reference to non-epistemic or even other epistemic features of your situation.

---

[9] For general semantic and pragmatic claims that explain the validity of this probabilistic inference, see my discussion of nested probability operators in §3.4 and my discussion of epistemic expressions in parallel constructions in §4.5.

Just like propositional knowledge, probabilistic knowledge resists analysis in more basic terms.

That being said, our intuitions about probabilistic knowledge ascriptions fall into familiar patterns. For instance, it is a familiar fact that we are more sympathetic to the skeptic when the stakes are high. We are reluctant to say that you know that the bank is open on Sunday in cases where you will miss a critical deposit if it is not. Similarly, we are reluctant to say that you know that you probably have enough fuel to get to Hawaii in cases where you should make a critical fuel stop if you don't. Meanwhile, we are happy to say that you know that your share of a restaurant check is probably $43 in cases where nothing much turns on whether you are right. Different theories of knowledge ascriptions explain these observations in different ways. According to the contextualist, for instance, the truth of a knowledge ascription may depend on the stakes of decisions faced by the knowledge ascriber. According to the interest-relative invariantist, the truth of an ascription may depend on the stakes of decisions faced by the subject of the ascription. Whatever theory we accept, the upshot is that as long as the relevant stakes are low, we can truly say that disagreeing peers can have knowledge of probabilistic contents. The knowledge norm of disagreement can explain our willingness to say that it is permissible for them to believe those contents. The knowledge norm similarly explains why steadfast credences seem less acceptable as the stakes of the decisions based on those credences are increased. To sum up, the knowledge norm of belief may be perfectly consistent with steadfast and conciliatory views of disagreement. But the knowledge norm makes it harder to judge these views against our intuitions, since our intuitions may also reflect that what you should believe in some sense depends on what you know.

8.4 Statistical inference

Suppose you hear a bird singing in the forest. You look up into the trees as it flies away, and from the corner of your eye, you seem to catch a glimpse of yellow. On the basis of your perception, you do not know that the bird was yellow. But intuitively, you might be able to know that it was probably yellow. Compare this perceptual knowledge with a second example of probabilistic knowledge. You hear another bird singing. You cannot see the bird, but you can tell from its song that it is a canary. In addition, you happen to know that almost all canaries are yellow. On the basis of this knowledge, you do not know that the bird you hear is yellow. But again, you might be able to know that it is probably yellow. This is not knowledge by perception, but knowledge by inference. A *direct inference* starts with a claim about the frequency of a feature in a population, and ends with a claim about some member of that population. This form of argument is also called *statistical syllogism*, and it is one of the most basic forms of non-deductive inference.

In the literature on direct inference, there are two competing interpretations of exactly what form these inferences take. The distinction between these interpretations is significant, although it sometimes goes unnoticed. In order to pull apart the two interpretations, it is helpful to focus on two questions. First, what sort of belief gains justification from a direct inference? Second, what sort of justification does that belief gain? According to one interpretation, direct inferences provide some justification for *full beliefs*. For instance, POLLOCK 2008 identifies statistical syllogism as having roughly the following form: "From 'This is an *A* and the probability of an *A* being a *B* is high', infer defeasibly, 'This is a *B*'" (451). According to Pollock, a direct inference does not fully justify belief in its conclusion, but merely provides some degree of justification for this belief. COHEN 2010 endorses this interpretation of direct inference, illustrating it with the following example:

> Now consider the defeasible rule of Statistical Syllogism
>
> > Most *F*s are *G*s
> > *a* is *F*
> > ———————
> > *a* is *G*...
>
> I suppose that most pit bulls are dangerous. Relying on my background knowledge that Fido is a Pit Bull, I infer by statistical syllogism, that Fido is dangerous. (152–3)

The conclusion of Cohen's pit bull inference is the proposition that Fido is dangerous. The pit bull inference does not fully justify belief in this proposition. Rather, the full belief that Fido is dangerous is justified to some intermediate degree, namely a degree that reflects the known proportion of dangerous dogs among pit bulls.

According to a second interpretation, direct inferences provide justification for *probabilistic beliefs*.[10] Direct inferences include arguments of the following form:

> Most *F*s are *G*s
> *a* is *F*
> ———————
> *a* is probably *G*

If most pit bulls are dangerous, and Fido is a pit bull, it follows by direct inference that Fido is probably dangerous. The conclusion of this second inference is not a

---

[10] For further discussion of the distinction between *degrees of justification of full beliefs* and *justification of probabilistic beliefs*, see §5.6.

proposition, but a probabilistic content. The inference does not directly justify any full belief about Fido. Rather, it justifies having greater than .5 credence that Fido is dangerous. As WHITE 2010 puts it, "setting one's credence to known frequencies seems clearly correct. The general principle at work here . . . goes by the names Statistical Syllogism or Direct Inference" (169).

Is one interpretation of direct inference better than the other? There are at least some important facts that can be captured only by the second. Suppose you know that exactly half of all pit bulls are dangerous. Then intuitively, you can form some justified opinions about the pit bull Fido. The second interpretation of direct inference accounts for this fact, namely by saying that you are justified in having .5 credence that Fido is dangerous. By contrast, the first interpretation of direct inference is at best silent about your opinions. There is no degree to which you are justified in forming the outright belief that Fido is dangerous, just as there is no degree to which you are justified in forming the outright belief that he is not. For present purposes, I shall adopt the second interpretation of direct inference. The conclusions of direct inferences are probabilistic contents, and direct inferences provide defeasible justification for believing these conclusions.

Having settled that direct inferences can justify probabilistic beliefs, we can take up an important question: when do these probabilistic beliefs constitute knowledge? An initial simple observation is that direct inferences do not generate knowledge from mere justified beliefs, but only from premises that themselves constitute knowledge. For instance, consider the following variation on the fake barn example from GOLDMAN 1976:

> *Photographs*: Henry is driving through fake barn country. As he drives, he occasionally stops to take photos of structures along the road. He takes a few photos of libraries and schoolhouses, but mainly he takes photos of structures that look like barns. At the end of the day, Henry believes that most of the structures featured in his photographs are barns. As it happens, Henry is right. Although there are very few real barns in fake barn country, Henry managed—by remarkable coincidence— to stop and photograph all of them. Later, Henry learns that his uncle built one of the structures in his photographs, though he doesn't learn which one. On that basis, Henry has high credence that his uncle built a barn.

Henry is justified in believing that the structure built by his uncle is probably a barn. After all, Henry derived this belief by direct inference from his true justified belief that most of the structures in his photographs are barns. But since the premise of his direct inference isn't knowledge, the conclusion isn't knowledge either. Direct inference is just like other forms of inference. Knowledge in, knowledge out. But direct inference from mere justified beliefs is not sufficient to yield probabilistic knowledge.

Suppose that you know the premises of a direct inference. A difficult question still remains: when does the inference itself succeed in grounding knowledge of its conclusion? This question resembles a difficult question addressed in §8.3, namely when steadfast or conciliatory credences constitute knowledge. In both cases, it is important to approach these questions with modest aims. There is no simple rule for when we find it natural to say that certain credences amount to knowledge in peer disagreement cases. Rather, our assessments of credences generally fall into familiar patterns, such as the fact that we find it harder to count beliefs as knowledge when those beliefs matter for high-stakes decisions. Similarly, there is no simple rule for when we find it natural to say that the conclusions of direct inferences amount to knowledge, although our assessments of these credences again fall into some familiar patterns.

Before discussing patterns in our assessments of these probabilistic beliefs, let us make a small detour to observe some patterns in our assessments of full beliefs based on statistical evidence. Here is one observation: ordinary speakers are often reluctant to say that full beliefs based on statistical evidence constitute knowledge. Suppose you have entered a fair lottery with one million tickets. Even though your odds of winning are incredibly small, we are reluctant to say that you know that you will not win the lottery. Here is a second observation: in rare cases, ordinary speakers are happy to say that lottery beliefs can be knowledge. HAWTHORNE 2004 describes one such example:[11]

> It is relatively easy to get ourselves in the frame of mind where we reckon ourselves to know that we will not win the New York State lottery each of the next thirty years (even if we expect to buy a ticket each year). Just ask people. They will happily claim to know that that will not happen. (20)

Taken together, these two observations raise a puzzle. Under a certain description, the event of winning thirty lotteries appears nearly equivalent with the event of winning one very large lottery. If the odds are bad enough, the former event might even be more likely than the latter. If you do not have enough knowledge to rule out the possibility of winning a very large lottery, then how could you have enough knowledge to rule out the more likely event of winning thirty smaller lotteries?

As many have noted, this puzzle about compound lotteries has a lot in common with a puzzle about lotteries introduced in HARMAN 1973, often called the *lottery*

---

[11] For additional examples, see the rookie cop case in VOGEL 1987, the Heartbreaker case in VOGEL 1999, and the typing monkey case in GRECO 2007.

paradox.[12] Suppose you have a lottery ticket in your back pocket. Harman points out that it seems natural to say that you do not know that your ticket will lose the lottery. But it can also seem natural to say that you know that you will not be able to afford to go on an expensive holiday vacation this year. These intuitions clearly stand in tension with one another. On the one hand, your belief that you will not be able to afford the vacation should be no better than your belief that you will lose the lottery, epistemically speaking, since you know that the former strictly entails the latter given your circumstances. On the other hand, it appears that the former belief is knowledge, while the latter belief is not.

When it comes to vindicating ordinary ascriptions of probabilistic knowledge, it doesn't matter how we solve the lottery paradox, as long as we resist giving an error theory of ordinary knowledge ascriptions. Any charitable theory of knowledge ascriptions should help explain familiar patterns in our ordinary assessments of statistical beliefs, including patterns in our ascriptions of lottery knowledge. Jennifer Nagel defends one especially compelling explanation for these patterns in NAGEL 2011. According to Nagel, our intuitions about lottery knowledge are best explained by dual-process theories of reasoning developed in cognitive and social psychology. As we consider lottery paradoxes, we make apparently conflicting ascriptions of knowledge when we are using different modes of cognition. In short, we are more willing to ascribe knowledge when our epistemic assessments are *automatic* rather than *controlled*. Citing SCHWARZ 1998, Nagel describes the difference between these modes of cognition by saying that "what automatic judgment could accept unconditionally, controlled judgment can accept only subject to qualification, conscious of certain limitations of its evidence, where the evidence available to controlled judgment is not necessarily the same as the evidence available to automatic judgment" (15). According to Nagel, when we assess your belief that you will lose a given lottery, our assessment is controlled, which is why we are reluctant to say that your belief is knowledge. By contrast, when we assess your belief that you will not win thirty lotteries, our assessment is automatic, which is why we are willing to say that your belief is knowledge.

Having made this detour to discuss full beliefs, we may now turn to consider probabilistic beliefs, including probabilistic beliefs that result from direct inferences. When we say that you know you will *probably* lose the lottery, we are not

---

[12] A distinct lottery paradox is introduced by KYBURG 1961 as a challenge for the claim that rational acceptance is closed under conjunction. NAGEL 2011 uses the label 'Harman-Vogel paradox' for the sort of lottery paradox discussed here, which is introduced in §10.2 of HARMAN 1973 and developed at length in VOGEL 1990.

making a controlled judgment about whether you have ruled out possibilities inconsistent with this content. In short, our assessment of your high credence does not raise the same alarm bells as our assessment of your full belief that you will lose. With respect to its intuitive epistemic status, your high credence that you will lose the lottery resembles your belief that you will not be able to afford an expensive vacation. When we assess probabilistic beliefs formed by direct inference, our assessments are often automatic, and hence we are often willing to say that these probabilistic beliefs constitute knowledge.

Assessments of probabilistic beliefs based on statistics are often automatic, but they are not *always* automatic. Accordingly, we are not always willing to say that probabilistic beliefs based on statistics constitute knowledge. Suppose that Jones knows that there are 8,000 canaries in a certain forest and that 5,000 of those canaries are yellow. She hears a bird in the forest, and recognizes its call as the mating call of a young canary. Jones could easily know that it is more likely than not that the canary is yellow. But could she just as easily know that it is exactly .625 likely that the canary is yellow? The second question raises more alarm bells than the first. What if mating canaries are more likely than average to be yellow? What if young canaries are less likely than average to be yellow? The claim that the overheard canary is exactly .625 likely to be yellow is true only if that canary is exactly as likely to be yellow as a canary chosen at random from the 8,000 canaries in the forest. But Jones may not be able to rule out that the canary is just as likely to be yellow as arbitrary members of an alternative reference class, such as the class of mating canaries. This is an instance of the notorious *reference class problem*, introduced by VENN 1866 and developed by REICHENBACH 1949. When alternative reference classes are salient, our epistemic assessments are controlled. The fact that Jones does not rule out conclusions of alternative direct inferences prevents us from saying that she knows the conclusion of the direct inference she performs. By contrast with many other probabilistic beliefs based on statistics, probabilistic beliefs based on statistics that raise alternative reference classes to salience are often assessed in a frame of mind that does not favor knowledge.

Let us sum up our observations so far. Some but not all statistical beliefs are judged by ordinary speakers to be knowledge. Statistical full beliefs are rarely judged using automatic reasoning, and hence rarely judged to be knowledge. By contrast, statistical probabilistic beliefs are often judged using automatic reasoning, and hence often judged to be knowledge. It is a familiar fact that whether we are willing to say that you know some proposition based on statistics may depend on facts about our context, such as whether some unlikely event is salient. In the same way, whether we are willing to say that you know the probabilistic conclusion of a direct inference may depend on facts about our context, such as whether alternative reference classes are salient.

These observations raise an important question: should we perhaps trust only controlled assessments, and endorse an error theory of automatic assessments of knowledge ascriptions?[13] After considering traditional lottery paradoxes, it is tempting to conclude that our automatic assessments are wrong. It is tempting to say that you do not in fact know that the expensive vacation will be unaffordable, and that you do not know that you will not win thirty lotteries. Should the reference class problem also lead us to conclude that you can never know by direct inference that some particular canary is probably yellow? Should we conclude that many probabilistic beliefs based on statistics are not in fact knowledge?

When it comes to our assessments of whether beliefs are knowledge, automatic assessments are not obviously less trustworthy than controlled assessments. As Nagel puts it, "we may grant the legitimacy of automatic and controlled epistemic assessments without accepting the correctness of the particular controlled assessments that seem to support contextualism; perhaps in these cases our natural tendency towards increased stringency is inappropriate" (23). In addition, it is important to appreciate that once we embrace an error theory of our automatic assessments of whether beliefs are knowledge, there is no principled end in sight. As HAWTHORNE 2004 argues at length, adopting an error theory of our automatic assessments of beliefs in lottery cases means adopting an error theory of many ordinary knowledge ascriptions. In short, my response to the skeptic about direct inference is similar to my response to the skeptical argument from closure in §7.3. The automatic reasoning that grounds ascriptions of knowledge by direct inference is the very same automatic reasoning that grounds many ordinary knowledge ascriptions. The rejection of this reasoning may be tempting, but it comes at the price of denying that many of our everyday beliefs constitute knowledge.

8.5 Responses to skepticism about perceptual knowledge

As demonstrated in chapter 7, many traditional arguments for skepticism about propositional knowledge can be extended to support skepticism about probabilistic knowledge. In many cases, the existence of probabilistic knowledge does not

---

[13] For comparison, see GREENE 2014 for a defense of the view that we should distrust characteristically deontological judgments, on the grounds that they are preferentially supported by automatic emotional responses.

make it any easier to answer the skeptic. However, in some cases, probabilistic knowledge allows us to give novel answers to traditional skeptical arguments. These answers illustrate the optimistic conclusion of §5.8, namely that we can strengthen the institution of traditional epistemology by recognizing probabilistic contents as knowledge.

Consider the following familiar challenge for perceptual knowledge: "Perhaps you know that you *seem* to have hands. But how can you thereby know that you have hands, without antecedently knowing that things are as they seem? And how could you ever possibly know this further claim, or more generally, that your perceptual faculties are reliable?" Following SILINS 2007, we may usefully distinguish two families of responses to this challenge. According to the *rationalist*, you can know independently of experience that your perceptual faculties are reliable. For instance, you might have some default justification for assuming that your perceptual faculties are reliable, where this justification is sufficient to ground knowledge. According to the *dogmatist*, your experience can itself ground knowledge of the claim that your perceptual faculties are reliable. In response to the skeptic, we may deny that you know you have hands only if you antecedently know that your experience of hands is veridical, since you could come to know the latter claim by experience, just as you come to know the former.

Against the rationalist response, DOGRAMACI 2014 objects that rationalists fail to vindicate many basic ordinary knowledge claims. For instance, Dogramaci argues that it is hard for the rationalist to explain how you can know by perception that you have hands. Suppose for sake of argument that the rationalist succeeds in proving that you have default justification for believing that almost all of your perceptual experiences are veridical, where this justification is sufficient to ground knowledge. This is indeed a victory against the skeptic, since it follows that you can know by perception that the external world exists, for instance, and that you are not a brain in a vat. But does it follow that you can know by perception that you have hands? Dogramaci argues that there is only one way you could gain armchair knowledge that your experience of hands is veridical—namely, by direct inference from the claim that almost all of your perceptual experiences are veridical. But according to Dogramaci, if you infer that your perceptual experience as of having hands is veridical "just on the basis of the premise that most of [your] experiences are veridical, then this will be a case of *statistical inference*," and "whatever justification the inferred conclusion in such an inference may enjoy, it is not knowledge" (6). Even if you know that almost all of your experiences are veridical, you cannot know by direct inference that any particular experience is veridical. As Dogramaci puts it, "Just as I can't use a statistical inference to know that my ticket in the million-ticket lottery will lose,

I can't use such an inference to know that its appearing to me that p isn't that one-in-a-million misfire" (6). Hence the rationalist has still failed to explain how your perception can give you knowledge that you have hands. The rationalist victory against the skeptic is a partial victory at best.

The theory of direct inference in §8.4 provides the rationalist with a strong response to this objection. The rationalist should concede that you do not know that it is absolutely certain that you have hands on the basis of your knowledge that almost all of your experiences are veridical. But the rationalist should also be happy to settle for your having some slightly more modest probabilistic knowledge, namely that your experience of hands is almost certainly veridical. The correct conclusion for the rationalist is that you can know that you almost certainly have hands on the basis of the following direct inference:

(1) a. Almost all of the contents of my perceptual experience are true.
     b. That I have hands is a content of my perceptual experience.
     c. Therefore, that I have hands is almost certainly true.

In other words, just as you can know that your lottery ticket *almost certainly* lost the lottery, you may know that your perception of your hands is *almost certainly* veridical. This thoroughly probabilistic conclusion is appropriately modest, but nevertheless still powerful knowledge to have from the armchair. For many practical purposes, knowing that you almost certainly have hands is just as good as knowing that you have hands.

In addition to defending rationalist responses to skepticism about perceptual knowledge, probabilistic knowledge can also be used to defend dogmatist responses. Let *Seems* be the conjunction of all of your evidence propositions, and let *Hands* be the proposition that you have hands. Let *Fake* be the conjunction of *Seems* and *not Hands*. As interpreted by some authors, the dogmatist says that when you learn *Seems*, you can gain justification for *not Fake*. For instance, when it appears to you that there is a hand in front of you, you can gain justification for your belief that your evidence is not misleading you about whether you have hands. However, several authors have recently put forward a serious challenge for this dogmatist response to skepticism, namely that it seems to be at odds with some basic Bayesian reasoning. This challenge is discussed at length by HAWTHORNE 2004, WHITE 2006, and WEATHERSON 2008, among others. As developed in WHITE 2006, the objection proceeds:

P1. If you gain justification for a claim, your credence in it should not decrease.
P2. When you learn *Seems*, your credence in *not Fake* should decrease.
 C. Hence when you learn *Seems*, you do not gain justification for *not Fake*.

The Bayesian reasoning behind (P2) is simple: since *Fake* entails *Seems*, *Seems* confirms *Fake*. Intuitively, when you learn *Seems*, you learn that things are just as *Fake* predicted they would be. By the same token, *Seems* disconfirms *not Fake*. As long as your credence in *Seems* increases when you learn *Seems*, your credence in *Fake* will also increase, and your credence in *not Fake* will decrease. From (P1), it follows that you cannot gain justification for *not Fake* when you learn *Seems*.[14]

Accepting probabilistic knowledge provides a compelling response to this challenge. In short, (P2) is false. If your evidence merely consisted of propositions, then you would update your credence by conditionalizing on those propositions. But not all evidence is propositional evidence. In particular, when you learn *Seems*, you could get probabilistic evidence. As you update on probabilistic evidence, your resulting beliefs are not determined by conditionalization. They are determined by generalized updating rules, which subsume conditionalization as a special case.[15] The dogmatist argues that experience provides you with a certain sort of evidence, namely evidence about evidential relationships. This is not propositional evidence, but rather probabilistic evidence about the conditional likelihood of hypotheses given various propositions. For instance, you could come to know by perception that if *Seems* is true, then *not Fake* is almost certain. Learning the probabilistic content of this conditional will directly affect your conditional credence in *Fake* given *Seems*. In light of this probabilistic evidence, your credence in *not Fake* should increase rather than decrease as you learn *Seems*. Hence (P2) is false. In other words, the dogmatist claims that you could learn from experience that *Seems* is better evidence for *Hands* than you had originally supposed.

How does my argument compare with other defenses of perceptual dogmatism? An alternative response to the Bayesian objection is developed at length in WEATHERSON 2008. Weatherson also argues on behalf of the dogmatist that you should not simply update your credences by conditionalizing them on your evidence propositions. But for Weatherson, this is not because your evidence is probabilistic in nature. As Weatherson sees it, rational credences are imprecise. According to the usual procedure for updating imprecise credences, each member of your representor is independently updated by conditionalization on your evidence propositions. But Weatherson rejects this theory in favor of an unorthodox updating procedure. According to Weatherson, the first step of

---

[14] For sake of argument, let us grant an underlying assumption of this challenge for dogmatism, namely that *Seems* does not logically entail *Hands*. In other words, we are exploring whether we can defend dogmatism against the Bayesian challenge without availing ourselves of the claim that in the good case where you have hands, your evidence includes the proposition that you have hands.

[15] See DIACONIS AND ZABELL 1982 for an introductory discussion of generalized updating rules.

rational updating involves throwing out certain members of your representor, before conditionalizing the remaining members on what you learn. For example, before you conditionalize on *Seems*, you may throw out representor members according to which *Seems* is not good evidence for *Hands*. If you update in this way when you learn *Seems*, your rational credence in *not Fake* may fail to decrease. According to Weatherson, that is why (P2) is false.

Both Weatherson and I reject the thought that you should update your beliefs by conditionalizing precise probability measures on the propositions that you learn. We also agree that roughly speaking, you can learn about evidential relationships. But our theories model this learning in very different ways. According to Weatherson, your learning about evidential relationships is modeled by your culling your representor before you update on your evidence. According to my theory, your learning about evidential relationships is modeled by your directly updating your credences on probabilistic contents that encode these relationships. There are several reasons to prefer my defense of dogmatism over Weatherson's defense. First, my defense does not foreclose on the possibility that rational agents must have precise credences. Second, my defense appeals to an antecedently motivated theory of updating. There is an extensive literature on generalized updating rules, which may be independently required by the sort of learning described in JEFFREY 1965 and VAN FRAASSEN 1980a. By contrast, there is no precedent for updating an imprecise credal state by throwing out some of its members before updating each remaining member on your propositional evidence. Finally, and most importantly, my defense adequately recognizes that learning about evidential relationships is just a special case of learning conditional information. According to Weatherson, learning about evidential relationships involves culling your representor, while ordinary learning is an entirely distinct step of rational updating. By contrast, on my theory, you learn the information that *Hands* is almost certain given *Seems* in just the same way that you learn any other conditional information, which is just a special case of learning any sort of information at all.

This concludes my argument against premise (P2) of the Bayesian challenge for dogmatism. In the remainder of this section, I want to also argue against (P1). In other words, I have just argued that if you learn *Seems*, your credence in *not Fake* need not decrease. But even if it does decrease, it does not follow that you do not gain justification for *not Fake*. Let us start by imagining the following situation in which you form some unjustified beliefs:

> *Three Lotteries*: There are three lotteries being held in your city, each with an enormous jackpot. You have been given a lottery ticket selected by a chance process, such that there was an equal objective chance of your ticket coming from each

lottery. Lottery A has just two tickets. Lottery B has one million tickets. Lottery C has one billion tickets. You have a pessimistic hunch that your ticket is not from Lottery A. In fact, you are almost certain that your ticket is from Lottery C.

Suppose that in light of your pessimism about your ticket, you believe that you will not be able to afford an expensive holiday vacation this year. For instance, as you wander the local library, you pass up the travel section and head to the home improvement section, since you believe you are going to have a lousy vacation spent repairing some leaks in your basement. You are not justified in forming the outright belief that you will not be able to afford an expensive vacation. After all, you have no good reason to believe that your ticket is from Lottery C. In fact, you have good reason to believe that there is a significant objective chance that you are about to win an enormous amount of money.

Now suppose that you later learn that your ticket is from Lottery B. Accordingly, you still believe that you will not be able to afford an expensive holiday vacation this year. As you walk through the library, your belief that you are going to have a lousy vacation may indeed be justified. As discussed in §8.4, we may even say it is knowledge. Let *Lousy* be the proposition that you are going to have a lousy vacation. As time passes in *Three Lotteries*, your attitudes about *Lousy* exhibit a surprising combination of features. When you learn that you have a ticket from Lottery B, your belief in *Lousy* goes from being unjustified to being justified. Hence you gain justification for your belief in *Lousy*. At the same time, you update your credence in *Lousy*. In particular, your credence in *Lousy* decreases, as it should in light of your new evidence. In short, your attitudes are a counterexample to the claim that "if one *gains* justification for an outright belief in P, then it is not the case that one's degree of belief in P, insofar as one has one, should *decrease*" (WHITE 2006, 554). The first premise of the Bayesian argument against dogmatism is false. In fact, it is indeed possible for your experience to justify belief in some proposition, while simultaneously making it the case that your credence in that proposition should decrease.[16]

According to the dogmatist, experience could in principle play roughly this sort of justificatory role for the proposition that you do not have fake hands. Apart from what you learn from experience, you do not have much knowledge about how likely it is that you have hands, fake hands, or neither. From the armchair, your credence that you have fake hands should be imprecise, and you should suspend judgment about whether you have fake hands. But when

---

[16] KUNG 2010 argues for a similar conclusion using his example of the *Third Alien Card Game*. However, it is not clear that you ever have any justification for having an outright belief in the proposition that plays the role of *Lousy* in his example, since that proposition is essentially just the proposition that you lost a small lottery.

you learn that you seem to have hands, you should come to have a very high credence that you do not have fake hands. In addition, you gain justification for believing that you do not have fake hands, just as you gain justification for believing that you are going to have a lousy vacation after you learn that your ticket is from Lottery B.

The *Three Lotteries* case helps us pull apart two evidential relations that are sometimes conflated. The first relation obtains when some evidence makes you gain justification for a hypothesis. The second obtains when some evidence justifies your having greater credence in a hypothesis than you did before. On reflection, these justification and confirmation relations come apart. The fact that you gain justification for some hypothesis is a fact about your full belief in that hypothesis, whereas the fact that you should raise your credence in a hypothesis is a fact about your thoroughly probabilistic beliefs. The independence of these facts highlights an important theme of this chapter. Throughout this chapter, I have described several applications of probabilistic knowledge, each of which motivates my central thesis that probabilistic beliefs can be knowledge. At the same time, my arguments have reinforced a theme that is more general than this central thesis. The more general theme is that thoroughly probabilistic beliefs should be recognized as attitudes with an epistemic status that is independent of the epistemic status of full beliefs, and on a par with it. I have argued that whether your full belief gains justification is independent of whether higher credences in the traditional propositional content of that belief are justified. This is another important respect in which epistemic facts about full beliefs and probabilistic beliefs are equally basic in nature.

9

Knowledge and action

9.1 Knowledge norms of action

In the previous chapter, I defended a probabilistic knowledge norm of belief. In this chapter, I develop and defend two probabilistic knowledge norms of action. After introducing both norms in this section, I raise and answer some objections for them in §9.2. The first norm that I develop is a knowledge norm for practical reasons. According to this norm, you may treat a probabilistic content as a reason for action if and only if you know it. In §9.3, I argue that this norm can account for certain intuitive judgments about what you may treat as a reason for action, while other norms fail to account for these judgments. In §9.4, I add that my knowledge norm for reasons can help us rethink alleged instances of pragmatic encroachment that are often cited as challenges for existing knowledge norms of action. The second norm developed in this chapter is a knowledge norm for decisions. According to this norm, an action is permissible for you if and only if it is considered permissible for an agent with certain imprecise credences, namely an agent whose beliefs exactly match your probabilistic knowledge. I end this chapter by arguing in §9.5 that my norm for decisions provides a valuable interpretation of a widely discussed thesis defended by PAUL 2014, namely that standard decision theory cannot guide our decisions about whether to have transformative experiences.

In recent literature on knowledge norms, the most commonly defended connection between knowledge and action concerns what propositions you may treat as reasons for action. According to a number of authors, you may treat a proposition as a reason for action if and only if you know it. For instance, HYMAN 1999 states that "A knows that p if and only if the fact that p can be A's reason for doing, refraining from doing, believing, wanting or doubting something" (442). HAWTHORNE AND STANLEY 2008 argue that among the contents on which a given decision depends, you know a content just in case it is appropriate for you to treat it as a reason for action.[1] These knowledge norms were formulated with

---

[1] HAWTHORNE 2004, STANLEY 2005, and WILLIAMSON 2005b defend similar knowledge norms.

propositional contents in mind, but they apply equally well to probabilistic contents. Just as you may treat propositions as reasons, you may also treat probabilistic contents as reasons. As discussed in §2.2 and argued at length in STAFFEL 2013, you can reason with probabilistic beliefs in just the same way that you reason with full beliefs. This probabilistic reasoning includes not only the theoretical reasoning that provides you with reasons for belief, but also the practical reasoning that provides you with reasons for action. For example, suppose you are driving to a restaurant and you come to an intersection. Just as you may turn left on the basis of your belief that the restaurant is to the left, you may turn left on the basis of your high credence that the restaurant is to the left. Similarly, you may grab an umbrella as you leave the house on the basis of your .4 credence that it will rain later in the day. In general, you may treat probabilistic beliefs as reasons for action, as long as they constitute knowledge for you.[2]

The knowledge norm for reasons states necessary and sufficient conditions for when it is permissible to treat something as a reason for action. In addition to this norm, it is natural to look for a second more comprehensive knowledge norm of action, namely a norm that states necessary and sufficient conditions for the permissibility of actions of any sort. According to standard decision theory, an action is permissible for you just in case it maximizes expected utility according to your utility function and your credences. According to a knowledge norm for decisions, whether an action is permissible for you should instead depend on what you know. In recent literature on knowledge norms, the most commonly defended norm for decisions replaces the notion of credence in standard decision theory with the notion of evidential probability. For sake of argument, let us assume that you have a unique evidential probability function that records the objective probability of any proposition given your evidence, and let us define the *epistemic expected utility* of an action for you as the expected utility of that action according to your utility function and your evidential probability function.[3] According to some authors, an action is permissible for you just in case it maximizes your epistemic expected utility. For instance, HAWTHORNE AND STANLEY 2008 express sympathy with the idea that one may "exploit epistemic probabilities (where, inter alia, knowledge delivers probability 1) as the ground of expected utility" (580).

---

[2] The difference between acting on full beliefs and acting on thoroughly probabilistic beliefs is not as great as it may seem at first, since—as argued in §3.6—full beliefs have thoroughly probabilistic loose contents. For the purposes of this chapter, though, my arguments are independent of this controversial account of full belief.

[3] The reader should be careful to distinguish *epistemic expected utility* from the notion of *expected epistemic utility*, as discussed by GREAVES AND WALLACE 2006 and others in the context of arguments for probabilism, as well as from the notion of *evidential expected utility*, as discussed by GIBBARD AND HARPER 1978 and others in the context of challenges for causal decision theory.

SCHULZ 2015 defends maximizing epistemic expected utility as a special case of his level-adjusted expected utility theory, which in general recommends that you choose the action with highest expected utility according to the likelihood of hypotheses given either your knowledge or a certain degree of higher-order knowledge.

The rule that you should maximize epistemic expected utility is a propositional knowledge norm for decisions. According to this norm, what you should do depends on what your evidential probabilities are, which depends on which of your full beliefs constitute knowledge. As an alternative to this propositional knowledge norm, we may state a similarly comprehensive probabilistic knowledge norm for decisions. Let us define your *epistemic representor* as the set of probability spaces compatible with your probabilistic knowledge. In other words, your epistemic representor is just the intersection of all the probabilistic contents that you know. This representor resembles the set of probability spaces representing your imprecise credences, except it corresponds to the probabilistic contents that you know, as opposed to those that you merely believe. According to my probabilistic knowledge norm for decisions, what you should do depends on your epistemic representor. Here is my preferred knowledge norm for decisions: an action is permissible just in case it is considered permissible for an imprecise agent who has your utility function and whose imprecise credences are given by your epistemic representor.

For example, suppose that you come to an intersection where you know that it is at least .9 likely that a certain restaurant is on the left. The members of your epistemic representor might disagree about exactly how likely it is that the restaurant is on the left. The restaurant might be .92 likely to be on the left according to one of your epistemic representor members, .95 likely according to another, and .98 likely according to another. But your epistemic representor members will unanimously agree that it is at least .9 likely that the restaurant is on the left. Given some natural assumptions about your utility function and your knowledge—that you want to find the restaurant soon, for instance, and that you know that turning left will not cause your car to explode—turning left will maximize expected utility according to each precise credence function in your epistemic representor. As a result, turning left will be permissible for you.

What if your epistemic representor members are not unanimous? In general, when is an action considered permissible for an agent with imprecise credences? The phrase 'considered permissible' in my knowledge norm for decisions refers to what is permissible according to the correct extension of standard decision theory to agents with imprecise credences. The jury is still out about what actions are permissible for imprecise agents, and different theories give rise to different versions of my knowledge norm for decisions. For instance, according to permissive decision theories defended by LEVI 1985 and others, an action is permissible for you just in case it maximizes expected utility given your utility function and *at least one* member of your imprecise credal state. According to a second decision theory for imprecise agents defended by RINARD 2015, the permissibility of an action can be determinately decided only by the unanimous vote of your representor members. An action is permissible for you just in case it maximizes expected utility given your utility function and *every* member of your imprecise credal state, and impermissible just in case it uniformly fails to maximize expected utility. If an action maximizes expected utility given some but not all members of your imprecise credal state, then it is indeterminate whether the action is permissible or impermissible for you.

The probabilistic knowledge norm for decisions defended in this chapter is closely related to the probabilistic knowledge norm of belief defended in chapter 8. According to the knowledge norm of belief, your imprecise credal state should match your epistemic representor. According to the knowledge norm for decisions, you should act like an agent whose imprecise credal state matches your epistemic representor. In short, my knowledge norm for decisions says that you should act like an agent whose beliefs satisfy the knowledge norm of belief, where that agent has your probabilistic knowledge. There is a sense in which your actions are good only insofar as they issue from epistemically good beliefs.

9.2   Addressing objections

Having spelled out my preferred knowledge norms of action, I will now address some objections that have been raised for existing knowledge norms. One common objection is that knowledge norms fail to account for the fact that it is permissible to act on the basis of credences. For instance, SCHIFFER 2007 argues that knowledge norms fail to explain why it is rationally permissible for you to carry around an umbrella on the basis of your .4 credence that it is going to rain. CRESTO 2010 develops a similar objection in her reply to Hawthorne and Stanley, arguing that their knowledge norm cannot account for the fact that "partial beliefs enter into the business of giving and asking for reasons," intuitively serving as perfectly acceptable grounds for rational action (328). This is a straightforward objection to the knowledge norm for reasons. Given my probabilistic knowledge norm, it has a straightforward answer. Rational action can be based on credences and also based on knowledge, since rational action can be based on probabilistic knowledge.

In addition to this initial objection, though, advocates of knowledge norms face another challenge. There is an intuitive sense in which it is permissible to carry an umbrella on the basis of your .4 credence that it is going to rain, precisely because carrying it has greater expected utility than leaving it behind. DOUVEN 2008b spells out this objection, rejecting knowledge norms on the grounds that you should choose whatever act has maximal expected utility given your credences. In response, advocates of knowledge norms should grant that there is some sense in which you should act on the basis of your credences, regardless of whether they constitute knowledge. Knowledge norms need not entail the radical conclusion that the verdicts of standard decision theory are false. What matters is that there is at least one sense in which subjects acting on mere probabilistic beliefs could be doing better, some sense in which their actions are deficient.

Suppose that you are driving to a restaurant and you come to an intersection, and suppose that you firmly believe that the restaurant is on the left, even though your evidence suggests that it is on the right. There is an intuitive sense in which you should turn left, since that is what maximizes expected utility given what you believe. But there is also an intuitive sense in which you should turn right, since your evidence suggests that turning right will take you to your destination. The first sense of 'should' may be salient in some contexts, while the second is salient in others. In addition, there is a third sense in which you should act only on the basis of knowledge. As STANLEY 2007b puts it, "There may be multiple norms governing rational action, which sometimes conflict . . . one sometimes acts on beliefs that are not knowledge, because there are other rational pressures on our behavior" (205). The rules of standard decision theory not only differ from knowledge norms, but also from moral norms, legal norms, social norms, and so on. An action might be impermissible according to one of these norms and permissible according to another. This combination of verdicts does not mean that at least one norm is false. Each norm spells out consistent considerations that might figure in rational deliberation, perhaps even incommensurable considerations that fail to determine what actions are permissible all things considered.[4]

The knowledge norm for reasons and the knowledge norm for decisions themselves spell out distinct conditions on rational action, so that an action may be permissible according to one norm but not the other. Suppose you know that Jones likes cats. For this reason, you give her a kitten for her birthday. Suppose you also know that Jones already has many more cats than she wants, and that she has recently been struggling to give some cats away. The knowledge norm for reasons

---

[4] This pluralism about norms of action is analogous to the pluralism about norms of belief discussed in §8.1.

fails to forbid your choice of birthday present, since you give the kitten to Jones on the basis of a reason that constitutes knowledge. By contrast, the knowledge norm for decisions accounts for our intuition that the birthday present is impermissible. Because you know that Jones almost certainly does not want another cat, each member of your epistemic representor agrees that the kitten is a bad choice, and any decision theory for imprecise agents will entail that it is impermissible for you to give the kitten to Jones.

Conversely, sometimes the knowledge norm for decisions fails to forbid bad actions that are forbidden by the knowledge norm for reasons. For instance, the knowledge norm for decisions fails to forbid dumb risks that happen to turn out well.[5] Consider the following example from ELGA 2008, as recounted in SCHOENFIELD 2014:

> *Hypoxia*: You are a pilot flying to Hawaii. You suddenly realize that you might not have enough fuel to get there. If you don't have enough fuel, you should land right away. You do some calculations and breathe a sigh of relief. It looks like you'll make it. You then get a message from ground control: "You are flying at an altitude that puts you at great risk for hypoxia. People flying at your altitude only do the relevant sort of calculations correctly 50% of the time." (1)

Suppose that after hearing the message from ground control, you do not know that you almost certainly have enough fuel to get to Hawaii. As a result, you suspend judgment about the likelihood that you have enough fuel, admitting that it might well be that your plane is likely to crash if you keep flying. Nevertheless, you keep flying. As it happens, you luck out: the plane has enough fuel, and so you and your passengers survive. There is a clear sense in which you were wrong to keep flying the plane. It turned out well in the end, but it was still a dumb risk that in some sense you should not have taken.

The knowledge norm for decisions fails to yield this result. Since you have enough fuel to get to Hawaii, there is not some small chance that you don't. Since knowledge is factive, you do not know that there is at least some small chance that you don't have enough fuel. Hence some member of your epistemic representor endorses an optimistic probabilistic claim, namely that there is at most some small chance that you don't have enough fuel to get to Hawaii. For sake of argument, assume that your utility function is such that this optimistic claim entails that continuing to fly the plane maximizes your expected utility. Also, assume that the best decision theory for imprecise agents only forbids actions that are uniformly forbidden by every member of your representor. In other words, an imprecise

---

[5] Thanks to Brian Weatherson for calling my attention to this point.

agent is not forbidden to do anything that maximizes utility according to her utility function together with some member of her imprecise credal state. From these assumptions, it follows that the probabilistic knowledge norm for decisions fails to forbid you from flying the plane.

Although my knowledge norm for decisions cannot explain our intuitive judgment that you are required to land the plane, my knowledge norm for reasons can explain it. In light of your ignorance, there is nothing that you may treat as a sufficient reason for continuing to fly the plane. When it comes to the likelihood that you have enough fuel to get to Hawaii, the strongest content you know is that there is at least some small chance that you do have enough fuel, not that there is at most some small chance that you don't. Only the latter content is strong enough to license your continuing to fly the plane. But only the former content is such that you may treat it as a reason for action. This example highlights one respect in which the knowledge norm for reasons is stronger than the knowledge norm for decisions. The knowledge norm for decisions requires roughly that your actions are consistent with your knowledge, while the knowledge norm for reasons requires that your actions are based on knowledge. In cases where you do not have much knowledge, the knowledge norm for reasons can yield more stringent verdicts.

Although the knowledge norm for decisions does not forbid you from flying the plane in a case where you happen to have enough fuel, the sort of person who takes dumb risks often ends up acting in ways that are forbidden by the knowledge norm for decisions. This may help explain why we are strongly inclined to say that you were wrong to keep flying the plane. LASONEN-AARNIO 2010 argues that in such cases, our assessment of your particular action is clouded by our negative assessment of the general epistemic policies on which you are acting.[6] In this connection, it is also worth noting that the knowledge norm for decisions does not enable agents to know in advance that it is permissible to take dumb risks. As you are deciding whether to keep flying the plane, you do not know that you have enough fuel, so you do not know that flying the plane is permissible according to the knowledge norm for decisions. At best, you may appeal to the knowledge norm for decisions in order to excuse your lucky actions in hindsight.

Like many other knowledge norms of action, my knowledge norm for decisions allows for a practical analog of moral luck. Say you keep flying and land safely in Hawaii. In a nearby world, your confident doppelganger keeps flying and runs out of fuel somewhere over the Pacific. According to the knowledge norm, it could turn out that you did something permissible and your doppelganger did not.

---

[6] For further development of this sort of defense of knowledge norms, see WILLIAMSON 2015.

The verdicts of the knowledge norm for decisions fail to supervene on facts about your internally accessible mental states, or indeed on any facts that you are in a position to know. This raises a final objection, namely that the knowledge norm for decisions will therefore fail to be useful in guiding your action. In defense of similar knowledge norms, WILLIAMSON 2005a points out that the same objection applies equally to more familiar norms that have nothing to do with knowledge. According to WILLIAMSON 2000, you do not have any *luminous* mental states, i.e. states such that you are always in a position to know that they obtain when they obtain. *A fortiori*, the rationality of your actions cannot be determined by your luminous mental states. Nevertheless, knowledge norms—like many other norms—may be practically useful without providing subjects with complete decision procedures for action. As HAWTHORNE AND SRINIVASAN 2013 put it, "it is far from clear that there is anything *ipso facto* wrong about articulating an imperfectly operationalizable norm as advice. After all, there can be instances in which one can't incorporate a norm in knowledgeable practical reasoning but nonetheless has good evidence about what a norm recommends" (16). In addition, the knowledge norm for decisions may guide your assessments of the actions of others, as well as your retrospective assessments of your own actions, even in cases where it could not have usefully guided your actions directly.[7]

9.3 Applying knowledge norms of action

As mentioned in §9.1, HAWTHORNE AND STANLEY 2008 defend a propositional knowledge norm for reasons. They use several examples to motivate this norm, starting with the following case:

> *Restaurant*: Hannah and Sarah are trying to find a restaurant, at which they have time-limited reservations. Instead of asking someone for directions, Hannah goes on her hunch that the restaurant is down a street on the left. After walking for some amount of time, it becomes quite clear that they went down the wrong street. A natural way for Sarah to point out that Hannah made the wrong decision is to say, "You shouldn't have gone down this street, since you didn't know that the restaurant was here." (571)

Hawthorne and Stanley suggest that their knowledge norm can account for our judgment that there is a sense in which Hannah does the wrong thing, while standard decision rules cannot account for this judgment. Their knowledge norm

---

[7] For further relevant discussion of the objection that knowledge norms are not sufficiently action-guiding, see HAWTHORNE AND SRINIVASAN 2013.

says that Hannah acts badly because she treats the restaurant being on the left as her reason for turning left, even though she does not know that the restaurant is on the left. According to standard decision theory, by contrast, turning left is permissible as long as Hannah has high enough credence that the restaurant is on the left, even if her high credence is not justified.

As an argument for the knowledge norm for reasons, *Restaurant* is suggestive but not decisive. In particular, it is not clear that Hannah's action is bad because it is based on a belief that is not *knowledge*. As the story is told, it is natural to assume that Hannah is not even *justified* in forming the outright belief that the restaurant is on the left. Hence the impermissibility of her action could just as well be explained by the norm that you should act only on justified beliefs. Against the knowledge norm for reasons, BROWN 2008 argues that you may rely on a justified true belief that an express train will leave the local station at 12:20 when deciding when to head for the station, even if your belief fails to constitute knowledge. LITTLEJOHN 2009 and NETA 2009 offer further examples in a similar spirit.

In response to this objection, advocates of knowledge norms should endorse the pluralist view of practical normativity described in §9.2. There is a sense in which you should act as if an express train will leave at 12:20 when that is what your timetable says, but there is also another sense in which actions should be based on knowledge. When it comes to catching trains, we may often care about the former norm as opposed to the latter. For advocates of knowledge norms, the important point is that in at least some cases, we care that you act on knowledge. *Restaurant* does not prove this point. But another example does. Consider the following example from BUCHAK 2013a:

> *Cell Phone*: You leave the seminar room to get a drink, and you come back to find that your iPhone has been stolen. There were only two people in the room, Jake and Barbara. You have no evidence about who stole the phone, and you don't know either party very well, but you know (let's say) that men are 10 times more likely to steal iPhones than women . . . you should have a high credence that Jake stole the phone: if you had to place a bet with only monetary gain and loss at stake, it is clear that you should bet on Jake. (292)

Suppose you only have the ability to investigate either Jake or Barbara, say by following one of them after seminar to see if they pull the stolen phone from their backpack. Also, suppose that based on your statistical evidence, you have high credence that Jake stole your phone. According to standard decision theory, it is permissible for you to act on your high credence. But intuitively, there is also another important sense in which you should not act on that high credence. Compare *Cell Phone* with a case in which you return to the seminar room just in time to see for yourself that it is very likely that Jake stole your phone. There is something intuitively better about acting as if Jake probably stole your phone on the basis of direct perceptual evidence, as opposed to acting as if he probably stole your phone on the basis of statistics about his gender. The probabilistic knowledge norm for reasons explains the contrast between these cases. When you see that Jake probably stole your phone, your high credence that Jake stole your phone is knowledge, and you may treat it as a reason for action. By contrast, it is intuitive to say that you do not know that Jake probably stole your phone on the basis of facts about other members of his gender. Given that you do not have this knowledge, the knowledge norm for reasons correctly predicts that it is impermissible for you to act on your high credence that Jake stole your phone.

As compared with *Restaurant*, *Cell Phone* provides a stronger case for the knowledge norm for reasons. The verdict that you should not act on your credences in *Cell Phone* is not explained by norms that say you should always act on your credences. But in addition, the verdict is not explained by norms that say you should act on your justified beliefs. Although you are not justified in forming the full belief that Jake stole your phone, you are in some sense justified in having high credence that he stole it. In particular, your high credence that Jake stole your phone may exactly match your evidential probability that he stole it. But insofar as your credence is justified by merely statistical evidence, it is impermissible for you to act on it. Justified belief norms fail to account for this intuition about *Cell Phone*, whereas the knowledge norm for reasons succeeds.

This account of *Cell Phone* raises an important question: why are we reluctant to say that you can know by statistical inference that Jake probably stole your phone? The problem with your credences about Jake is not simply that they result from a statistical inference. As discussed in §8.4, statistical inferences do sometimes yield probabilistic knowledge. The problem is that as we consider this case, there is a certain possibility that is salient—namely, that Jake is not exactly as likely to have stolen your phone as an arbitrary member of his gender. There is a possibility that your having high credence that Jake stole your phone would amount to falsely suspecting an innocent person on the basis of their gender. As we consider this possibility, our assessment of your high credence is *controlled* rather than *automatic*, in the sense described in §8.4. As a result, the belief that Jake probably stole your phone has the same intuitive epistemic standing as your belief that you will lose the lottery. Although some statistical beliefs do intuitively count as knowledge, your high credence that Jake stole your phone does not. I further develop this line of thought in §10.4. In response to similar cases described in that section, I introduce a moral rule regarding our consideration of others, and then use this rule to help explain why credences fail to constitute knowledge when they are based on acts of profiling.

There are modest limits to the support that *Cell Phone* provides for the knowledge norm for reasons. For starters, our judgments about *Cell Phone* do not establish that there is some sense in which *every* reason for action must be knowledge. Is action based on bad belief always *ipso facto* bad action? Or is there a distinctive class of actions that must be based on good beliefs? For simplicity, I did not restrict the knowledge norm for reasons in my original exposition of this norm in §9.1. But strictly speaking, I remain neutral on whether this norm is a universal norm applying to all reasons for action. The same goes for the knowledge norm for decisions. As compared with standard decision theory, the knowledge norm for decisions may be more restricted in scope. Furthermore, I have not argued that knowledge norms are the only norms that could account for the sense in which you act badly in *Cell Phone*. For all I have argued, some alternative to my knowledge norms may do just as well with *Cell Phone* and even better with further cases. If some other rule in the neighborhood does a better job predicting our judgments, it may turn out that my knowledge norms are simply elegant rules of thumb, useful in virtue of being both reasonably accurate and extremely simple in nature.

Before concluding that our intuitions about *Cell Phone* support my central thesis that probabilistic beliefs can be knowledge, we should not only attempt to explain these intuitions using the belief norms mentioned above, but also using norms according to which agents should act on their propositional knowledge. Could a more traditional propositional knowledge norm for reasons explain our intuitions about cases in which it seems permissible to act on probabilistic beliefs? Hawthorne and Stanley have some suggestions. In response to objections from Schiffer and others, Hawthorne and Stanley hold the line and insist that it is not ever permissible for agents to act on credences. They say that whenever it appears as if you may act on credences, "the normative role of partial beliefs is replaced by beliefs about chances" (581). For example, Hawthorne and Stanley do not accept that you may carry around an umbrella on the basis of your .4 credence that it is going to rain. Instead they say that you may carry an umbrella on the basis of the full belief that there is .4 objective chance that it will rain, or the full belief that you have .4 evidential probability that it will rain, or the full beliefs that ground your .4 evidential probability, or full beliefs of some other sort. According to Hawthorne and Stanley, the fact that you may carry around an umbrella is explained by the norm that you should act on your propositional knowledge, together with the claim that you are carrying your umbrella on the basis of some proposition that you know.

Unfortunately, the most natural application of this line of reasoning fails to draw a principled distinction between permissible actions based on knowledge and your impermissible action in *Cell Phone*. Just as you have .4 evidential probability that it will rain when you grab an umbrella, we can stipulate that it is very likely given your evidence that Jake stole your phone, and also that you know that it is very likely given your evidence that he stole it. The propositional knowledge norm does not say anything distinctively critical about actions based on knowledge about evidential probabilities that result from problematic statistical evidence, as opposed to actions based on knowledge about evidential probabilities resulting from other sorts of evidence. By contrast, my knowledge norm can distinguish your statistical evidence about Jake from other sorts of evidence, namely by saying that your statistical evidence fails to ground probabilistic knowledge.

Accepting my knowledge norm for reasons has an additional advantage over insisting that it merely appears permissible to act on credences. As explained in §2.2, you may reason using credences, just as you may reason using full beliefs. For instance, you may reason from your high credence that the restaurant is on the left to the conclusion that you should turn left. After you complete this reasoning, it is permissible for you to treat a certain probabilistic content as your reason for turning left, namely the very same content that played a role in your reasoning about which way to turn. To restate the point using thoroughly probabilistic vocabulary, you can turn left on the basis of your belief that the restaurant is probably on the left. My knowledge norm for reasons explains this fact, while the propositional knowledge norm does not. Similarly, my account explains how you can rationally act on a combination of full beliefs and probabilistic beliefs. For example, suppose you buy some cigarettes for your friend Jones on the basis of your full belief that she carries a cigarette lighter, together with your probabilistic belief that if she carries a lighter then she probably smokes. As far as the rationality of your action is concerned, there is nothing special about your buying cigarettes for Jones on the basis of practical reasoning from these premises, as opposed to premises that include only full beliefs. Accepting probabilistic knowledge enables us to give a unified normative theory governing action based on full beliefs, action based on probabilistic beliefs, and action based on both sorts of beliefs at once.

9.4 Pragmatic encroachment

I have responded to the objection that knowledge norms of action should be replaced by justified belief norms. Another significant objection against knowledge norms of action is that they entail that what you know is *interest relative*.[8] For example, consider the classic bank cases introduced in DeRose 1992: you believe that your local bank is open on Saturday mornings. In most contexts, you may

---

[8] For detailed discussion of this objection, see HAWTHORNE 2004, STANLEY 2005, and WEATHERSON 2005.

treat your belief as a reason for action. For instance, you may act on your belief as you drive past the bank on Friday night, intending to return to deposit your paycheck on Saturday. But you may not treat that same belief as a reason for action if some crucial financial transaction depends on the bank being open on Saturday. This raises a concern for the knowledge norm for reasons: if you may treat a belief as a reason if and only if it is knowledge, it follows that your knowledge that the bank will be open on Saturday suffers from *pragmatic encroachment*. In other words, what you know depends not only on facts traditionally treated as epistemic, but also on facts about your practical interests. This result is sometimes identified as one of the most costly consequences of knowledge norms of action. As STANLEY 2007a puts it, pragmatic encroachment undermines "a powerful and perhaps non-negotiable theoretical commitment of many philosophers" (169).[9]

Accepting probabilistic knowledge allows us to say that rational action in bank cases requires knowledge, without saying that knowledge is interest relative. Say that you believe that it is at least .5 likely that the local bank will be open on Saturday, but you do not believe that it is at least .999 likely that it will be open. In most ordinary contexts, you may treat the former probabilistic content as a reason for driving past the bank on Friday night. "I hate waiting in the long lines at the bank on Friday. The bank will probably be open tomorrow. And even if it isn't, nothing much depends on whether I deposit my paycheck this weekend. I should just come back in the morning." In high stakes cases, this same reasoning fails. The very same probabilistic content—namely, that the bank will probably be open on Saturday—no longer supports the same action of postponing your trip to the bank. If you must deposit your paycheck before Sunday to complete some crucial financial transaction, then your driving past the bank is licensed only by much stronger contents, such as the claim that it almost certain that the bank will be open on Saturday. And you do not know these stronger contents, which is why you should not drive past the bank.

According to my alternative account of bank cases, what you know does not depend on your practical interests. Whether the stakes are low or high, the very same probabilistic beliefs constitute knowledge for you. In particular, you know the weaker content that it is at least .5 likely that the bank will be open on Saturday, regardless of your interests, and you do not know the stronger content that it is at least .999 likely that the bank will be open. As the stakes are raised, these epistemic facts stay the same. What changes is which contents are strong enough to license your postponing your trip to the bank. The content that the bank will probably

---

[9] The extent to which pragmatic encroachment conflicts with folk intuitions about knowledge is a matter of controversy. See BUCKWALTER AND SCHAFFER 2015 for an opinionated overview of relevant empirical studies.

be open on Saturday is no longer strong enough to serve as a premise in your practical reasoning to the conclusion that you should postpone your trip. That is why your knowledge no longer includes any content that you could treat as a reason to postpone your trip until Saturday. To sum up, my knowledge norm for reasons can explain familiar intuitions about how you should act in bank cases, without entailing that knowledge is subject to pragmatic encroachment. Facts about probabilistic knowledge may account for many similar intuitions that have been considered challenging for knowledge norms of action.[10]

This defense of knowledge norms of action is limited in scope. I have not aimed to prove that knowledge is not interest relative. In fact, probabilistic knowledge may itself turn out to be interest relative. Recall the case of Judy Benjamin from VAN FRAASSEN 1981 discussed in §5.2:

> [Judy Benjamin and her soldiers are] hopelessly lost. Using their radio they are at one point able to contact their own headquarters. After describing what they remember of their movements, they are told by the duty officer 'I don't know whether or not you have strayed into Red Army territory. But if you have, the probability is 3/4 that you are in their Headquarters Company Area.' (377)

Does Judy Benjamin know the probabilistic content asserted by the duty officer? For all I have argued, it may depend on how much is at stake. Suppose that several critical tactical questions depend on the conditional probability that Judy is in the Red Army Headquarters Area if she is in Red Army territory. Then her conditional credences may not constitute knowledge, even if they would constitute knowledge in more ordinary circumstances. The argument in this section is merely intended to limit pragmatic encroachment, not eradicate it.[11] The valuable upshot of this argument is that in many familiar cases cited as examples of pragmatic encroachment, subjects may be acting on beliefs that constitute knowledge and that continue to constitute knowledge even as the stakes are raised. Advocates of my knowledge norm for reasons can resist one sort of widespread pragmatic encroachment that other knowledge norms require.

9.5 Transformative experience

A basic fact about decisions is that some are harder than others. It is one thing to decide to brush your teeth after dinner. It is quite another to decide to become a

---

[10] For further discussion, see my account of Barry and the genie in MOSS 2013, which answers a similar argument for pragmatic encroachment put forward by WEATHERSON 2012.

[11] See §7.3 for another potential example of pragmatic encroachment on probabilistic knowledge. For discussion of a closely related phenomenon, see my account of *moral encroachment* in §10.4.

parent, emigrate to a new country, or fight in a war. L. A. Paul argues that these major experiences are often *transformative experiences*, radically new experiences that change you in a deep and fundamental way. The central theme of PAUL 2014 is that there is a sense in which decisions about transformative experiences are not just hard, but impossible. According to Paul, standard decision theory can tell you whether you should brush your teeth after dinner, but not whether you should become a parent. Paul argues that this is because when you decide whether to have a transformative experience, you lack some knowledge that is necessary for your choice. Standard decision theory says that you should do whatever action has the greatest expected value. But when you decide whether to have a transformative experience, "you don't know enough about the structure of the values of the outcome space to use a standard model for decision-making under ignorance to make a choice organized around these outcomes" (35), and "decision-theoretic models will fail in contexts where we cannot know the relevant values" (33). In short, Paul's critique of standard decision theory can be condensed into three claims:

(KNOWLEDGE)   Decisions should be based on knowledge that is represented by standard decision tables.

(IGNORANCE)   When deciding whether to have a particular transformative experience, we lack this knowledge.

(INADEQUACY)   Hence the resources of standard decision theory are inadequate for decisions about whether to have transformative experiences.

Paul's theory of transformative experience has attracted both extensive praise and extensive criticism. In this section, I develop an interpretation of PAUL 2014 that can answer several recent objections to her view. In particular, I spell out a precise interpretation of the three claims stated above, and I answer objections that have been raised for each of these claims.

Against (KNOWLEDGE), Paul's opponents have argued that decision-making does not in fact require *knowledge* of anything represented by standard decision tables. Rather, what you should do depends on your credences and your utilities, neither of which is essentially tied to what you know. Paul claims that when you make decisions about transformative experiences, "you are like the agent who cannot rationally determine the value of winning the lottery because he cannot determine the value of the prize, so he cannot decide whether he should pay to play" (32). According to Paul's opponents, though, standard decision theory is meant for agents who are coping with just this sort of ignorance. If you consider various hypotheses about how much you would value winning the lottery and you cannot determine which is correct, then whether you play the lottery should depend on how much credence you give to each of those hypotheses. The same goes for deciding whether to have a transformative experience, when you are not certain about exactly how valuable that experience will be. As DOUGHERTY ET AL. 2015 put it, "From the fact that an experience is epistemically transformative, it only follows that the agent is not antecedently in a position to know what the experience would be like. This is consistent with the agent being able to rationally estimate the experience's value" (307).

Against (IGNORANCE), Paul's opponents have argued that sometimes you can know whether standard decision theory says that you should have particular transformative experiences. For instance, sometimes you can get evidence about your credences and your utility function, where you can infer from that evidence that certain experiences have greater expected utility than others. PETTIGREW 2015 argues that this evidence may include facts about the opinions of other agents: "when I use statistical evidence to set my credences about my own utilities and then use these credences to make a decision . . . I am using the opinions of others as evidence about my own utility function" (4). Dougherty et al. argue that in addition to getting testimony from other agents, you can rationally estimate the value of a transformative experience by observing the behavior of others, or by drawing inferences from similar experiences you have had. For example, suppose you teach kindergarten for several years, and thereby discover that you deeply love caring for children and that you do not mind the drudgery of some tasks that come along with it; this experience may give you evidence about how much you will enjoy parenting (313).

Against (INADEQUACY), Paul's opponents have argued that her challenge for standard decision theory proves too much, undermining the application of standard decision theory to even the most ordinary decisions. It is argued that Paul must say that even some easy decisions are impossible, since they concern experiences that are novel and formative, just as transformative experiences are. For instance, KRISHNAMURTHY 2015 worries that insofar as decisions about parenting are phenomenally unique, "each experience that we have is both transformative and unique. Each experience that we have changes us in some way and is unlike any other experience we have had before it," including experiences as mundane as eating some particular serving of chocolate ice cream (177). In addition, Paul's opponents point out that for nearly any decision you make, you will believe that there is some small chance that it will result in a genuinely transformative experience. Dougherty et al. observe that when someone is asked out on a date, they may have some miniscule credence that accepting the invitation will one day lead them into parenthood. If Paul says that standard decision theory gives out in any such decision situation, her critique of standard decision theory is much more radical and much less intuitive than it first appears.

These are difficult objections for Paul. The good news is that accepting probabilistic knowledge enables us to develop a compelling interpretation of each of her three central claims. According to my knowledge norm for decisions, there is a sense in which your decisions must be based on knowledge. But this is not because you must know that the decision table for your decision has a certain feature. Rather, what is required is that some probabilistic beliefs represented by that table constitute knowledge for you. Since knowledge entails belief, the features of your epistemic representor members that determine what you should do will be features of the credences that appear in the standard decision table for your decision. In many cases where you are deciding whether to have a transformative experience, your epistemic representor members will disagree about the expected value of the transformative experience, and hence disagree about what you should do. In other words, your probabilistic knowledge will not be strong enough to settle whether you should have the experience. For example, suppose you do not know how likely it is that you would enjoy parenting. Suppose that one member of your epistemic representor assigns very high probability to the claim that you would enjoy it, while another assigns very low probability to that claim. Then becoming a parent will maximize expected value according to the first representor member but not the second. In this situation, what you should do will depend on the best extension of standard decision theory to imprecise agents. This is an important sense in which the resources of standard decision theory are inadequate for your decision about whether to become a parent.

This precise interpretation of PAUL 2014 provides answers to the objections raised for each of her central claims. In defense of (KNOWLEDGE), recall from §9.2 that the probabilistic knowledge norm for decisions is one among many norms of rational action. Dougherty et al. are indeed correct that there is some intuitive sense in which what you should do is determined by your credences and utilities. If your credences are precise, for instance, standard decision theory will deliver a verdict about which actions are permissible for you. According to my interpretation of Paul, though, the norm that she is investigating is independent of this verdict. Paul is concerned with another way of evaluating actions, another intuitive sense in which one action can be better than another. Unlike the rules of standard decision theory, the norm that Paul is investigating requires knowledge.

Suppose that your credences are precise, but that your epistemic representor isn't. You believe it is very likely that you will enjoy being a parent, but you don't *know* that it is very likely. Do you bring a child into existence on the basis of your mere belief that it is for the best? Standard decision theory says that you *must* become a parent. By contrast, the knowledge norm for decisions says that the decision is not so simple. Insofar as you must act on knowledge, you are in a *credal dilemma* in the sense of Moss 2014. That is, your decision is like a moral dilemma, in which you have incommensurable values that recommend different actions— only in this case, the different actions are recommended by different members of your epistemic representor. According to some imprecise decision theories, it is therefore indeterminate whether you should become a parent. According to other decision theories, either choice is determinately permissible. In such situations, making a choice is partly an act of self-determination.[12]

In defense of (IGNORANCE), it is worth noting that as Paul discusses transformative experiences, she creates a context in which she can truly say that your probabilistic beliefs about those experiences fail to constitute knowledge. Paul raises possibilities that you cannot rule out, where these possibilities are inconsistent with whatever knowledge you might hope to gain by experience or by the observation of others. These challenging alternative possibilities are sometimes described in vivid detail, as the reader is asked to "imagine a constantly screaming, colicky child, and the relentless drudgery of changing diapers, combined with months of sleepless nights" (151), or "how awful, or heart-wrenching, [parenting] could be (if for example, your child is born severely disabled, in great pain, with only a few months to live)" (152). Considering these possibilities leads us to consider certain probabilistic contents, including the contents that you would end up believing if you had a child and came to regret it. In particular, Paul encourages us to consider probabilistic contents that would recommend against your becoming a parent according to standard decision theory. These probabilistic contents are incompatible with contents that would license your becoming a parent. After making the former contents salient, Paul can truly deny that you know the latter contents.[13] In short, Paul is playing the role of the skeptic. Having raised the possibility that you are looking at a cleverly disguised mule, the skeptic can truly deny that you know that it is a zebra. Having raised the possibility that you will almost certainly regret being a parent, Paul can truly deny that you know that you will probably enjoy it. From the knowledge norm for decisions, it follows that your decision to become a parent falls outside the scope of standard decision theory. It is governed by the correct decision theory for agents in credal dilemmas,

---

[12] This consequence of my interpretation of Paul is similar to a proposal briefly described in §5 of DOUGHERTY ET AL. 2015, namely that decisions about transformative experiences might be intractable insofar as you are not even justified in having precise credences about those experiences.

[13] For present purposes, I assume that knowledge ascriptions are false as uttered in skeptical contexts.

for agents who suspend judgment about contents that make a difference to what they should do.

Finally, in defense of (INADEQUACY), there is an important disanalogy between becoming a parent and eating some chocolate ice cream. Paul does not vividly describe possibilities where you eat some chocolate ice cream and then deeply regret it. Decisions about whether to eat ice cream do not usually involve a lot of careful consideration of remote possibilities. In many contexts when you are deciding whether to eat ice cream, you simply know that you will probably enjoy eating it. Similarly, decisions about whether to go on a first date with someone generally do not involve consideration of the possibility that the date will lead you to become a parent of a severely disabled child with only a few months to live. By contrast, the decision whether to become a parent often has high stakes and salient emotional costs, features that naturally prompt consideration of skeptical possibilities. The same goes for many paradigmatic transformative experiences. Hence in many contexts where people are deciding whether to have these experiences, they may truly deny that they have enough knowledge to determine what they should do.

According to my interpretation of Paul, it is not *necessarily* the case that you lack sufficient knowledge to determine whether you should have a transformative experience. Similarly, you may not always have sufficient knowledge to determine whether you should have some everyday experience. Rather, it is an empirical fact that parenting decisions are generally belabored in a way that decisions about ice cream are not. It is an empirical fact that our assessments of credences about transformative experiences are generally less *automatic* than our assessments of credences about everyday decisions, in the sense described in §8.4. According to my interpretation of Paul, not every transformative experience necessarily poses a challenge to standard decision theory. As I see it, this is a significant advantage of my interpretation. Consider the following passage from BARNES 2015:

> I have never wanted kids. Neither has my partner . . . we've never had the slightest desire to have them, and other peoples' strong desire to have them is somewhat mystifying to us . . . Given my and my partner's preferences, deciding not to have kids seemed pretty rational. Indeed, it seemed like one of the most rational, clearest choices we've ever made. So it would be a surprising result, to say the least, if it turned out not to have been rational at all. (1–2)

In this passage, Barnes claims that not having children is a rational decision for her. My interpretation of Paul can make sense of this intuitive claim. Barnes has enough knowledge to determine that she should not have kids. For instance, she knows that it is very unlikely that having kids would be a desirable experience for her and her partner. As a result, the decision to avoid the transformative experience of becoming a parent is just as straightforward for her as an ordinary decision about whether to eat some ice cream.

The argument of this section has some limits. I have not aimed to remain faithful to everything that Paul has said about transformative experience, and I suspect that Paul might favor a more radical interpretation of her critique of standard decision theory. The modest goal of my discussion has been to develop a precise interpretation of PAUL 2014 that can answer several recent objections to her account. The extensive praise of Paul's account of transformative experience suggests that there is something deeply right about it. The probabilistic knowledge norm for decisions vindicates this suggestion, and thereby provides further motivation for my central thesis that probabilistic beliefs can be knowledge.

10

Knowledge and persons

10.1 Statistical evidence

In the context of a criminal trial, what does it mean to say that something has been *proved beyond a reasonable doubt*? Jurors routinely raise this question, but many appellate courts strongly discourage judges from answering it. In some jurisdictions, giving any definition of proof beyond a reasonable doubt constitutes an error of law. To quote one representative opinion from the Oklahoma Court of Criminal Appeals, "We are at a loss to understand why trial courts in this jurisdiction continue to give such an instruction when we have condemned them from territorial days to the present . . . it is error for the trial judge to try to define reasonable doubt."[1] Given the importance of this standard of proof in common law countries, it is perhaps disconcerting that there is widespread uncertainty among jurors and judges—as well as widespread disagreement among legal scholars—about what exactly it consists in. As Judge Posner puts it, "The question whether the prosecution has proved the defendant guilty beyond a reasonable doubt is central to every criminal trial. Can it be that the term should *never* be defined? Is it a mystical term, a talisman, somehow tarnished by attempts at definition?"[2] In the first half of this chapter, I defend an account of the notion of proof beyond a reasonable doubt. At a first pass, a defendant has been proved guilty beyond a reasonable doubt just in case the factfinder—the judge or jury—knows a certain probabilistic content, namely that it is beyond a reasonable doubt that the defendant is guilty.

An account of *proof beyond a reasonable doubt* should be divided into two parts. First, we can ask what it means to consider some fact to be *beyond a reasonable doubt*. Second, we can ask what is required by the relevant notion of *proof*. A compelling reason to distinguish these questions is that unlike the first question, the second question is relevant to the interpretation of many standards

---

[1] *Jones v. Oklahoma*, 554 P.2d 830, 835 (1976).
[2] *United States v. Hall*, 854 F.2d 1036, 1043 (1988).

of proof. In civil trials, for instance, the defendant must be proved liable merely *by a preponderance of the evidence* or *by a balance of the probabilities*. This standard is commonly understood to require proof that it is more likely than not that the defendant is liable.[3] In special situations, such as when terminating parental rights, claims must be proved according to the higher standard of *clear and convincing evidence*, commonly interpreted as requiring proof that a claim is highly probable, or much more likely than not.[4] By contrast, the standard of proof needed for a grand jury to indict a suspect is merely that there is *probable cause to believe* that the suspect committed the crime in question, where this standard is commonly identified with a probability threshold lower than .5. In this chapter, I defend a general account of legal proof that has implications for each of these standards. According to my account, proof by any of these standards requires that the factfinder have some specific probabilistic knowledge.

In the rest of this section, I identify four constraints on an adequate account of proof beyond a reasonable doubt. In §10.2, I develop and defend my thesis that legal proof requires probabilistic knowledge. I apply my account of legal proof to the reasonable doubt standard and argue that the resulting account satisfies the constraints identified in this section. I also use my account of legal proof to address some familiar questions about the value of statistical evidence in the courtroom, arguing that my account explains why merely statistical evidence is often not enough to license a verdict of guilt or liability. In §10.3, I talk about what distinguishes statistical evidence from testimonial evidence, and about why some kinds of statistical evidence are considered better than others.

In §10.4, I shift from discussing legal standards to discussing moral and epistemic norms—in particular, norms according to which it is wrong to engage in racial profiling. I argue that there is something wrong about forming or acting on beliefs about a person merely on the basis of statistics about his or her race. The same goes for beliefs and actions based on statistics about gender, class, sexual orientation, and disability status, among other features. There are a number of existing accounts according to which such acts of profiling are morally wrong. According to my account, acts of profiling are not merely morally wrong. They also exhibit a distinctive epistemic failure. In §10.5, I end by discussing applications and attractive features of my epistemic argument against profiling.

Before I talk more about the standard of proof beyond a reasonable doubt, a brief clarification is in order. Strictly speaking, the burden of proof at issue

---

[3] For an overview and history of the preponderance standard, see LEUBSDORF 2015. For an introductory discussion comparing several standards of proof, see CLERMONT 2013.

[4] *Santosky v. Kramer*, 455 U.S. 745 (1982).

in many criminal trials is not merely the claim that it is beyond a reasonable doubt that the defendant is guilty of some crime. In 1970, the United States Supreme Court held that every element of a crime must be proved beyond a reasonable doubt.[5] For example, in order to convict a defendant of a hate crime, the prosecution must not only prove beyond a reasonable doubt that the defendant committed the crime in question, but also prove beyond a reasonable doubt that the crime was motivated by prejudice. This point is often left implicit by legal scholars discussing the reasonable doubt standard. Accordingly, in this chapter, I often simplify my discussion by focusing on the claim that a defendant has been proved guilty beyond a reasonable doubt, though my arguments extend to the several facts that may constitute this claim.

There are four constraints that must be satisfied by any account of proof beyond a reasonable doubt. The first constraint concerns the relevant notion of proof. For any standard of proof to be met, the factfinder must have certain subjective opinions. For instance, the reasonable doubt standard cannot simply require that a defendant is convicted if and only if they are guilty. The United States Supreme Court has repeatedly insisted on this point, saying that the standard "impress[es] upon the factfinder the need to reach a *subjective state* of near certitude of the guilt of the accused" (my emphasis).[6] In his concurring opinion in *In re Winship*, Justice Harlan clarifies that each standard of proof imposes a condition on the credence assigned by the factfinder to the proposition under dispute:

> [A] standard of proof represents an attempt to instruct the fact-finder concerning the degree of confidence our society thinks he should have in the correctness of factual conclusions for a particular type of adjudication. Although the phrases 'preponderance of the evidence' and 'proof beyond a reasonable doubt' are quantitatively imprecise, they do communicate to the finder of fact different notions concerning the degree of confidence he is expected to have in the correctness of his factual conclusions.[7]

This condition on legal proof has a long history. For instance, BENTHAM 1843 argues that in a legal context, proof "admits of, and exists in, different degrees of strength," and clarifies that "the practice of wagering affords at the same time a proof of the existence, and a mode of expression or measurement for [these] quantities or degrees" (223). In short, each standard of proof requires that the factfinder's credence in the relevant proposition exceed some threshold, and some standards of proof require higher credences than others.

---

[5] *In re Winship*, 397 U.S. 358, 364 (1970).
[6] *Jackson v. Virginia*, 443 U.S. 307, 315 (1979). For further discussion, see chapter 2 of LAUDAN 2006.
[7] *In re Winship*, 397 U.S. 358, 370 (1970).

A second constraint on our account of proof beyond a reasonable doubt concerns the reasonable doubt standard in particular. Proof of guilt beyond a reasonable doubt must require the factfinder to have at least some high credence that the defendant is guilty, without requiring absolute certainty of guilt. According to one statement about reasonable doubt approved by Justice Ginsburg, for instance, proof beyond a reasonable doubt requires that "the prosecution must prove its case by more than a mere preponderance of the evidence, yet not necessarily to an absolute certainty."[8] The Supreme Court of Canada has clarified the standard by saying that it "falls much closer to absolute certainty than to proof on a balance of probabilities."[9] These observations are reflected by numerous empirical studies. MCCAULIFF 1982 reports that among 171 federal judges and United States Supreme Court justices, the average probability threshold associated with proof beyond a reasonable doubt was .90. According to MAGNUSSEN ET AL. 2014, trial judges report intentions to return guilty verdicts in mock trial settings when their credences in guilt exceed .83. The expression 'beyond a reasonable doubt' has also been interpreted using the same experimental methods commonly used to interpret natural language probability operators. According to one such study by DHAMI 2008, subjects associated 'beyond a reasonable doubt' with an average probability threshold of .96. To sum up the second constraint on our account of the reasonable doubt standard: a defendant is proved guilty beyond a reasonable doubt only if the factfinder has at least some threshold credence that the defendant is guilty, where the relevant threshold is greater than .5 and in some sense less than 1.

A third constraint on our account requires more extensive discussion. The constraint is that proof beyond a reasonable doubt generally cannot be supplied by merely statistical evidence.[10] For instance, consider this classic example from NESSON 1979:

> *Prison Yard*: In an enclosed yard are twenty-five identically dressed prisoners and a prison guard. The sole witness is too far away to distinguish individual features. He sees the guard, recognizable by his uniform, trip and fall, apparently knocking himself out. The prisoners huddle and argue. One breaks away from the others and goes to a shed in the corner of the yard to hide. The other twenty-four set upon the

---

[8] *Victor v. Nebraska*, 511 U.S. 1, 27 (1994) (Ginsburg, J., concurring). This statement is taken from an interpretation of reasonable doubt originally proposed in 1987 by the Federal Judicial Center, the research arm of the federal judicial system.

[9] *R. v. Starr* 2 S.C.R. 144 (2000).

[10] There is a vast legal literature on "naked statistical evidence," especially concerning the question of why merely statistical evidence often fails to license a verdict of guilt or liability. For recent surveys of relevant literature, see HO 2008, REDMAYNE 2008, and ENOCH AND FISHER 2015.

fallen guard and kill him. After the killing, the hidden prisoner emerges from the shed and mixes with the other prisoners. When the authorities later enter the yard, they find the dead guard and the twenty-five prisoners. Given these facts, twenty-four of the twenty-five are guilty of murder. (1192–93)

Whatever sort of evidence it takes to prove guilt beyond a reasonable doubt, the merely statistical evidence in *Prison Yard* does not have what it takes. Furthermore, the problem with the *Prison Yard* evidence is not merely that the threshold of credence required for proof beyond a reasonable doubt is greater than .96. At least at first glance, it is natural to say that a defendant cannot be proved guilty beyond a reasonable doubt on the basis of merely statistical evidence of this sort, no matter how unfavorable the odds.

The second and third constraints on our account of the reasonable doubt standard appear to be in tension with each other. The tension arises because statistical evidence can justify a factfinder in having an arbitrarily high credence that a defendant is guilty. In fact, the only credence that could not be justified by merely statistical evidence is credence 1. But according to our second condition, this credence cannot be required by the reasonable doubt standard. Picking up on this tension, a number of legal scholars and judges have made the almost paradoxical observation that even though there is one sense in which the reasonable doubt standard does not require absolute certainty of guilt, there must also be some sense in which it does require certainty of guilt after all. This observation appears even in very early texts on the criminal standard of proof, as BECCARIA 1764 argues that convictions require "nothing but a probability, though a probability of such a sort to be called certainty" (34). This observation is echoed centuries later in the opinion of Judge Posner in *United States v. Hall*: "'proof beyond a reasonable doubt' requires, and is (I believe) understood to require, that the jury be certain of the defendants' guilt, with this proviso: complete certainty . . . is never attainable with respect to the question whether a criminal defendant is guilty."[11] Along similar lines, the Supreme Court originally defined reasonable doubt in 1970 as requiring the factfinder to reach "a subjective state of *certitude* of the facts in issue," before stating in 1979 that proof beyond a reasonable doubt requires only "a subjective state of *near certitude* of the guilt of the accused" (my emphasis).[12] To sum up the challenge for our account of the reasonable doubt standard: in light of the fact that one cannot convict on the basis of merely statistical evidence, it seems that there must be at least some sense in which the reasonable doubt standard for conviction requires the factfinder to be certain that the defendant is guilty.

[11] *United States v. Hall*, 854 F.2d 1036, 1044 (1988).
[12] See *In re Winship*, 397 U.S. 358, 364 (1970) and *Jackson v. Virginia* 443 U.S. 307, 315 (1979).

But at the same time, there must be some sense in which proving guilt beyond a reasonable doubt does not require proving that it is *absolutely* or *completely* certain that the defendant is guilty.

This challenge for our account of the reasonable doubt standard should feel very familiar to readers of chapter 3 of this book. The attitude that is required by the standard of proof beyond a reasonable doubt seems just like the attitude of *full belief* described at length in that chapter, also commonly known among epistemologists as the attitude of *outright belief*. Full belief requires much more than merely believing that some claim is more likely than not. As I argue in §3.5, there is a fundamental tension in our intuitions about exactly what stronger attitude full belief requires. On the one hand, full belief seems significantly weaker than absolute certainty, since full belief may be justified in cases where absolute certainty is not. On the other hand, full belief seems to be just as strong as certainty, insofar as both attitudes seem equally inconsistent with doubt. In §3.6, I defended a theory of full belief that vindicates both of these intuitions. According to my theory, full belief strictly requires certainty, but loosely requires merely having a credence that is close enough to certainty for practical purposes.

These observations support an extremely tempting proposal about what proof beyond a reasonable doubt requires, recently suggested by the work of ROTH 2010 and BUCHAK 2013b, among others.[13] The tempting proposal is that a defendant is proved guilty beyond a reasonable doubt just in case the factfinder is *justified in fully believing* that the defendant is guilty. This proposal satisfies each of our first three constraints on an account of proof beyond a reasonable doubt. According to the tempting proposal, proof of guilt beyond a reasonable doubt requires that the factfinder have certain subjective opinions. In particular, having the full belief that the defendant is guilty requires the factfinder to have high credence that the defendant is guilty, without requiring absolute certainty of guilt. Finally, the proposal successfully predicts that the *Prison Yard* evidence cannot supply proof of guilt beyond a reasonable doubt, since this evidence cannot justify the strong attitude of full belief that the defendant is guilty. Both Roth and Buchak appeal to the categorical nature of full belief to explain why verdicts cannot be based on merely statistical evidence. As ROTH 2010 puts it, "naked statistical evidence of guilt is incapable of inspiring a juror's actual belief in guilt, which is more than a mere acknowledgment of a high likelihood of guilt—and therefore cannot inspire the 'moral certainty' underlying the modern reasonable doubt standard" (1158). BUCHAK 2013a points out that we cannot blame someone on the basis of merely statistical evidence, and argues that "this is best explained by the fact that we need

---

[13] For additional proposals in a similar spirit, see FERRER BELTRÁN 2006 and HO 2008.

a *belief* in someone's guilt to blame her, and that merely statistical evidence cannot give rise to a belief in these cases" (303).

So far, so good. But unfortunately, there is a serious problem for this tempting explanation of why statistical evidence fails to license a conviction in *Prison Yard*. The problem is that the explanation is not general enough. Statistical evidence also fails to license verdicts in cases where the reasonable doubt standard does not apply. Here is one classic example from COHEN 1977:

> *Gatecrasher*: [I]t is common ground that 499 people paid for admission to a rodeo, and that 1,000 are counted on the seats, of whom *A* is one. Suppose no tickets were issued and there can be no testimony as to whether *A* paid for admission or climbed over the fence. So by any plausible criterion of mathematical probability there is a .501 probability, on the admitted facts, that he did not pay. (74)

Just as in *Prison Yard*, the merely statistical evidence in *Gatecrasher* is intuitively insufficient to license a verdict against the defendant. As COHEN 1981 puts it, "our intuitions of justice revolt against the idea that the plaintiff should be awarded judgment" on the grounds of the statistical evidence described above (627). Yet *Gatecrasher* is not a criminal case, but a civil case. As mentioned above, the civil standard of proof is not proof beyond a reasonable doubt, but merely proof by a preponderance of the evidence. Hence the *Gatecrasher* case demonstrates that the insufficiency of statistical evidence should not be explained by any feature of the reasonable doubt standard in particular, but rather by some feature that all standards of proof have in common. In other words, the problem of statistical evidence should be solved by our more general account of what legal proof requires. This observation finally brings us to our fourth constraint on our account of proof beyond a reasonable doubt. Whatever explains why the evidence in *Prison Yard* fails to prove guilt beyond a reasonable doubt, there must be some feature of this evidence that also explains why the evidence in *Gatecrasher* fails to prove liability by a preponderance of the evidence.

This fourth constraint cannot be satisfied by the tempting account of the reasonable doubt standard mentioned above. Suppose the criminal standard of proof requires a justified full belief that the defendant is guilty. If this is correct, then what attitude does the civil standard require? In response to cases like *Gatecrasher*, it is sometimes suggested that proof by a preponderance of the evidence requires the factfinder to have a justified full belief that the defendant is liable.[14] But this strong interpretation of the civil standard fails to distinguish it

---

[14] For an early statement of this suggestion, see *Sargent v. Massachusetts Accident Co.* 307 Mass. 246, 250 (1940).

from the criminal standard of proof. As a result, the interpretation fails to explain why verdicts of liability can be licensed by case-specific evidence that merely justifies the factfinder in believing that the defendant is more likely than not to be liable, without justifying the stronger subjective attitude that the criminal standard requires. To give a simple example, the interpretation does not explain why someone may be acquitted of a crime while being found liable for the same act in a civil case—for instance, why someone may be acquitted of murder, and yet still be successfully sued for wrongful death.

At the same time, proof by a preponderance of the evidence cannot merely require that the factfinder be justified in having greater than .5 credence that the defendant is liable. For the factfinder in *Gatecrasher*, the epistemic probability that the defendant is liable is greater than .5. In this straightforward sense, the factfinder is indeed justified in having greater than .5 credence that the defendant is liable—and yet the civil standard of proof is not met in this case. To sum up, *Gatecrasher* demonstrates that there is still something missing from our explanation of why merely statistical evidence is often insufficient to prove guilt beyond a reasonable doubt, as we have not yet explained why merely statistical evidence is often insufficient for proof by any standard at all.

10.2 An account of legal proof

Having introduced the problem of statistical evidence, let us briefly review several proposals that others have put forward about how to solve it. THOMSON 1986 argues that statistical evidence cannot license a verdict of liability because the standard of proof in civil trials imposes a requirement that is *incompatible with luck*:

> [I]t is required of a jury that it not impose liability unless it has, not merely good reason, but reason of a kind which would make it not be just luck for the jury if its verdict is true. (214)

ENOCH ET AL. 2012 argue that proof requires *sensitivity*:

> [W]hat we need is an epistemological vindication of the distinction between statistical and individual evidence. And focusing attention on Sensitivity does just that, for noticing the epistemic significance of Sensitivity explains why there is something suspicious about statistical evidence across the board. (208)

PRITCHARD 2015 argues that proof requires *safety*:

> [W]e should construe knowledge as incorporating an anti-risk condition, such that if one knows then one's cognitive success is not subject to a high level of

epistemic risk (i.e., it is not an easy possibility that one's belief could have been false)...an adequacy condition on the total evidence presented at trial in support of the defendant's guilt ought to be such that it satisfies the epistemic anti-risk condition. (457)

PARDO 2010 argues that whatever proof requires is *absent in Gettier cases*:

[A]n appropriate connection among (1) fact finders' conclusions (however conceived), (2) the epistemic support they require, and (3) their truth, matters for legal proof. This connection arises in non-Gettier cases and is missing in Gettier cases. The verdicts of legal fact finders achieve an additional level of cognitive success when they possess this connection, and this additional requirement matters for legal proof...the goal of legal proof is *non-Gettier-ized* true and justified conclusions. (55, 57)

NESSON 1985 argues that proof requires the factfinder to reach a conclusion that *can be treated as a reason for action*:

[T]he object of judicial factfinding is the generation and projection of acceptable verdicts—verdicts that the public will view as statements about what actually happened, which the legal system can then use as predicates for imposing sanctions. (1358)

DUFF ET AL. 2007 argue that proof requires *truth*:

[T]he conviction of an innocent person is not a successful outcome of the trial, even if he is believed to be guilty... What is fundamental, in other words, is the truth and its significance: whatever 'dispute' there is matters only because the truth matters, and its resolution is, constitutively and not contingently, achieved by establishing the truth. (69)

Almost all of these conditions on legal proof were originally proposed as solutions to the problem of statistical evidence. Why is merely statistical evidence insufficient for legal proof? According to these authors, it is because legal proof requires something that is incompatible with luck, sensitive, safe, absent in Gettier cases, and so on. The common thread running throughout this literature speaks for itself. An elegant explanation of these several observations is that legal proof requires *knowledge*.

The idea that proof requires knowledge has been defended by a small handful of scholars as a necessary condition for proof beyond a reasonable doubt.[15] But absent the notion of probabilistic knowledge, it has proved difficult to extend this

---

[15] For relevant discussion, see DUFF ET AL. 2007 and PARDO 2011. Also, see THOMSON 1986 for an early attempt to solve the problem of statistical evidence by appealing to conditions required for knowledge.

idea to other standards of proof, such as proof by a preponderance of the evidence. REDMAYNE 2008 makes just this point in a recent paper on statistical evidence. Redmayne admits that parallels between legal and philosophical examples "suggest that verdicts require knowledge" (299). But then he goes on to object that this solution to the problem of statistical evidence cannot be extended to civil cases. Redmayne explains his objection as follows:[16]

> There is an obvious problem with this view, however. It is plausible that whatever prevents a liability verdict in Prisoners also prevents a liability verdict in [the civil case] Blue Bus. If Prisoners is explained by a knowledge requirement for proof, then Blue Bus is too. But that would involve arguing that civil as well as criminal verdicts require knowledge, and that is not easy to accept. Civil verdicts require no more than proof on the balance of probabilities. This standard seems too low to satisfy the degree of justification required for knowledge. (299)

As Redmayne sees it, proof by a preponderance of the evidence cannot require knowledge, since this standard merely requires that the factfinder have greater than .5 credence that the defendant is liable. Redmayne is correct that proof of liability by a preponderance of the evidence cannot require that the factfinder know *that the defendant is liable.* But there is another option available—namely, that proof by a preponderance of the evidence requires knowledge of a significantly weaker probabilistic content. This is the option I want to defend: proof of liability by a preponderance of the evidence requires that the factfinder know *that the defendant is probably liable.* In other words, the belief that must be knowledge according to this standard of proof is the very same subjective opinion that the standard itself requires. A defendant is proved liable by a preponderance of the evidence only if the factfinder has greater than .5 credence that the defendant is liable, *and that probabilistic belief constitutes knowledge.*

For instance, suppose you are the factfinder in *Gatecrasher.* The plaintiff proves that an arbitrary person at the rodeo is more likely than not to have climbed over the fence. Meanwhile, the defendant claims that he is an exception to this statistical generalization. He denies that it is more likely than not that he climbed over the fence, insisting that he did not climb over the fence at all. The statistical evidence of the case may justify your having .501 credence that the defendant is liable. But on the basis of this statistical evidence, your credence does not constitute knowledge. You do not know that the defendant is exactly as likely to have climbed over the fence as an arbitrary person at the rodeo, because you cannot rule out a certain possibility that is inconsistent with this content—namely,

---

[16] The *Blue Bus* case mentioned here by Redmayne is an infamous hypothetical case modeled after *Smith v. Rapid Transit* 58 N.E.2d 754 (1945). For a detailed description of this case, see §10.3.

that the defendant is an exception to the statistical generalization presented by the plaintiff. As a result, you do not know that it is more likely than not that the defendant is liable for trespass. According to my account of legal proof, it follows that the plaintiff has failed to prove that the defendant is liable by a preponderance of the evidence.

Probabilistic knowledge is not only required for proof by a preponderance of the evidence, but also for proof according to many other standards. As explained above, standards of proof come in degrees. That is, some standards of proof are stronger than others. As I see it, this is not because legal proof itself comes in degrees. Rather, it is because different standards of proof require knowledge of different probabilistic contents. Each standard of proof corresponds to a distinct threshold of probability. A standard of proof is met just in case the factfinder knows a certain probabilistic content—namely, the set of probability spaces according to which the probability of guilt or liability exceeds the corresponding threshold. To give another specific example, proof of liability by clear and convincing evidence requires the factfinder to know that it is *highly* probable that the defendant is liable. An informal study conducted by Judge Weinstein found that judges in the Eastern District of New York associated this standard with probability thresholds ranging from .6 to .75, for instance, and a subsequent study by MCCAULIFF 1982 found that hundreds of federal judges and United States Supreme Court justices associated this standard with an average probability threshold of .75.[17] Compared with the preponderance standard, proof of liability by clear and convincing evidence requires knowledge of a strictly stronger probabilistic content.

The idea that legal proof requires probabilistic knowledge can also be derived from the idea that legal proof is a special case of a more general notion of proof. The context of the courtroom is only one of many contexts in which speakers argue for some content with the aim of proving it to someone else. Having a proof is a factive mental state, and as argued at length by WILLIAMSON 2000, factive mental states require knowledge. For example, suppose that it is correct that a defendant is proved liable by a preponderance of the evidence just in case the factfinder has a proof of the probabilistic content that the defendant is probably liable. Then from the general idea that proof requires knowledge, it follows that a defendant is proved liable by a preponderance of the evidence only if the factfinder knows that the defendant is probably liable. And to a first approximation, nothing more is required by the civil standard of proof. Compare the following account

---

[17] For further discussion of the former study, see *United States v. Fatico*, 458 F. Supp. 388, 410 (1978).

of mathematical proof offered by WILLIAMSON 2000: "to a first approximation, in mathematics one knows *p* if and only if one has a proof of *p*" (263).

Before applying my account of legal proof to the reasonable doubt standard in particular, there are four clarificatory points that deserve attention. First, given the empirical studies mentioned above, it may be reasonable to conclude that some standards of proof are vague. As far as my arguments go, it remains an open question whether standards of proof ultimately correspond to vague or determinate probability thresholds. Second, it also remains an open question whether any standards of proof are context sensitive. For all I have argued, a single standard of proof might impose different requirements on factfinders in the context of different trials. A third point of clarification is that in jury trials, the factfinder is a group of people. Among social epistemologists, it is a familiar observation that groups of people can have knowledge, and it is an open question how exactly this knowledge is related to the knowledge of the individual group members.[18] Theories of collective knowledge may be useful in guiding our understanding of what it means to say that a jury knows some probabilistic content. A final point of clarification is that strictly speaking, the factfinder having certain probabilistic knowledge is only a necessary condition for the satisfaction of a given standard of proof. This necessary condition for proof is also sufficient, provided that the knowledge in question is based on the evidence admitted at trial. For instance, a defendant cannot be proved liable by a preponderance of the evidence merely because the judge happens to know that he is probably liable, if the grounds for that knowledge have nothing to do with anything that has happened in court. This feature of my account of legal proof is nothing out of the ordinary. Any account of legal proof that requires the factfinder to have certain subjective attitudes should also require these attitudes to be grounded in the evidence admitted at trial. For ease of exposition, this qualification will be left implicit throughout this chapter.

Having clarified these four points, we can return to the question of what is required by the standard of proof beyond a reasonable doubt. According to my account, proving a defendant is guilty beyond a reasonable doubt requires the factfinder to know some probabilistic content, namely that the likelihood that the defendant is guilty exceeds a certain threshold. This threshold is greater than .5 and in some sense less than 1—and as long as the reasonable doubt threshold satisfies these conditions, my account of the reasonable doubt standard satisfies each of the four adequacy constraints introduced in §10.1. Most notably, my account provides a sufficiently general explanation of why the evidence in *Prison*

---

[18] For introductory discussions of recent literature on group knowledge, see MATHIESEN 2007 and KERR 2013.

Yard cannot by itself prove guilt beyond a reasonable doubt. Suppose you are the factfinder in *Prison Yard*. Although you may believe that the defendant is .96 likely to be guilty, the prosecution cannot provide you with knowledge of this content merely by proving that 24 of the 25 prisoners in the yard are guilty, since there is a certain possibility that you cannot rule out—namely, that the defendant is less likely to be guilty than an arbitrary prisoner in the yard. This diagnosis of the problem with your evidence in *Prison Yard* holds equally for the evidence in *Gatecrasher*. As the factfinder in *Gatecrasher*, you may believe on the basis of merely statistical evidence that the defendant is probably liable. But the plaintiff cannot provide you with knowledge of this content merely by proving that most people at the rodeo are liable. There is a certain possibility that you cannot rule out, namely that the defendant is less likely to have climbed over the fence than an arbitrary person at the rodeo. By contrast, if a witness testifies that she saw the defendant climb over the fence, and you know that she is probably telling the truth, you can thereby come to know the probabilistic content that the defendant is probably liable, and accordingly, you may return a verdict of liability on the basis of her testimony.[19]

The foregoing account of *proof beyond a reasonable doubt* does not settle exactly what probabilistic knowledge this standard requires. A compelling conjecture is that the standard requires knowledge of the thoroughly probabilistic content of the full belief that the defendant is guilty, as described and defined in §3.6. Buchak and Roth may be correct when they say that justified full belief is a necessary condition for proof of guilt beyond a reasonable doubt, even though this necessary condition does not solve the problem of statistical evidence. According to this conjecture, it is overdetermined that the *Prison Yard* evidence is insufficient to prove guilt beyond a reasonable doubt. The evidence in *Prison Yard* not only fails to provide the factfinder with knowledge, but also fails to even justify the belief that would have to constitute knowledge in order for the reasonable doubt standard to be met. In other words, proof beyond a reasonable doubt requires evidence that is strong in two respects—namely, with respect to the strength of the probabilistic belief it justifies, and with respect to the strength of the justification that it provides. The first of these respects is distinctive to the reasonable doubt standard, and the second is common to every standard of proof. I leave further exploration of this conjecture for future research.

I have defended my account of legal proof with three arguments. The account provides an appropriately general solution to the problem of statistical evidence. It identifies legal proof as a special case of proof in general. And finally, my account

---

[19] For a more detailed comparative discussion of statistical evidence and testimonial evidence, see §10.3.

explains patterns in existing solutions to the problem of statistical evidence, namely patterns that suggest that legal proof requires knowledge. A natural objection to my third argument is that even if standards of proof require knowledge, they may not require probabilistic knowledge. It is prudent to consider and reject conventional proposals before embracing revisionary ones. A natural alternative knowledge account is that legal proof does not place requirements on the probabilistic knowledge of the factfinder, but rather on their *epistemic probabilities*. That is, one might argue that the burden of proof according to a given standard is met just in case the epistemic probability of guilt or liability exceeds a certain threshold.

Unfortunately, the epistemic probability account fails to satisfy the first adequacy constraint introduced in §10.1, namely that proving a claim must require the factfinder to have certain subjective opinions. According to the epistemic probability account, a defendant can be proved liable by a preponderance of the evidence even if the factfinder does not believe that the defendant is probably liable, namely in cases where the credences of the factfinder do not match their epistemic probabilities. Similarly, the epistemic probability account will sometimes require the conviction of defendants that are believed by the factfinder to be innocent. These objective standards of proof are perfectly consistent, and perhaps even reasonable, but they are not adequate interpretations of the standards of proof that we actually have.

Another problem for the epistemic probability account of legal proof is that it fails to forbid—and indeed sometimes requires—the conviction of an innocent person. Ho 2008 rejects the account on exactly these grounds:

> If all that a positive finding of fact expresses is a proposition of epistemic probability, a finding of guilt cannot be shown to be false by any post-conviction introduction of newly discovered exculpatory evidence. That we do think of the conviction as wrongful suggests that we do not read a finding of facts as merely expressing a proposition of epistemic probability. (116)

By contrast, my knowledge account reflects the fact that the state of being *proved* is a factive state. A defendant is *proved* guilty beyond a reasonable doubt only if they *are* guilty beyond a reasonable doubt. Let us say that a claim is *almost certainly* true just in case its probability exceeds the reasonable doubt threshold. If a convicted defendant is actually innocent, then they are not almost certainly guilty, and so they cannot have been proved almost certainly guilty. In other words, they cannot have been proved guilty beyond a reasonable doubt, and their conviction may correctly be identified as wrongful on these grounds. In a related discussion of the reasonable doubt standard, LAUDAN 2003 argues that whether this standard is met must be "an *objective* question about logical relations between events, not merely or primarily a question about the subjective state of the jurors' minds" (321). By requiring both belief and truth, my account of legal proof places both subjective and objective constraints on the mental states of the factfinder, simultaneously accommodating internalist and externalist intuitions about what each standard of proof requires.

A second potential objection to my general account of legal proof is that standards of proof should not require any sort of knowledge at all. This claim is defended at length by ENOCH ET AL. 2012, among others.[20] According to Enoch et al., using knowledge to explain why merely statistical evidence often fails to license a verdict is "resorting to knowledge fetishism" (221). To defend this claim, they argue that "to insist that the law should after all care about knowledge is (pretty much) to be willing to pay a price in accuracy" (212), and they give a thought experiment intended to demonstrate that this price is unreasonably high:

> Suppose you have to choose the (criminal) legal system under which your children will live, and you can choose only between systems A and B. System A is epistemo-logically better: perhaps its courts only convict when they know (or think that they know) the accused is guilty . . . But System B is more accurate, so that the chances of System B convicting an innocent are lower than the chances of System A doing so.
>
> (212–13)

Enoch et al. argue that you ought to choose System B for your children. They conclude that when it comes to the question of what our standards of legal proof ought to require, the value of knowledge is at best lexically inferior to the value of accuracy.

In response to this thought experiment, it is important to distinguish the value of convicting only the guilty from the value of acquitting only the innocent. The thesis that legal proof requires knowledge is consistent with the claim that one should avoid convicting innocent people at any cost. The relevant cost in accuracy of my account is that factually guilty defendants may be acquitted in cases where they might have been convicted according to less stringent standards of proof. This cost in accuracy is not unreasonably high. According to my account, defendants have the right to be convicted on the basis of nothing less than knowledge. It is defensible to value protecting this right, over and above maximizing the rate at which factually guilty defendants are convicted. This sort of trade-off between rights and accuracy is perfectly familiar. As we uphold the right against self-incrimination, for instance, and various other evidentiary privileges, we value the protection of these rights at the price of just the same sort of accuracy.

---

[20] See PUNDIK 2011 and ENOCH AND FISHER 2015 for related arguments.

10.3   Applying knowledge standards of proof

At the start of the previous section, I outlined several similarities between knowledge and whatever is required by legal proof. In addition to these similarities, it is often noted that certain paradoxes about legal proof resemble familiar paradoxes about knowledge, namely paradoxes concerning knowledge of lottery propositions. For instance, you cannot know that your ticket will lose the lottery. But at the same time, it seems natural to say that you can know that you will not be able to afford to go on an expensive holiday vacation this year.[21] As many have noted, a similar difficulty arises given our intuitions about what evidence suffices for legal proof. A defendant cannot be proved liable on the basis of the statistical evidence in *Gatecrasher*. But at the same time, it seems natural to say that a defendant can be proved liable on the basis of testimony, even though testimonial evidence is often far from perfectly reliable. In an influential study of jurors in mock trial settings, WELLS 1992 confirms that subjects are less likely to make judgments of liability on the basis of statistical evidence as opposed to other sources of evidence, even when they believe these sources of evidence to be equally reliable.

It is difficult to reflectively endorse our ordinary intuitions about what you know in lottery cases, especially when the content you seem to know is just as probable as the content you don't know. In the same way, it is difficult to reflectively endorse our ordinary intuitions about what evidence suffices for legal proof. Faced with this difficulty, many legal scholars have concluded that there is no principled distinction between testimony and statistical evidence. As ALLEN 1991 puts it, "the assumption that there are two qualitatively distinct types of evidence, statistical and non-statistical, is essentially false" (1093).[22] This sentiment is sometimes echoed in court opinions. For instance, Judge Posner claims that "All evidence is probabilistic, and therefore uncertain; eyewitness testimony and other forms of 'direct' evidence have no categorical epistemological claim to precedence over circumstantial or even explicitly statistical evidence."[23] These claims about statistical evidence resemble a familiar claim about lottery knowledge—namely, that there is no principled distinction between lottery knowledge and a lot of ordinary knowledge. As MCGRATH 2004 puts it, "we enter a lottery when we leave our parked cars (winners have their cars stolen), and even just by being alive (winners die of a heart attack next year, or tomorrow)."

---

[21] See §8.4 for further background discussion of lottery paradoxes.
[22] For similar arguments, see TRIBE 1971, KOEHLER AND SHAVIRO 1990, and SCHAUER 2003.
[23] *Milan v. State Farm Mutual Automobile Insurance Co.*, 972 F.2d 166, 170 (1992).

Are these skeptical conclusions correct? Should we ultimately reject intuitive distinctions between statistical evidence and other evidence, and between lottery knowledge and other knowledge? This is one of many questions that my account of legal proof does not answer. As explained in §8.4, giving an error theory of ascriptions of lottery knowledge requires accepting some counterintuitive consequences. But for all I have argued in this chapter, philosophical reflection might ultimately lead us to accept that you cannot ever really know that you will not be able to afford an expensive vacation next year, without also knowing that you will lose the lottery. Similarly, we might accept that you cannot ever really know on the basis of testimony that a defendant is almost certainly guilty, without being able to know the same probabilistic content on the basis of equally reliable statistical evidence. Accordingly, we might embrace the revisionary conclusion that our legal standards of proof cannot be met by testimonial evidence whenever they cannot be met by equally reliable statistical evidence. As far as my account of legal proof is concerned, I am not defending any solution to paradoxes concerning lottery knowledge and statistical evidence. Rather, my aim is to explain the parallels between these paradoxes. In the context of the courtroom, it is difficult for your statistical beliefs to constitute knowledge when you cannot rule out the possibility that the defendant is unlike an arbitrary member of the reference class grounding your statistical inference. And without ruling out this possibility, you do not have the knowledge that legal proof requires.[24] The modest upshot of my account is that whatever conclusions we reach after philosophical reflection, claims about lottery knowledge and claims about statistical evidence should stand or fall together.

So far I have discussed parallels between our general reluctance to ascribe lottery knowledge and our general reluctance to convict on merely statistical evidence. In addition, there are parallels between our selective willingness to ascribe lottery knowledge and our selective willingness to convict on merely statistical evidence. As far as our ordinary intuitions are concerned, some beliefs about lotteries have better epistemic standing than others. As discussed in §8.4, it seems natural to say that you know that you will not win the New York State Lottery every year for the next thirty years. Given my account of legal proof, one should expect to find cases where we are willing to ascribe statistical knowledge of guilt beyond a reasonable doubt, and hence willing to say that defendants may be convicted accordingly. And there are indeed such cases. Since the development of DNA typing and its rapid acceptance as a valid forensic technology, there

---

[24] For further discussion of the reference class problem for knowledge by statistical inference, see §8.4.

have been a number of "cold hit" cases in which defendants are convicted almost entirely on the basis of the fact that their DNA profile matches that of a sample found at the crime scene.[25]

Again, it may be difficult to reflectively endorse our ordinary intuitions about what sort of evidence can provide knowledge or license legal verdicts. The odds of winning the New York State Lottery every year for thirty years might be greater than the odds of winning one very large lottery, in which case it is hard to see how your knowledge could rule out the former possibility but not the latter. The odds of a wrongful conviction based on DNA evidence might be greater than the odds of a wrongful conviction based on the sort of statistical evidence presented in *Prison Yard*, so it is hard to see how a verdict could be licensed by the former evidence but not the latter. I am not evaluating whether we should ultimately reject our ordinary intuitions in either case, but explaining the parallels between these intuitions. According to my account, defendants are proved guilty beyond a reasonable doubt just in case the factfinder knows that it is beyond a reasonable doubt that they are guilty. As far as our ordinary intuitions are concerned, DNA evidence is sufficient for both, while other apparently similar evidence is insufficient for either. The modest upshot of my account is that whatever conclusions we reach after philosophical reflection, claims about New York State Lottery knowledge and claims about DNA evidence should stand or fall together.

Here is another respect in which our ordinary intuitions about statistical evidence are somewhat nuanced: statistical evidence comes in different flavors, and it is not clear that all flavors of statistical evidence have equal epistemic standing. The evidence in *Gatecrasher* is a claim about a reference class that contains the defendant as a member. But statistical evidence is not limited to claims of this sort; for instance, it also includes claims about reference classes that contain *inanimate objects* as members. A well-known example is the following *Blue Bus* case:

> *Blue Bus*: A car is negligently run off the road by a blue bus. The driver of the car cannot identify the exact bus that caused the accident, but she can prove that the Blue Bus Company operates 80 percent of the blue buses in town, while another company operates only the remaining 20 percent.[26]

---

[25] See ROTH 2010 for further discussion of these cases and their implications for theories of statistical evidence.

[26] The original inspiration for this case is *Smith v. Rapid Transit* 58 N.E.2d 754 (1945). For an early discussion of the implications of the case for theories of statistical evidence, see TRIBE 1971.

As compared with cases like *Gatecrasher*, cases like *Blue Bus* often inspire more controversy, both in our intuitions and in actual court opinions. For instance, in *Kaminsky v. Hertz Corp.*, the plaintiff was in an accident caused by a passing yellow truck with a Hertz logo.[27] As a matter of fact, Hertz Corporation owns only 90% of trucks fitting this description. The remaining 10% are either owned by licensees or franchisees, or were sold without removal of the Hertz logo and colors. The statistical inference at work in this case is not that Hertz is probably liable for the accident because it belongs to some reference class of companies, most of which are liable for the accident. Rather, the inference is that the yellow truck in question was probably owned by Hertz, because it belongs to a reference class of trucks, most of which are owned by Hertz. The trial court for this case ruled that the merely statistical evidence against Hertz was insufficient to bring the case to a jury. But the Michigan Court of Appeals later overturned this ruling, saying that the question of whether Hertz Corporation was liable should proceed to trial.[28]

As I see it, conflicting verdicts about cases like *Blue Bus* reflect conflicting intuitions about whether the statistical evidence in these cases can in fact ground probabilistic knowledge. According to the Michigan Court of Appeals, but not according to the original trial court, the statistical evidence presented by the plaintiff in *Kaminsky v. Hertz Corp.* could in principle provide the factfinder with knowledge that the truck involved in the accident was probably owned by Hertz. By contrast, the statistical evidence in *Gatecrasher* more clearly fails to provide the factfinder with knowledge that the defendant is probably liable. In short, courts are sometimes willing to act as if statistical inferences about *objects* can ground knowledge, whereas they are more reluctant to act on similar inferences about *people*. In §10.5, I defend an explanation of this contrast. Statistical inferences about people often face special epistemic challenges. As a result, my account of statistical evidence has an unusual strength: it can explain why verdicts against the defendants in *Prison Yard* and *Gatecrasher* seem especially intolerable in comparison with other verdicts that might or might not be licensed by statistical evidence.

A final question left open by my account of legal proof concerns the communication of standards of proof to jurors. For example, although some studies suggest that jurors identify the reasonable doubt standard with a relatively high probability threshold, other studies suggest that jurors identify it with a threshold

---

[27] *Kaminsky v. Hertz Corp.* 288 N.W.2d 426 (1979).

[28] In a similar spirit, the doctrine of market-share liability allows a plaintiff to bring a suit against multiple product manufacturers for an injury caused by a product, and allows the court to assign liability to manufacturers in proportion with their share of the market for that product. For instance, see *Sindell v. Abbott Laboratories* 26 Cal. 3d 588 (1980).

that is dramatically lower than any that would be considered viable by legal experts. As reported in MAGNUSSEN ET AL. 2014, studies of more than 1200 participants over a time span of ten years revealed that "a majority of jury-eligible young and elderly participants, and police officers, were willing to convict a defendant when the judged probability of guilt exceeded .6" (196). These studies raise a serious concern about jury instruction. By refusing to clarify the reasonable doubt standard for jurors, courts may be allowing them to interpret it in a way that is determinately wrong. The account of legal proof that I have defended does not itself provide any solution to this urgent practical problem. In short, epistemology papers cannot be translated into jury instructions, not least because the crafting of jury instructions should be informed by empirical results far out of reach of the epistemologist's armchair. However, the process of instructing juries on standards of proof should reflect our best efforts to get clear about exactly when these standards are met. If my account of legal proof is correct, it is in these efforts that contemporary epistemology has an important role to play. This conclusion is good news for epistemology. At first glance, the lottery paradox might appear to be an idle question, with nothing much turning on whether we reflectively sanction ordinary knowledge ascriptions as being strictly speaking true or false. But as it turns out, theories of lottery knowledge matter for theories about what sort of statistical evidence can license verdicts of guilt and liability. It is good for epistemology that our investigations of knowledge are tethered by the substantive role that knowledge plays in legal contexts. And of course, it is deeply motivating to see that these academic investigations may have significant practical import.

10.4 Racial and other profiling

Suppose you know that most canaries are yellow. Intuitively, when you hear a canary in the forest, there is nothing wrong with believing on the basis of your statistical evidence that it is probably yellow, and there is nothing wrong with acting as if it is probably yellow. By contrast, suppose you know that most women who work in a certain office building are administrative assistants. Intuitively, when you see a woman working in that office building, is there something wrong with believing that she is probably an administrative assistant? Is there something wrong with acting on the belief that she is probably an administrative assistant? In what follows, I will argue that there is indeed something wrong with forming and acting on this probabilistic belief. More generally, I argue that there is something wrong with *profiling*: forming or acting on beliefs based on certain statistical evidence about a person, including statistical evidence about their race, gender, class, sexual orientation, or disability status. Racial profiling is the most widely discussed form of profiling, but my arguments in this chapter extend to profiling on the basis of membership in many other groups.

A word of caution: in mainstream discussions of racial profiling, and even in academic contexts, authors sometimes talk about "the problem with racial profiling," as if there is just one distinctive problem with racial profiling that we must diagnose and solve. This presupposition is unfounded and unhelpful. Acts of profiling are wrong for a whole host of reasons, including demeaning and stigmatizing people, promoting harmful ideologies, and causally contributing to violence and oppression. In addition to these moral concerns, acts of profiling raise multiple epistemic concerns. Someone who forms a belief by profiling often has no good reason for relying on statistics about one particular reference class as opposed to another, and this problem is compounded by the fact that subjects using profiling can suffer from implicit biases which cause them to adopt irrational priors or ignore relevant evidence. Insofar as profiling involves these sorts of failures, it violates familiar and general epistemic norms.

The rest of this chapter discusses a problem with profiling that is partly epistemic in nature, but more focused in its scope than the epistemic problems mentioned above. The reference class problem not only challenges your statistical inferences about people, but your statistical inferences about canaries as well. The same goes for epistemic injunctions against adopting irrational priors and ignoring relevant evidence. Just as your beliefs about people should be the rational product of your total evidence, the same goes for your beliefs about canaries. The goal of my discussion is to identify an epistemic failing exhibited by a broad range of acts of profiling directed at people, but not by similar acts directed at canaries. The act of profiling a person violates a norm that involves both moral and epistemic considerations. In short, I argue that if you act on certain moral reasons that you have, your beliefs about people based on profiling will be epistemically deficient in virtue of failing to be knowledge. This particular argument against profiling relies on the following moral norm, which I call the *rule of consideration*: in many situations where you are forming beliefs about a person, you morally should keep in mind the possibility that they might be an exception to statistical generalizations. To give an intuitive example, as you form beliefs about a woman in an office building, you should keep in mind the possibility that she is unlike the average woman in the building with respect to whether she is probably an administrative assistant. That is, you should keep in mind the possibility that she probably has some other position.

The moral rule of consideration is not an epistemic norm. But it does have epistemic consequences. In particular, you may fail to know some probabilistic contents in virtue of keeping other probabilistic contents in mind. The intended reading of the rule of consideration requires a certain sort of consideration of contents, where this consideration precludes knowledge of the contents they are inconsistent with. For example, suppose you meet Jones in the office building, and you are keeping in mind the possibility that she is unlike the average woman in the building with respect to whether she is probably an administrative assistant. Then you are giving this possibility the sort of consideration that precludes your knowing that Jones is probably an administrative assistant on the basis of statistical inference. This sort of failure to have knowledge is not anything unusual. In just the same sense, you may fail to know that you are looking at a zebra in virtue of keeping in mind the possibility that you are looking at a cleverly disguised mule. As you pay attention to possibilities that you cannot rule out, you fail to know contents that are inconsistent with those same possibilities.

According to the knowledge norm of belief defended in chapter 8, you should believe some content only if you know it. In this sense, you should refrain from believing that Jones is probably an administrative assistant, assuming you have no further decent evidence on the matter. The knowledge norm of belief and the moral rule of consideration together entail a constraint on your beliefs, namely that it morally should be the case that it epistemically should not be the case that you believe that Jones is probably an administrative assistant. The simultaneous satisfaction of these moral and epistemic norms requires that you suspend judgment about Jones.

To illustrate with an analogy, imagine that you are visiting a zoo with a philosopher friend of yours. The friend has been asking you to take certain skeptical hypotheses more seriously. You promise your friend that for the next fifteen minutes, you will pay careful attention to the possibility that the animals in the zebra cage are cleverly disguised mules. In order to keep your promise, you morally should consider this skeptical possibility. As you consider it, you may fail to know that the caged animals are indeed zebras. According to the knowledge norm of belief, it follows that you should suspend judgment about whether they are zebras. Hence it morally should be the case that it epistemically should not be the case that you believe that the animals in the zebra cage are zebras. In the same way, the moral rule of consideration gives you reason to consider certain possibilities, and thereby affects what it is epistemically permissible for you to believe.

Although the knowledge norm of belief and the moral rule of consideration together require you to suspend judgment about whether Jones is probably an administrative assistant, they do not require you to suspend judgment about whether a particular canary is probably yellow. Canaries are not people, and they generally do not demand the sort of consideration that the moral rule requires. The rule of consideration spells out one modest interpretation of the thought that we should *treat people as individuals*. This thought is both compelling and familiar, though it is not always precisely defined by theorists who endorse it. As LIPPERT-RASMUSSEN 2011 observes, "However popular the idea that we have a right to be treated as individuals is, it is also clear that it is hard to specify in any convincing way what exactly treating someone as an individual amounts to" (49).[29] As I see it, there are actually several moral norms corresponding to the rough idea that people should be treated as individuals, and the rule of consideration is among the least demanding of these norms. Although it is modest, the rule nevertheless grounds a valuable distinction between different statistical inferences. Since the rule says only that we should treat *people* as individuals, it allows that we can form and act on statistical beliefs about canaries.

This difference between beliefs about people and beliefs about canaries highlights a surprising consequence of my discussion, namely that knowledge may be subject to *moral encroachment*.[30] The moral features of a belief may make a difference to whether it constitutes knowledge. If there is an object that acquires or loses the moral status of a person over time, for instance, such changes may affect whether morally responsible agents can have knowledge about it on the basis of certain statistical inferences. And more importantly, whether you should form a belief by statistical inference may depend partly on what is at stake if your belief turns out to be false. By comparison, it is a common observation that we are reluctant to say that you know that the bank will be open on Saturday in situations where there would be a financial cost to your getting it wrong. As the financial cost of an error increases, so does our reluctance to say that your belief constitutes knowledge. This same sort of observation can help clarify the scope of the moral rule of consideration: in just the same way, we should be reluctant to say that a belief based on profiling is knowledge in situations where there would be some significant cost to your getting it wrong.

The argument against profiling developed in this section leaves open many questions, including exactly how to define the potentially significant cost of forming a false belief by statistical inference. But without giving an extensive analysis of this notion, we can make some commonsense observations about it. For instance, suppose you believe that someone probably has brown eyes, on the grounds that most people have brown eyes. There may not be much at stake in whether your belief turns out to be false, and so morally speaking, your belief

---

[29] For sympathetic discussion of the idea that acts of profiling fail to treat people as individuals, see SINGER 1978, ADLER 1993, MILLER 1999, and EIDELSON 2013.

[30] For a review of relevant literature and further discussion of moral encroachment, see Moss 2018.

may be no different from your statistical beliefs about canaries. By contrast, if you were to mistakenly believe that someone is heterosexual, on the grounds that most people are heterosexual, you would thereby be falsely stereotyping someone in a historically disadvantaged group. This fact may make a difference to what is morally required of you as you form beliefs about the sexual orientations of other people. Again, it may be useful to compare your situation with the situation of subjects in bank cases. If someone would lose large amounts of money if their bank is closed on Saturday, then they pragmatically should consider the possibility that their bank may have recently changed its hours. For purposes of my argument against profiling, it is important that sometimes you morally should consider certain possibilities, such as the possibility that someone you are profiling has a minority sexual orientation. As you consider this possibility, your belief that they are probably heterosexual may fail to be knowledge. The same goes for many beliefs formed by profiling on the basis of race, gender, class, sexual orientation, or disability status. Whatever the relevant notion of stakes, an important feature of the moral rule of consideration is that it generally requires consideration of possibilities about people, namely that individual people differ in relevant respects from arbitrary members of reference classes to which they belong. The moral status of a person can thereby make a difference to the epistemic status of our statistical beliefs about them, whereas this sort of difference rarely extends to our statistical beliefs about canaries.

Another important open question concerns the relationship between the rule of consideration and other moral norms. For instance, in some situations, probabilistic beliefs formed by profiling could make a difference to the best choice of medical treatment for a victim. In such situations, is it morally permissible for an emergency room doctor to act on the basis of beliefs that are impermissible by the lights of the rule of consideration? For example, is it permissible for the doctor to believe that you are more likely than average to have a certain medical condition, merely on the basis of statistics about your gender? Is it permissible for her to act as if you are more likely than average to have had an alcoholic beverage in the past eight hours, merely on the basis of statistics about your racial group? Another difficult set of questions concerns the permissibility of acts of profiling in the context of affirmative action policies. Can a person consent to being profiled, and thereby defeat moral reasons generated by the rule of consideration? I leave these questions open for future research. For instance, it may turn out that the moral rule of consideration simply generates *pro tanto* moral reasons against profiling, reasons that could be defeated in cases of emergency, as a result of consent, or in the service of more important moral aims. Without defining the exact scope and strength of the rule of consideration, it is still possible to appreciate the consequences of this rule for many ordinary acts of profiling. With these consequences in mind, we can conclude that it is epistemically impermissible to form and act on beliefs in situations where moral considerations compel us to remain agnostic about their contents.

10.5 Applying the rule of consideration

In the previous section, I discussed questions about the relationship between the rule of consideration and other moral norms. A final open question concerns the relationship between knowledge norms of action and other practical norms, such as the norm to maximize expected utility. For sake of argument, suppose that in some situations, maximizing expected utility requires acting on beliefs formed by profiling. For example, suppose that in emergency situations, acting on the basis of mere justified beliefs often saves lives. If that is right, then it is important to recall from §9.2 that our actions are governed by a plurality of practical norms. Different norms govern our evaluation of actions in different contexts, and sometimes our evaluations reflect our application of standard decision theoretic norms. Against the background of this pluralist view, it is natural to wonder when knowledge norms are relevant, and it is helpful to observe that there are at least some special categories of actions for which it seems especially appropriate to supplement standard decision theory with more demanding knowledge norms.

For example, consider acts of assertion. There is something wrong with simply asserting that your ticket lost the lottery when you do not know that it lost, even if you are justified in believing that it lost. In just this same sense, there is something wrong with asserting that a particular woman is probably an administrative assistant when you do not know that she is probably an administrative assistant, even if your statistical evidence justifies your belief that she is probably is an administrative assistant. According to the knowledge norm of assertion, these two assertions exhibit the same sort of failing—namely, a lack of epistemic humility. In Moss 2012a, I argue that it is epistemically irresponsible to assert a content that is incompatible with salient possibilities that you cannot rule out. If you satisfy the moral rule of consideration with respect to the woman in the office building, your assertion that she is probably an administrative assistant will be epistemically irresponsible, as it will be incompatible with the salient possibility that she is not just as likely to be an administrative assistant as an arbitrary woman in the building.

In addition to acts of assertion, there is an intuitive sense in which actions related to the blame and punishment of others should be based on nothing less than knowledge. To return to an example from BUCHAK 2013a discussed in §9.3, suppose that your cell phone was stolen, and you know that either Jake or Barbara is the thief. You also know that men are ten times more likely to steal iPhones than women. There is something wrong with your acting as if Jake probably stole your phone merely on the basis of general facts about members of his gender, given that you cannot rule out that he is an exception to the statistical generalization grounding your probabilistic belief. This fact might be explained by a knowledge norm governing actions related to the blame and punishment of others. To sum up so far, there are certain sorts of everyday actions for which knowledge norms seem especially appropriate. As mentioned in §9.3, I leave it as an open question whether knowledge norms of action target only actions in these categories, or whether there is some sense in which every action should be based on knowledge.

In addition to everyday actions of blame and punishment, I have argued that formal verdicts of blame and punishment must be based on nothing less than knowledge. As a result, the moral rule of consideration has indirect implications for the solution to the problem of statistical evidence defended in the first half of this chapter. For example, it is natural to say that the jury cannot return a verdict of liability in *Gatecrasher* because the jury does not know that the defendant is probably liable. As we reflect on this case, we judge that the jury does not have this knowledge because we are paying attention to a certain possibility that the jury cannot rule out, namely that the *Gatecrasher* defendant is an exception to the relevant generalization about people at the rodeo. As theorists, we are paying attention to the possibility that the defendant is less likely to have climbed over the fence than an arbitrary person at the rodeo. It is predictable that we would pay attention to this possibility, given a certain reasonable assumption about legal contexts—namely, that the jurors themselves are in fact legally required to pay attention to just this same possibility. That is, it is reasonable to assume that treating people as individuals is not merely recommended by the moral rule of consideration, but required by legal rules governing factfinders in the context of a courtroom. Justice Coyne of the Minnesota Supreme Court makes this point in a criminal context, saying that "it seems to me wrong to confine any person on the basis not of that person's own prior conduct but on the basis of statistical evidence regarding the behavior of other people."[31] This opinion is shared by a number of scholars who have argued that verdicts based on statistical evidence are unacceptable because they fail to treat people as individuals.[32]

It is important to distinguish the legal requirement to treat people as individuals from hypothetical legal requirements that would, if adopted, threaten

---

[31] *In re Linehan* 518 N.W.2d 609, 616 (1994), Coyne J. dissenting.
[32] For instance, see TRIBE 1971, ZUCKERMAN 1986, COHEN 1987, and WASSERMAN 1991.

to undermine any verdict against a defendant. For instance, the factfinder in a criminal case is not required to consider absolutely any possibility according to which a defendant is definitely innocent. The legal requirement to treat people as individuals does prohibit certain inferences, such as the inference from the claim that most defendants of a certain sort are guilty to the claim that some particular defendant is probably guilty. In this respect, the requirement resembles the legal requirement of the presumption of innocence. But the requirement to treat people as individuals applies in a much broader range of contexts than the presumption of innocence, including in the context of civil trials, and even in legal contexts where a defendant has already been found guilty of a crime. For instance, consider the following description of an actual court case:

> *United States v. Shonubi*: In October 1992, Charles Shonubi was convicted of drug smuggling, after being found to have swallowed balloons containing 427.4 grams of heroin on the date of his arrest. There was substantial evidence that Shonubi had made seven previous drug smuggling trips, but there was no evidence as to how much heroin he carried on these trips. Based on information about 124 other Nigerian balloon swallowers, the prosecution concluded that Shonubi was at least .99 likely to have smuggled over 2000 grams of heroin on his previous trips combined.[33]

Although Shonubi was originally sentenced according to the statistical evidence presented by the prosecution, the Second Circuit Court of Appeals later ruled that in the absence of case-specific evidence, Shonubi could be sentenced only according to the amount of heroin in his possession on the date of his arrest. A plausible explanation for this verdict is that the standards of proof at sentencing require probabilistic knowledge. Although the statistical evidence in *United States v. Shonubi* may justify the belief that Shonubi almost certainly smuggled over 2000 grams of heroin into the United States, it is not enough to yield knowledge of this probabilistic content. Whether at trial or at sentencing, the law requires that defendants and convicted persons be treated as individuals. This requirement is satisfied by the appropriate consideration of certain contents, namely alternatives to the conclusions of statistical inferences. As a result, there exists a modest form of legal encroachment on knowledge of probabilistic contents. According to my knowledge account of legal proof, the epistemic phenomenon of legal encroachment has significant legal consequences. As a factfinder considers various epistemic alternatives, they will be legally forbidden from returning a verdict of guilt or liability on the basis of statistical evidence, namely because they will not have the probabilistic knowledge required by the relevant standard of proof.

---

[33] *United States v. Shonubi* 895 F. Supp. 460 (1995).

Having explored potential legal implications of the rule of consideration, I want to end by discussing some practical implications of the rule as it figures in my argument against racial profiling. In informal discussions of racial profiling, it is sometimes suggested that instances of profiling present a dilemma between moral and epistemic concerns. The suggestion is that racial profiling catches us in a situation where we morally should refrain from making epistemically good inferences. As KELLY AND ROEDDER 2008 put it:

> Our point is that it can sometimes be unkind or uncompassionate to believe ill of a person, even if it is rational to do so. Thus it can sometimes be immoral to hold a belief that is, in fact, rational. (530)

GENDLER 2011 elaborates on this idea, arguing that to be perfectly rational, you must sometimes act on the basis of statistical beliefs about racial groups:

> In short, as long as there's a differential crime rate between racial groups, a perfectly rational decision maker will manifest different behaviors, explicit and implicit, towards members of different races. This is a profound cost: living in a society structured by race appears to make it impossible to be both rational and equitable. (57)

These remarks encourage a certain line of thought, namely that even if profiling is morally impermissible, doing without it requires subjects to violate epistemic norms by ignoring perfectly good evidence. According to this line of thought, the epistemically virtuous subject believes that the woman in the office building is probably an administrative assistant, and treats this belief as a potential reason for action. The morally virtuous subject remains agnostic. But her moral virtue comes only at the price of her rationality.

Some members of profiled groups, myself included, find this line of thought unsatisfying. There may be many moral reasons to reject profiling. But it is important that there is at least some sense in which the rejection of profiling does not require epistemic compromise. An attractive feature of my epistemic argument against profiling is that it does not posit any conflict between moral and epistemic norms. According to my argument, it is not the case that moral norms require you to refrain from profiling and thereby flaunt epistemic norms that require it. Indeed, my argument against profiling turns this thought on its head. If you satisfy the moral rule of consideration, then acts of profiling are in fact *forbidden* by certain epistemic norms.

A second attractive feature of my argument against profiling is that my argument identifies a problem that individuals have the power to change. Advocates of profiling sometimes object that it is impossible to do without it. Abandoning the practice of profiling is seen as requiring you to deliberately ignore evidence, to forget about certain statistics as you are forming beliefs. This requirement may seem unreasonably demanding. By contrast, the rule of consideration does not demand that subjects deliberately ignore anything at all. The rule of consideration does not *prohibit* paying attention to possibilities. The rule *requires* paying attention to possibilities. As compared with the act of ignoring possibilities, the act of paying attention to possibilities is not unreasonably demanding. The attitude of attention that the rule of consideration requires can be cultivated with time and effort. This attitude can be taught and learned and practiced. In short, this particular problem of profiling is a problem that we can solve.

In conclusion, it has long been assumed by epistemologists that only certain sorts of beliefs get to be knowledge—namely, propositional beliefs that have a fundamentally different character from our thoroughly probabilistic beliefs. Throughout this book, I have argued that this assumption is false, and that epistemology is better off without it. Probabilistic knowledge is supported by our best theories of the contents that we can believe, assert, and know. In this chapter, I have argued that our reasons to accept probabilistic knowledge extend far beyond these academic concerns. Probabilistic knowledge is also supported by compelling theories about what legal proof requires and about what norms are violated by acts of profiling. Accepting probabilistic knowledge helps us better understand the nature of our own mental states. But in addition, it helps us better understand the nature of our responsibilities to each other.

Appendix: A formal semantics for epistemic vocabulary

A.1 Background

A probabilistic semantics requires the introduction of a new semantic type $\mathcal{P}$. The denotations of type $\mathcal{P}$ expressions are sets of probability spaces. Formally, a probability space $S = \langle \Omega_S, \mathcal{F}_S, m_S \rangle$ is an ordered triple consisting of a set Ω_S of possible worlds, an algebra $\mathcal{F}_S$ over Ω_S, and a probability measure m_S on $\mathcal{F}_S$. A proposition p is *possible according to* S just in case $p \cap \Omega_S \neq \varnothing$, and *certain according to* S just in case $\Omega_S \subseteq p$.[1] The *probability of p according to S* is the value $m_S(p \cap \Omega_S)$. Finally, we define the result of updating S on p as follows: $S|_p = \langle \Omega_S \cap p, \{q \cap p : q \in \mathcal{F}_S\}, m_S|_p \rangle$, where $m_S|_p$ is the conditional probability assigned by m_S conditional on p, assumed to satisfy $m_S|_p(q) = m_S(q \cap p)/m_S(p)$ whenever $m_S(p) > 0$.

In this appendix, the lexical entry for each expression states the extension of that expression as uttered at a context. Following HEIM AND KRATZER 1998, we take the context c in which a sentence is uttered to determine an assignment function g_c that assigns a value to each index in that sentence. Each epistemic expression has an index i, and the value $g_c(i)$ is the partition that context provides for the interpretation of that expression as uttered in c.

A.2 Epistemic modals and probability operators

Epistemic modals have semantic type $\langle \mathcal{P}, \mathcal{P} \rangle$. An epistemic modal introduces quantification over propositions in a partition that context provides for its interpretation, namely the partition that results from applying the assignment function to the index of the modal:

---

[1] In the tradition of MONTAGUE 1969, I use 'proposition' in this appendix to refer to a set of possible worlds.

$$[\![\textbf{might}_i]\!]^c = [\lambda \mathcal{S} . \{S : \exists p \in g_c(i) \text{ such that } p \cap \Omega_S \neq \varnothing \text{ and } S|_p \in \mathcal{S}\}]$$

$$[\![\textbf{must}_i]\!]^c = [\lambda \mathcal{S} . \{S : \forall p \in g_c(i) \text{ such that } p \cap \Omega_S \neq \varnothing, S|_p \in \mathcal{S}\}]$$

Probability operators also have semantic type $\langle \mathcal{P}, \mathcal{P} \rangle$. Like epistemic modals, each probability operator is interpreted relative to a partition, namely the value of the assignment function on the index of that operator. For example, 'probably' may be defined as follows:

$$[\![\textbf{probably}_i]\!]^c = [\lambda \mathcal{S} . \{S : m_S(\bigcup \{p \in g_c(i) : S|_p \in \mathcal{S}\}) > .5\}]$$

In each of the lexical entries given above, the variable 'p' ranges over propositions, 'S' ranges over probability spaces, and '$\mathcal{S}$' ranges over sets of probability spaces. For simplicity, the lexical entry for 'probably' follows KRATZER 1991 in taking 'probably' to be synonymous with 'more likely than not'. This condition may easily be made more sophisticated. For instance, one might modify the condition in light of arguments by LASSITER 2011 that 'likely' is a relative adjective whose unmarked positive form compares the probability of a proposition with a contextually determined threshold. Also, the lexical entry for 'probably' may be modified to create lexical entries for other probability operators, as well as for epistemic comparatives.

As explained in §3.4, sentences containing nested epistemic expressions have just the same semantic type as sentences containing one epistemic expression. At first glance, it is tempting to say that sentences containing nested epistemic expressions should have a higher semantic type. For instance, the content of a sentence containing a string of two epistemic expressions could be a property of an *imprecise* credal state, represented by a set of *sets of* probability spaces. For example, the content of 'it might be probable that Jones smokes' could contain a set of probability spaces just in case some probability space in that set assigns high probability to Jones smoking.[2]

Although this proposal is tempting, it does not provide a compelling interpretation of arbitrary strings of epistemic expressions. The most natural extension of the proposal says that sentences containing three nested epistemic modals denote sets of sets of sets of probability spaces, for instance, and that sentences containing epistemic modals can have arbitrarily high semantic types. In addition, extending the proposal to epistemic expressions embedded under probability operators requires sentences to denote sets of probability spaces *defined over sets of probability spaces*. This extensive proliferation of semantic types is a significant theoretical cost. A key strength of my semantics is that it exploits the fact that

---

[2] Thanks to Malte Willer and Thony Gillies for encouraging me to consider this proposal.

updating a probability space on a proposition yields another probability space. My semantics thereby provides interpretations for arbitrary strings of epistemic expressions, while allowing all sentences containing epistemic vocabulary to have the same semantic type. In addition, some theorists may prefer my semantics on the grounds that the contents of belief and assertion are sets of probability spaces, if there is no independent reason for taking them to be the more complex sorts of objects assigned as semantic values by the alternative proposed semantics.

The above lexical entries for epistemic possibility and necessity modals deliver both concord and cumulative readings of nested modals. For instance, it is easy to verify that when context provides the same partition for the interpretation of nested possibility modals, they are equivalent with a single possibility modal. The same result holds for nested necessity modals. But nested modals interpreted relative to different partitions are generally not equivalent to just one modal.[3]

In addition to delivering cumulative readings of nested modals, my semantics can deliver natural readings of sentences containing just one epistemic modal or probability operator, as mentioned in §4.5. For illustration, consider the following sentence:

(1)   It is [.3 likely]$_i$ that Jones smokes.

The extension of (1) as uttered in c contains a probability space S just in case S assigns .3 probability to the union of $g_c(i)$ elements that accept the probabilistic content of 'Jones smokes' relative to S. As discussed in Appendix A.3, these $g_c(i)$ elements are just the propositions $p \in g_c(i)$ such that it is certain that Jones smokes according to $S|p$. If $g_c(i)$ is decisive with respect to the proposition that Jones smokes, then this union of $g_c(i)$ elements is simply that proposition itself. Hence the extension of (1) is the set of probability spaces according to which it is .3 likely that Jones smokes. Analogous results hold for many sentences containing just one modal or probability operator. For instance, in many contexts, 'Jones might smoke' simply denotes the set of probability spaces according to which it is possible that Jones smokes. Hence my semantics delivers the intuitive verdict that 'might' sentences often *cause us to see possibilities* in roughly the sense of §2.3.2 of SWANSON 2006.

---

[3] The semantics I defend does not have any special consequences for the interpretation of nested modal auxiliaries such as 'I don't think I have any grants you might could apply for' (cf. DI PAOLO 1989). It seems reasonable to expect that nested auxiliaries would have the same distribution of interpretations as other nested modal operators, but my arguments are independent of this empirical claim.

A.3 Simple sentences

At a first pass, my semantics associates simple sentences with their traditional propositional semantic values. However, the denotations of epistemic modals, probability operators, and indicative conditionals take sets of probability spaces rather than propositions as arguments. As a result, there will be a semantic type mismatch between a simple sentence and an epistemic expression embedding it. This mismatch is resolved by shifting the semantic type of the simple sentence from a proposition to a set of probability spaces, namely by the application of the following type-shifting operator:

$$[\![\mathcal{C}]\!]^c = [\lambda p \,.\, \{S : \Omega_S \subseteq p\}]$$

For instance, 'it is .3 likely that Jones smokes' has the following logical form:

(2)   It is [.3 likely]$_i$ that $\mathcal{C}$ [Jones smokes].

The semantic value of the constituent '$\mathcal{C}$ [Jones smokes]' in (2) is the set of probability spaces according to which it is certain that Jones smokes.

If a sentence contains no epistemic vocabulary at all, then assertion itself forces the semantic type of that sentence to be shifted from a proposition to a set of probability spaces. Each unembedded simple sentence contains a constituent whose semantic value is the traditional propositional content of that sentence, together with a covert $\mathcal{C}$ operator that shifts the semantic type of that constituent. For instance, the sentence 'Jones smokes' has the following logical form:

(3) $\mathcal{C}$ [Jones smokes]

The semantic value of (3) is a nominally probabilistic content, namely the set of probability spaces according to which it is certain that Jones smokes. As discussed in §3.6, this nominally probabilistic content is the strict content that you use 'Jones smokes' to assert.

A.4 Indicative conditionals

Indicative conditionals have semantic type $\langle \mathcal{P}, \langle \mathcal{P}, \mathcal{P} \rangle \rangle$. An indicative conditional introduces a strict conditional over propositions in a partition that context provides for its interpretation, namely the partition that results from applying the assignment function to the index of the conditional operator:

$$[\![\mathbf{if}_i]\!]^c = [\lambda \mathcal{A} \,.\, \lambda \mathcal{C} \,.\, \{S : \forall p \in g_c(i) \text{ such that } p \cap \Omega_S \neq \varnothing \text{ and } S|_p \in \mathcal{A}, S|_p \in \mathcal{C}\}]$$

I argue in chapter 4 that my semantics accounts for several facts about what we use conditionals to assert. In addition, my semantics accounts for facts about what conditionals presuppose. It is a common observation that an indicative conditional carries the presupposition that its antecedent is possible. This simple observation admits of many precise interpretations. According to my semantics, an indicative conditional presupposes a thoroughly probabilistic content, namely that its antecedent might be the case.[4]

To give an example, imagine that you go see a doctor for help with a bad headache. The doctor examines you and says:

(4) If you have brain cancer, we will be discussing several treatment options.

If you had no idea that your headache might be a symptom of brain cancer, you might naturally respond by saying, 'Hey, wait a minute—I might have brain cancer?!' As communicated in (4), the content that you might have brain cancer exhibits the projection behavior typical of presuppositional content.[5] The same response would sound natural even if your doctor had not asserted (4) outright, but merely used this conditional in any of the following sentences:

(5) If you have brain cancer, will we be discussing several treatment options?

(6) Unfortunately, it's not the case that if you have brain cancer, we will be discussing several treatment options.

(7) If we will be discussing several treatment options if you have brain cancer, I should check my schedule to see whether we could meet again this afternoon.

In addition, as noted by DUDMAN 1994 and others, an indicative conditional often sounds bad when the negation of its antecedent is common ground:

(8) You don't have brain cancer. #If you have brain cancer, we will be discussing several treatment options.

The conditional in (8) improves only with the addition of focal stress, presumably indicating the retraction of presupposed content:

---

[4] This conclusion resembles a pragmatic constraint proposed by STALNAKER 1975, namely that it is appropriate to utter an indicative conditional only in a context compatible with its antecedent. As PERCUS 2006 would put it, an indicative conditional *antipresupposes* its antecedent. For further proposals in a similar spirit, see also WILLIAMS 2008 and LEAHY 2011.

[5] For discussion of the 'Hey, wait a minute!' test for presuppositional content, see VON FINTEL 2004. For an introductory discussion of presupposition projection, see KARTTUNEN 1973.

(9) You don't have brain cancer. But if you *do* have brain cancer, we will be discussing several treatment options.

These judgments are to be expected on the hypothesis that the conditional in (8) presupposes the probabilistic content that its antecedent might be the case, since this presupposition is inconsistent with the negation of its antecedent (cf. §3.6).

The presuppositions of conditionals are explained by my semantics. It is a familiar result that strong quantifiers presuppose that their domain is non-empty (cf. STRAWSON 1952, DE JONG AND VERKUYL 1985, GEURTS 2007). The content of a conditional is the set of probability spaces relative to which every possible partition element that accepts the antecedent of the conditional also accepts its consequent. Hence my semantics predicts that an indicative conditional carries the presupposition that some possible partition element accepts its antecedent. For instance, my semantics predicts that (4) presupposes that some possible partition element accepts that you have brain cancer:

(4) If you have brain cancer, we will be discussing several treatment options.

This presupposition is a thoroughly probabilistic content, namely the content of 'you might have brain cancer' interpreted relative to the same partition as 'if' in the context of (4) itself. In just this sense, a conditional presupposes that its antecedent might be the case. Facts about the presuppositions of indicative conditionals help to distinguish their behavior from the behavior of material conditionals, accounting for apparent failures of Antecedent Strengthening and other similar inference rules.

In addition to explaining the presuppositions of conditionals, my semantics for 'if' accounts for the valid reading of the probabilistic Sly Pete inference described in §4.3. This reading of the inference can be represented as follows:

(10) a. It is at least .9 likely$_1$ that if$_2$ Pete called, he won.
b. It is at least .9 likely$_1$ that if$_2$ Pete called, he lost.
c. Therefore, it is at least .8 likely$_1$ that Pete did not call.

As discussed in §4.5, it is reasonable to assume that the partition $g_c(2)$ is decisive with respect to the proposition that Pete called. Given this background assumption, the inference (10) is indeed valid. Suppose that your credences are contained in the content of each premise. Then you give at least .9 credence to $g_c(1)$ elements that accept the content of 'if Pete called, he won' relative to your credences, and at least .9 credence to $g_c(1)$ elements that accept the content of 'if Pete called, he lost' relative to your credences. From the probability axioms, it follows that you give at least .8 credence to $g_c(1)$ elements that accept both of these contents.

Any proposition accepting both contents has a peculiar property: if you update on that proposition and then on any element of the $g_c(2)$ partition that accepts that Pete called, the resulting credences must be contained in the content of 'Pete won' and also in the content of 'Pete lost'. But the intersection of these simple sentence contents is empty. Hence relative to your credences conditional on $g_c(1)$ elements that accept both embedded indicative conditionals, no element of $g_c(2)$ accepts that Pete called. From the fact that $g_c(2)$ is decisive with respect to whether Pete called, it follows that relative to these same conditional credences, each element of $g_c(2)$ accepts that Pete did not call. Hence any $g_c(1)$ element that accepts the contents of both embedded conditionals also accepts the content of 'Pete did not call'. The fact that you give at least .8 credence to such $g_c(1)$ elements entails that your unconditional credences are in the content of the conclusion of the probabilistic Sly Pete inference.

A.5 Other logical operators

According to my semantics, logical operators are polymorphic, taking arguments of multiple semantic types. As operators on sentential constituents denoting propositions, 'or', 'and', and 'not' have their traditional intensional semantic values. But as operators on sentences denoting probabilistic contents, these expressions have semantic type $\langle \mathcal{P}, \mathcal{P} \rangle$ or $\langle \mathcal{P}, \langle \mathcal{P}, \mathcal{P} \rangle \rangle$. Just like epistemic operators, each logical operator is interpreted relative to a partition, namely the value of the assignment function on the index of that operator:

$$[\![\mathbf{or}_i]\!]^c = [\lambda \mathcal{S} . \lambda \mathcal{T} . \{S : \forall p \in g_c(i), S|_p \in \mathcal{S} \text{ or } S|_p \in \mathcal{T}\}]$$

$$[\![\mathbf{and}_i]\!]^c = [\lambda \mathcal{S} . \lambda \mathcal{T} . \{S : \forall p \in g_c(i), S|_p \in \mathcal{S} \text{ and } S|_p \in \mathcal{T}\}]$$

$$[\![\mathbf{not}_i]\!]^c = [\lambda \mathcal{S} . \{S : \forall p \in g_c(i), S|_p \notin \mathcal{S}\}]$$

These semantic entries account for nuanced interpretations of logical operators embedding epistemic vocabulary. For example, in the context of a conversation about the outcome of rolling a fair die, speakers may naturally interpret 'or' in the sentence 'the number is low or probably even' relative to a partition containing two propositions—namely, that the number is low, and that it is high. If the first proposition accepts the content of the first disjunct relative to your credences, and the second proposition accepts the content of the second disjunct, the content of the disjunction will contain your credences, even if your credences are not themselves contained in the content of either disjunct.

As with many covert operators, one might naturally worry that the introduction of the $\mathcal{C}$ operator decreases the predictive strength of my semantics. Without any restrictions on the distribution of the $\mathcal{C}$ operator, my semantics would indeed generate unwanted readings of sentences. For example, my semantics would generate two readings of the simple sentence (11), namely (12) and (13):

(11) Jones does not smoke.

(12) not$_1$ [$\mathcal{C}$ Jones smokes]

(13) $\mathcal{C}$ [not Jones smokes]

This would be an unwelcome result. Intuitively, (12) is generally too weak to be an available interpretation of (11). Only (13) is an available interpretation of this sentence. To give another example, my semantics would generate multiple readings of the inference (14), including both (15) and (16):

(14) a. It is not the case that: Jones smokes and Smith drinks.
      b. Therefore, either Jones does not smoke or Smith does not drink.

(15) a. not$_1$ [$\mathcal{C}$ Jones smokes and$_2$ $\mathcal{C}$ Smith drinks]
      b. Therefore, [$\mathcal{C}$ not Jones smokes] or$_2$ [$\mathcal{C}$ not Smith drinks]

(16) a. $\mathcal{C}$ not [Jones smokes and Smith drinks]
      b. Therefore, $\mathcal{C}$ [[not Jones smokes] or [not Smith drinks]]

Again, this would be an unwelcome result. The inference (15) is generally invalid, and hence it should not be an available interpretation of (14). Only (16) is an available interpretation of this inference.

Fortunately, there are demanding and well-motivated restrictions on the distribution of the $\mathcal{C}$ operator. The semantic types of sentences are shifted from sets of worlds to sets of probability spaces if and only if such type shifting is forced. If a sentence contains no epistemic vocabulary, then the $\mathcal{C}$ operator takes scope over that sentence, shifting its type so that the resulting sentence denotes a content fit for assertion. If a sentence contains epistemic vocabulary, then the $\mathcal{C}$ operator appears only as it is required to make embedded sentences have the right type to serve as arguments of that vocabulary. To sum up, the arguments of the $\mathcal{C}$ operator include any sentential constituent denoting a proposition, when that constituent would otherwise be asserted or would be the argument of an epistemic expression. From these restrictions, it follows that (13) is the only available interpretation of (11), and (16) is the only available interpretation of (14), as desired.

These conditions on the distribution of the $\mathcal{C}$ operator are not ad hoc stipulations, but consequences of a general rule against unforced type shifting. According to this rule, embedded sentences are always interpreted according to the simplest types consistent with the coherent typing of the sentence in which they are embedded. In addition to uniquely determining the distribution of the $\mathcal{C}$ operator, the prohibition of unforced type shifting uniquely determines the semantic type of each logical operator in a sentence. In other words, there are never unforced choices about whether logical vocabulary operates on sets of worlds or on sets of probability spaces. PARTEE AND ROOTH 1983 point out that the prohibition of unforced type shifting mitigates the theoretical cost of assigning multiple semantic types to expressions, since "the potential disadvantage of having multiple interpretations…is offset by the processing strategy of trying the simplest type first" (341).

In addition to accounting for the validity of (14), my semantics for logical operators helps account for the invalidity of the inferences discussed in §4.4. The fact that logical operators are polymorphic provides a partial explanation for the invalidity of the following apparent instance of *modus tollens*:

(17) a. If it is low, it is probably odd.
      b. It is not probably odd.
      c. #Therefore, it is not low.

The negation operators in (17-b) and (17-c) have different semantic types, since the $\mathcal{C}$ operator is distributed throughout the inference as follows:

(18) a. if$_1$ [$\mathcal{C}$ it is low] [probably$_2$ $\mathcal{C}$ it is odd]
      b. not$_1$ [probably$_2$ $\mathcal{C}$ it is odd]
      c. Therefore, $\mathcal{C}$ not [it is low]

As uttered in the context of a conversation about the outcome of rolling a fair die, (18) is not a valid inference. But neither is it a genuine instance of *modus tollens*. As far as my semantics is concerned, the standard rule of inference by *modus tollens* remains in good standing.

The fact that logical operators are context sensitive helps explain the invalidity of the following apparent instance of constructive dilemma:

(19) a. If it is low, it is probably odd.
      b. If it is high, it is probably even.
      c. It is either low or high.
      d. #Therefore, either it is probably odd or probably even.

The most natural reading of (19) has the following logical form:

(20) a. if$_1$ [$\mathcal{C}$ it is low] [probably$_2$ $\mathcal{C}$ it is odd]
      b. if$_1$ [$\mathcal{C}$ it is high] [probably$_2$ $\mathcal{C}$ it is even]
      c. $\mathcal{C}$ [it is low or it is high]
      d. Therefore, [probably$_2$ $\mathcal{C}$ it is odd] or$_3$ [probably$_2$ $\mathcal{C}$ it is even]

As explained in §4.4, it is natural to imagine (19) as being uttered in a context such that the partition $g_c(1)$ contains two propositions—that the number rolled is low, and that the number is high—while the partition $g_c(3)$ contains just the trivial proposition. As uttered in this sort of context, (20) is not a valid inference. But neither is it a genuine instance of constructive dilemma. Again, this classically valid rule of inference remains in good standing.

In addition to the above inferences, my semantics accounts for the invalidity of another sort of inference not mentioned in §4.4. For instance, imagine being in a context where the following is true:

> It is several months before the 2016 United States presidential election. The Republican primaries are over, and it is settled that Donald Trump will be the Republican presidential candidate. However, there is much heated debate about whether Hillary Clinton or Bernie Sanders is more likely to be the Democratic nominee.

In this context, there is a natural reading on which (21) entails (22):

(21) The future president is either Trump or probably Clinton.

(22) It's not the case that the future president is either Trump or probably Sanders.

However, the reading of (22) that is entailed by (21) *does not* entail (23-b):

(23) a. It's not the case that the future president is either Trump or probably Sanders.

b. #Therefore, it's not the case that the future president is Trump.

The inference (23) illustrates an important point: when using epistemic vocabulary, we cannot blithely infer from the negation of a disjunction to the negation of one of its disjuncts. Like many standard inference rules, De Morgan's laws have plenty of apparent counterexamples involving sentences containing epistemic vocabulary.

However, it is also important to note that apparent instances of De Morgan's laws embedding epistemic vocabulary can also sound perfectly fine. For example, YALCIN 2014a observes that the following inference is intuitively valid:

(24) a. Bill is not handsome or likely to get a date.

b. Therefore, Bill is not handsome.

How should we account for the felicity of (24), and the contrast between (23) and (24)? A recurring theme of this book is that the interpretation of inferences containing epistemic vocabulary can depend on subtle features of context. In §4.4, I argue that whether an inference is valid depends on how context resolves the semantic values of the epistemic vocabulary it contains. In §7.5, I suggest that whether an inference is sound can depend on contextually determined ways of thinking about the objects that we are talking about or quantifying over. As I see it, (23) and (24) highlight a third reason why inferences may be good in some contexts and bad in others. In some contexts, the conclusion of an inference may be entailed by the premises together with some additional information that is presupposed. An especially useful hypothesis is that in some but not all contexts, speakers presuppose instances of *epistemic excluded middle*, namely that something either must be the case or couldn't be the case.

The disjunction operator in an instance of epistemic excluded middle should be interpreted relative to the partition containing just the trivial proposition. For instance, in the context of (24), the relevant presupposition of epistemic excluded middle is the union of two nominally probabilistic contents—namely, the set of probability spaces according to which it is certain that Bill is handsome, and the set of probability spaces according to which it is certain that he isn't. The union of these contents is a very strong content. If you believe it and you have precise credences, then either you are certain that Bill is handsome or you are certain that he isn't. But even if you do not believe this strong content yourself, you may nevertheless presuppose it for sake of conversation when you are talking with someone whom you know to believe it.

How does the presupposition of epistemic excluded middle account for the contrast between (23) and (24)? There is an important difference between what we naturally imagine about the contexts in which these sentences are uttered. In the context of (23), we naturally imagine that the speaker does not know whether Trump is the future president. But in the context of (24), we naturally imagine that the speaker *does* know whether Bill is handsome. Hence in the second context, it is more natural to imagine that it is presupposed that either Bill is certainly handsome or Bill is certainly not handsome. Together with this presupposition, the content of (24-a) does indeed entail the content of (24-b), provided that 'not' in (24-a) is interpreted using the partition containing just the trivial proposition, and 'or' in (24-a) is interpreted using the same partition as 'not' in (24-b).

The acceptability of (24) illustrates a more general conclusion: together with background assumptions of instances of epistemic excluded middle, probabilistic contents may indeed entail their *propositional closures*, in the sense of §7.3. It is natural to wonder whether applications of epistemic excluded middle might therefore have significant implications for our understanding of certain skeptical arguments, namely those that exploit the conflation of probabilistic contents and their propositional closures. I leave this question for future research, along with many other questions about the formal semantics and pragmatics of epistemic vocabulary. As we improve our understanding of the probabilistic contents of sentences containing epistemic vocabulary, we will also improve our understanding of the nature and extent of our probabilistic knowledge. This book is a progress report on my thinking about these topics. I hope that others might find it useful as a springboard for further research.

References

ADAMS, ERNEST. 1965. "The Logic of Conditionals." *Inquiry* vol. 8 (1–4): 166–97.
———. 1975. *The Logic of Conditionals*. Reidel, Dordrecht.
ADLER, JONATHAN. 1993. "Crime Rates by Race and Causal Relevance: A Reply to Levin." *Journal of Social Philosophy* vol. 24 (1): 176–84.
ALLEN, RONALD J. 1991. "On the Significance of Batting Averages and Strikeout Totals: A Clarification of the 'Naked Statistical Evidence' Debate, the Meaning of 'Evidence,' and the Requirement of Proof Beyond a Reasonable Doubt." *Tulane Law Review* vol. 65 (5): 1093–110.
ALONI, MARIA D. 2000. "Quantification Under Conceptual Covers." Ph.D. thesis, ILLC/Department of Philosophy, University of Amsterdam.
AUSTEN, JANE. 1818. *Persuasion*. Norton, New York. Ed. Patricia Meyer Spacks. Norton Critical Editions. 1995.
BARNES, ELIZABETH. 2015. "What You Can Expect When You Don't Want to Be Expecting." *Philosophy and Phenomenological Research* vol. 91 (3): 775–86.
BARNETT, DAVID. 2009. "Yalcin on 'Might'." *Mind* vol. 118 (471): 771–75.
BARNHOLDT, LAUREN. 2014. *Through to You*. Simon Pulse, New York.
BEAVER, DAVID. 2001. *Presupposition and Assertion in Dynamic Semantics*. CSLI Publications, Stanford.
BECCARIA, CESARE. 1764. "On Crimes and Punishments." In *'On Crimes and Punishments' and Other Writings*, RICHARD BELLAMY (ed.), 1–114. Cambridge University Press, Cambridge.
BENNETT, JONATHAN. 2003. *A Philosophical Guide to Conditionals*. Oxford University Press, Oxford.
BENTHAM, JEREMY. 1843. *The Works of Jeremy Bentham, vol. 6 (The Rationale of Judicial Evidence)*. JOHN BOWRING (ed.). William Tait, Edinburgh.
BLACKBURN, SIMON. 1984. *Spreading the Word: Groundings in the Philosophy of Language*. Oxford University Press, Oxford.
———. 1996. "Securing the Nots: Moral Epistemology for the Quasi-Realist." In *Moral Knowledge?: New Readings in Moral Epistemology*, WALTER SINNOTT-ARMSTRONG AND MARK TIMMONS (eds), 82–100. Oxford University Press, New York.
BLOCK, NED. 1986. "Advertisement for a Semantics for Psychology." *Midwest Studies in Philosophy* vol. 10 (1): 615–78.
———. 1991. "What Narrow Content Is Not." In *Meaning in Mind: Fodor and His Critics*, BARRY M. LOEWER (ed.), 33–64. Blackwell, Cambridge.
BLOME-TILLMANN, MICHAEL. 2013. "Contextualism and the Knowledge Norms." *Pacific Philosophical Quarterly* vol. 94 (1): 89–100.
BODANSKY, DAVID. 2005. *Nuclear Energy: Principles, Practices, and Prospects*. Springer-Verlag, New York.
BOGHOSSIAN, PAUL A. 1996. "Analyticity Reconsidered." *Noûs* vol. 30 (3): 360–91.

———. 1997. "What the Externalist Can Know *A Priori*." *Proceedings of the Aristotelian Society* vol. 97 (2): 161–75.

BRADLEY, P. H. 1981. "The Folk Linguistics of Women's Speech: An Empirical Examination." *Communication Monographs* vol. 48 (1): 73–90.

BRAUN, DAVID. 2016. "The Objects of Belief and Credence." *Mind* vol. 125 (498): 469–97.

BROGAARD, BERIT. 2011. "Do 'Looks' Reports Reflect the Contents of Perception?" Ms., Department of Philosophy, University of Miami.

BROOME, JOHN. 2009. *Rationality Through Reasoning*. Wiley-Blackwell, Malden, MA.

BROWN, JESSICA. 1995. "The Incompatibility of Anti-Individualism and Privileged Access." *Analysis* vol. 55 (3): 149–56.

———. 2008. "Subject-Sensitive Invariantism and the Knowledge Norm for Practical Reasoning." *Noûs* vol. 42 (2): 167–89.

BUCHAK, LARA. 2013a. "Belief, Credence, and Norms." *Philosophical Studies* vol. 169 (2): 285–311.

———. 2013b. *Risk and Rationality*. Oxford University Press, Oxford.

BUCKWALTER, WESLEY AND JONATHAN SCHAFFER. 2015. "Knowledge, Stakes, and Mistakes." *Noûs* vol. 49 (2): 201–34.

BYRNE, ALEX. 2009. "Experience and Content." *Philosophical Quarterly* vol. 59 (236): 429–51.

CANTWELL, JOHN. 2008. "Changing the Modal Context." *Theoria* vol. 74 (4): 331–51.

CAPPELEN, HERMAN AND JOHN HAWTHORNE. 2009. *Relativism and Monadic Truth*. Oxford University Press, Oxford.

CARLI, LINDA. 1990. "Gender, Language, and Influence." *Journal of Personality and Social Psychology* vol. 59 (5): 941–51.

CHALMERS, DAVID. 2011. "Frege's Puzzle and the Objects of Credence." *Mind* vol. 120 (479): 587–635.

———. 2012. *Constructing the World*. Oxford University Press, Oxford.

CHARLOW, SIMON AND YAEL SHARVIT. 2014. "Bound 'De Re' Pronouns and the LFs of Attitude Reports." *Semantics and Pragmatics* vol. 7 (3): 1–43.

CHISHOLM, RODERICK. 1957. *Perceiving: A Philosophical Study*. Cornell University Press, Ithaca.

CHRISTENSEN, DAVID. 2004. *Putting Logic in Its Place: Formal Constraints on Rational Belief*. Oxford University Press, Oxford.

———. 2007. "Epistemology of Disagreement: The Good News." *Philosophical Review* vol. 116 (2): 187–217.

CHRISTENSEN, DAVID AND JENNIFER LACKEY (eds). 2013. *The Epistemology of Disagreement: New Essays*. Oxford University Press, Oxford.

CLARKE, ROGER. 2013. "Belief Is Credence One (in Context)." *Philosophers' Imprint* vol. 13 (11): 1–18.

CLERMONT, KEVIN. 2013. *Standards of Decision in Law: Psychological and Logical Bases for the Standard of Proof, Here and Abroad*. Carolina Academic Press, Durham, NC.

COHEN, L. JONATHAN. 1977. *The Probable and the Provable*. Clarendon, Oxford.

———. 1981. "Subjective Probability and the Paradox of the Gatecrasher." *Arizona State Law Journal* vol. 2 (2): 627–34.

———. 1987. "On Analyzing the Standards of Forensic Evidence: A Reply to Schoeman." *Philosophy of Science* vol. 54 (1): 92–97.

COHEN, STEWART. 1988. "How to Be a Fallibilist." *Philosophical Perspectives* vol. 2 (1): 91–123.

———. 2010. "Bootstrapping, Defeasible Reasoning, and *A Priori* Justification." *Philosophical Perspectives* vol. 24 (1): 141–59.

———. 2013. "A Defense of the (Almost) Equal Weight View." In CHRISTENSEN AND LACKEY (2013), 98–117.

CRESTO, ELEONORA. 2010. "On Reasons and Epistemic Rationality." *Journal of Philosophy* vol. 107 (6): 326–30.

CRIMMINS, MARK. 1992. *Talk About Beliefs*. MIT Press, Cambridge.

CROSS, TROY. 2010. "Skeptical Success." In GENDLER AND HAWTHORNE (2010), 35–62.

CURTIS, JAMES T. 1997. *Lewis Grizzard Is Dead and I Don't Feel So Good Myself!* [author] Kindle DX version. Retrieved from Amazon.com.

DEROSE, KEITH. 1992. "Contextualism and Knowledge Attributions." *Philosophy and Phenomenological Research* vol. 52 (4): 913–29.

DEVER, JOSH AND HERMAN CAPPELEN. 2013. *The Inessential Indexical: On the Philosophical Insignificance of Perspective and the First Person*. Oxford University Press, Oxford.

DHAMI, MANDEEP K. 2008. "On Measuring Quantitative Interpretations of Reasonable Doubt." *Journal of Experimental Psychology: Applied* vol. 14 (4): 353–63.

DI PAOLO, MARIANNA. 1989. "Double Modals as Single Lexical Items." *American Speech* vol. 64 (3): 195–224.

DIACONIS, PERSI AND SANDY L. ZABELL. 1982. "Updating Subjective Probability." *Journal of the American Statistical Association* vol. 77 (380): 822–30.

DOGRAMACI, SINAN. 2014. "A Problem for Rationalist Responses to Skepticism." *Philosophical Studies* vol. 168 (2): 355–69.

DORR, CIAN AND JOHN HAWTHORNE. 2012. "Embedding Epistemic Modals." *Mind* vol. 122 (488): 867–913.

———. 2014. "Semantic Plasticity and Speech Reports." *Philosophical Review* vol. 123 (3): 281–338.

DOUGHERTY, TOM, SOPHIE HOROWITZ, AND PAULINA SLIWA. 2015. "Expecting the Unexpected." *Res Philosophica* vol. 92 (2): 301–21.

DOUVEN, IGOR. 2008a. "Kaufmann on the Probabilities of Conditionals." *Journal of Philosophical Logic* vol. 37 (3): 259–66.

———. 2008b. "Knowledge and Practical Reasoning." *Dialectica* vol. 62 (1): 101–18.

DOWELL, JANICE. 2011. "A Flexible Contextualist Account of Epistemic Modals." *Philosophers' Imprint* vol. 11 (14): 1–25.

DREIER, JAMES. 2009. "Practical Conditionals." In *Reasons for Action*, DAVID SOBEL AND STEVEN WALL (eds), 116–33. Cambridge University Press, Cambridge.

DRETSKE, FRED. 1970. "Epistemic Operators." *Journal of Philosophy* vol. 67 (24): 1007–23.

DUDMAN, V. H. 1994. "Against the Indicative." *Australasian Journal of Philosophy* vol. 72 (1): 17–26.

DUFF, ANTONY, LINDSAY FARMER, SANDRA MARSHALL, AND VICTOR TADROS. 2007. *The Trial on Trial (vol. 3): Towards a Normative Theory of the Criminal Trial*. Hart, Oxford.

DUMMETT, MICHAEL. 1964. "Bringing About the Past." *Philosophical Review* vol. 73 (3): 338–59.

———. 1973. *Frege: Philosophy of Language*. Gerald Duckworth, London.

DUTTON, D. G. AND A. P. ARON. 1974. "Some Evidence for Heightened Sexual Attraction Under Conditions of High Anxiety." *Journal of Personality and Social Psychology* vol. 30 (4): 510–17.

EASWARAN, KENNY. 2014. "Regularity and Hyperreal Credences." *Philosophical Review* vol. 123 (1): 1–41.

EDGINGTON, DOROTHY. 1986. "Do Conditionals Have Truth Conditions?" *Crítica: Revista Hispanoamericana de Filosofía* vol. 18 (52): 3–39.

———. 2000. "General Conditional Statements: A Response to Kölbel." *Mind* vol. 109 (433): 109–16.

EGAN, ANDY. 2007. "Epistemic Modals, Relativism, and Assertion." *Philosophical Studies* vol. 133 (1): 1–22.

EGAN, ANDY, JOHN HAWTHORNE, AND BRIAN WEATHERSON. 2005. "Epistemic Modals in Context." In *Contextualism in Philosophy: Knowledge, Meaning, and Truth*, GERHARD PREYER AND GEORG PETER, editors, 131–70. Oxford University Press, Oxford.

EGAN, ANDY AND BRIAN WEATHERSON (eds) 2011. *Epistemic Modality*. Oxford University Press, Oxford.

EIDELSON, BENJAMIN. 2013. "Treating People as Individuals." In *Philosophical Foundations of Discrimination Law*, DEBORAH HELLMAN AND SOPHIA MOREAU (eds), 203–27. Oxford University Press, Oxford.

ELGA, ADAM. 2008. "Lucky to be Rational." Ms., Department of Philosophy, Princeton University.

ELGIN, CATHERINE. 2002. "Take It from Me: The Epistemological Status of Testimony." *Philosophy and Phenomenological Research* vol. 65 (2): 291–308.

ENOCH, DAVID AND TALIA FISHER. 2015. "Sense and 'Sensitivity': Epistemic and Instrumental Approaches to Statistical Evidence." *Stanford Law Review* vol. 6/ (3). 557 611.

ENOCH, DAVID, LEVI SPECTRE, AND TALIA FISHER. 2012. "Statistical Evidence, Sensitivity, and the Legal Value of Knowledge." *Philosophy and Public Affairs* vol. 40 (3): 197–224.

EVANS, GARETH. 1979. "Reference and Contingency." In *Collected Papers*, JOHN McDOWELL (ed.) 178–213. Oxford University Press, Oxford.

FANTL, JEREMY AND MATTHEW McGRATH. 2010. *Knowledge in an Uncertain World*. Oxford University Press, Oxford.

FELDMAN, RICHARD. 2003. *Epistemology*. Prentice Hall, Upper Saddle River, NJ.

FERRER BELTRÁN, JORDI. 2006. "Legal Proof and Fact Finders' Beliefs." *Legal Theory* vol. 12 (4): 293–314.

FINE, KIT. 2009. *Semantic Relationism*. Oxford University Press, Oxford.

VON FINTEL, KAI. 2004. "Would You Believe It? The King of France is Back! Presuppositions and Truth-Value Intuitions." In *Descriptions and Beyond: An Interdisciplinary Collection of Essays on Definite and Indefinite Descriptions and Other Related Phenomena*, MARGA REIMER AND ANNE BEZUIDENHOUT (eds), 315–41. Oxford University Press, Oxford.

VON FINTEL, KAI AND ANTHONY GILLIES. 2007. "An Opinionated Guide to Epistemic Modality." In GENDLER AND HAWTHORNE (2007), 32–62.

———. 2008. "CIA Leaks." *Philosophical Review* vol. 117 (1): 77–98.

———. 2011. "*Might* Made Right." In EGAN AND WEATHERSON (2011), 108–30.

VON FINTEL, KAI AND SABINE IATRIDOU. 2003. "Epistemic Containment." *Linguistic Inquiry* vol. 34 (2): 173–98.

FODOR, JERRY A. 1987. *Psychosemantics*. MIT Press, Cambridge.

FOLEY, RICHARD. 1992. "The Epistemology of Belief and the Epistemology of Degrees of Belief." *American Philosophical Quarterly* vol. 29 (2): 111–24.

———. 2001. *Intellectual Trust in Oneself and Others*. Cambridge University Press, Cambridge.

FORREST, PETER. 1981. "Probabilistic Modal Inferences." *Australasian Journal of Philosophy* vol. 59 (1): 38–53.

FRANKISH, KEITH. 2009. "Partial Belief and Flat-Out Belief." In *Degrees of Belief*, FRANZ HUBER AND CHRISTOPH SCHMIDT-PETRI (eds), 75–93. Springer, Dordrecht.

FRIEDMAN, JANE. 2013. "Suspended Judgment." *Philosophical Studies* vol. 162 (2): 165–81.

GANSON, DORIT. 2008. "Evidentialism and Pragmatic Constraints on Outright Belief." *Philosophical Studies* vol. 139 (3): 441–58.

GENDLER, TAMAR SZABÓ. 2011. "On the Epistemic Costs of Implicit Bias." *Philosophical Studies* vol. 156 (1): 33–63.

GENDLER, TAMAR SZABÓ AND JOHN HAWTHORNE (eds). 2007. *Oxford Studies in Epistemology*, vol. 2. Oxford University Press, Oxford.

———. 2010. *Oxford Studies in Epistemology* vol. 3. Oxford University Press, Oxford.

GETTIER, EDMUND. 1963. "Is Justified True Belief Knowledge?" *Analysis* vol. 23 (6): 121–23.

GEURTS, BART. 1999. *Presuppositions and Pronouns*. Elsevier, Amsterdam.

———. 2007. "Existential Import." In *Existence: Semantics and Syntax*, ILEANA COMOROVSKI AND KLAUS VON HEUSINGER (eds), 253–71. Springer, Netherlands.

GEURTS, BART AND JANNEKE HUITINK. 2006. "Modal Concord." In *Concord Phenomena and the Syntax-Semantics Interface*, P. DEKKER AND H. ZEIJLSTRA (eds), 15–20. ESSLLI, Malaga.

GIBBARD, ALLAN. 1981. "Two Recent Theories of Conditionals." In *Ifs: Conditionals, Belief, Decision, Chance, and Time*, WILLIAM L. HARPER, ROBERT STALNAKER, AND GLENN PEARCE (eds), 211–47. D. Reidel Publishing Company, Dordrecht.

———. 1990. *Wise Choices, Apt Feelings*. Harvard University Press, Cambridge.

———. 2003. *Thinking How to Live*. Harvard University Press, Cambridge.

GIBBARD, ALLAN AND WILLIAM L. HARPER. 1978. "Counterfactuals and Two Kinds of Expected Utility." In *Foundations and Applications of Decision Theory*, C. HOOKER, J. LEACH, AND E. MCCLENNEN (eds), 123–62. Reidel, Dordrecht.

GINZBURG, JONATHAN. 1994. "An Update Semantics for Dialogue." In *Proceedings of the First International Workshop on Computational Semantics*, HARRY BUNT, REINHARD MUSKENS, AND GERRIT RENTIER (eds), 111–20. Tilburg, the Netherlands.

GOLDMAN, ALVIN. 1976. "Discrimination and Perceptual Knowledge." *Journal of Philosophy* vol. 73 (20): 771–91.

GOODMAN, NELSON. 1955. *Fact, Fiction, and Forecast*. Harvard University Press, Cambridge.

GREAVES, HILARY AND DAVID WALLACE. 2006. "Justifying Conditionalization: Conditionalization Maximizes Expected Epistemic Utility." *Mind* vol. 115 (459): 607–32.

GRECO, DANIEL. 2015. "How I Learned to Stop Worrying and Love Probability 1." *Philosophical Perspectives* vol. 29 (1): 179–201.

GRECO, JOHN. 2007. "Worries about Pritchard's Safety." *Synthese* vol. 158 (3): 299–302.

GREENE, JOSHUA D. 2014. "Beyond Point-and-Shoot Morality: Why Cognitive (Neuro)Science Matters for Ethics." *Ethics* vol. 124 (4): 695–726.

GRICE, PAUL. 1967. "Logic and Conversation." In *Studies in the Way of Words*. Harvard University Press, Cambridge.

HACQUARD, VALENTINE AND ALEXIS WELLWOOD. 2012. "Embedding Epistemic Modals in English: A Corpus-Based Study." *Semantics and Pragmatics* vol. 5 (4): 1–29.

HADDOCK, ADRIAN, ALAN MILLAR, AND DUNCAN PRITCHARD (eds). 2010. *Social Epistemology*. Oxford University Press, New York.

HÁJEK, ALAN. 2013. "Staying Regular." Ms., Research School of the Social Sciences, Australian National University.

———. 2015. "A Puzzle About Degree of Belief." Ms., Research School of the Social Sciences, Australian National University.

HALE, BOB. 1993. "Can There Be a Logic of Attitudes?" In *Reality, Representation, and Projection*, J. HALDANE AND C. WRIGHT (eds), 337–64. Oxford University Press, New York.

HAMBLIN, CHARLES. 1973. "Questions in Montague English." *Foundations of Language* vol. 10 (1): 41–53.

HANSEN, MATTHEW SCOTT. 2007. *The Shadowkiller: A Novel*. Simon & Schuster, New York.

HARE, R. M. 1970. "Meaning and Speech Acts." *Philosophical Review* vol. 79 (1): 3–24.

HARMAN, GILBERT. 1973. *Thought*. Princeton University Press, Princeton.

———. 1986. *Change in View: Principles of Reasoning*. MIT Press, Cambridge.

HAWTHORNE, JOHN. 2004. *Knowledge and Lotteries*. Oxford University Press, Oxford.

———. 2007. "Eavesdroppers and Epistemic Modals." *Philosophical Issues* vol. 17 (1): 92–101.

HAWTHORNE, JOHN AND AMIA SRINIVASAN. 2013. "Disagreement Without Transparency: Some Bleak Thoughts." In CHRISTENSEN AND LACKEY (2013), 9–30.

HAWTHORNE, JOHN AND JASON STANLEY. 2008. "Knowledge and Action." *Journal of Philosophy* vol. 105 (10): 571–90.

HEIM, IRENE AND ANGELIKA KRATZER. 1998. *Semantics in Generative Grammar*. Blackwell, Malden, MA.

HINTIKKA, JAAKKO. 1969. "Semantics for Propositional Attitudes." In *Philosophical Logic*, J. W. DAVIS, D. J. HOCKNEY, AND W. K. WILSON (eds), 21–45. Reidel, Dordrecht.

HO, HOCK LAI. 2008. *A Philosophy of Evidence Law: Justice in the Search for Truth*. Oxford University Press, Oxford.

HOLTON, RICHARD. 2014. "Intention as a Model for Belief." In *Rational and Social Agency: Essays on the Philosophy of Michael Bratman*, MANUEL VARGAS AND GIDEON YAFFE (eds), 12–37. Oxford University Press, New York.

HORWICH, PAUL. 2001. "Stipulation, Meaning, and Apriority." In *New Essays on the A Priori*, PAUL BOGHOSSIAN AND CHRIS PEACOCKE (eds), 150–69. Oxford University Press, New York.

HUMPHREY, JUDITH. 2015. "The Communication Style You Need To Break Into the Boys' Club." *Fast Company Magazine*, 12 March 2015. Available at <https://www.fastcompany.com/3043463>.

HYMAN, JOHN. 1999. "How Knowledge Works." *Philosophical Quarterly* vol. 49 (197): 433–51.

JACKSON, FRANK. 1977. *Perception: A Representative Theory*. Cambridge University Press, New York.

JEFFREY, RICHARD C. 1965. "Probability Kinematics." In *The Logic of Decision*, 164–83. University of Chicago Press, Chicago.

——. 1968. "Probable Knowledge." In *Probability and the Art of Judgment*, 30–43. Cambridge University Press, Cambridge. Originally published in *The Problem of Inductive Logic*, I. Lakatos (ed.), North-Holland Publishing Company, Amsterdam, 1968, pp. 166–80.

——. 1983. "Bayesianism with a Human Face." In *Testing Scientific Theories*, JOHN EARMAN (ed.), 133–56. University of Minnesota Press, Minneapolis.

DE JONG, FRANCISKA AND HENK VERKUYL. 1985. "Generalized Quantifiers: The Properness of Their Strength." In *Generalized Quantifiers in Natural Language*, ALICE TER MEULEN AND JOHAN VAN BENTHEM (eds), 21–43. Foris, Dordrecht.

JOYCE, JAMES. 2005. "How Probabilities Reflect Evidence." *Philosophical Perspectives* vol. 19 (1): 153–78.

KAPLAN, MARK. 1996. *Decision Theory as Philosophy*. Cambridge University Press, Cambridge.

KARTTUNEN, LAURI. 1973. "Presuppositions of Compound Sentences." *Linguistic Inquiry* vol. 4 (2): 169–93.

KAUFMANN, STEFAN. 2004. "Conditioning Against the Grain." *Journal of Philosophical Logic* vol. 33 (6): 583–606.

KELLY, DANIEL AND ERICA ROEDDER. 2008. "Racial Cognition and the Ethics of Implicit Bias." *Philosophy Compass* vol. 3 (3): 522–40.

KERR, ERIC. 2013. "Are You Thinking What We're Thinking? Group Knowledge Attributions and Collective Visions." *Social Epistemology Review and Reply Collective* vol. 3 (1): 5–13.

KHOO, JUSTIN. 2016. "Probabilities of Conditionals in Context." *Linguistics and Philosophy* vol. 39 (1): 1–43.

KNILL, DAVID C. AND ALEXANDRE POUGET. 2004. "The Bayesian Brain: The Role of Uncertainty in Neural Coding and Computation." *Trends in Neurosciences* vol. 27 (12): 712–19.

KOEHLER, JONATHAN J. AND DANIEL N. SHAVIRO. 1990. "Veridical Verdicts: Increasing Verdict Accuracy Through the Use of Overtly Probabilistic Evidence and Methods." *Cornell Law Review* vol. 75 (2): 247–79.

KOLODNY, NIKO AND JOHN MACFARLANE. 2010. "Ifs and Oughts." *Journal of Philosophy* vol. 107 (3): 115–43.

KONEK, JASON. 2016. "Probabilistic Knowledge and Cognitive Ability." *Philosophical Review* vol. 125 (4): 509–87.

KORSGAARD, CHRISTINE. 1996. *Sources of Normativity*. Cambridge University Press, Cambridge.

KRATZER, ANGELIKA. 1977. "What *Must* and *Can* Must and Can Mean." *Linguistics and Philosophy* vol. 1 (3): 337–55.

———. 1981. "The Notional Category of Modality." In *Words, Worlds, and Contexts: New Approaches in Word Semantics*, HANS JURGEN EIKMEYER AND HANNES RIESER (eds), 38–74. W. de Gruyter, Berlin.

———. 1991. "Modality." In *Semantics: An International Handbook of Contemporary Research*, ARNIM VON STECHOW AND DIETER WUNDERLICH (eds), 639–50. W. de Gruyter, Berlin.

KRETZMANN, NORMAN. 1966. "Omniscience and Immutability." *Journal of Philosophy* vol. 63 (14): 409–21.

KRIFKA, MANFRED. 2009. "Approximate Interpretations of Number Words: A Case for Strategic Communication." In *Theory and Evidence in Semantics*, ERHARD HINRICHS AND JOHN NERBONNE (eds), 109–31. CSLI Publications, Stanford.

KRIPKE, SAUL. 1979. "A Puzzle About Belief." In *Readings in the Philosophy of Language*, PETER LUDLOW (ed.), 875–920. MIT Press, Cambridge.

———. 1980. *Naming and Necessity*. Harvard University Press, Cambridge.

KRISHNAMURTHY, MEENA. 2015. "We Can Make Rational Decisions to Have a Child: On the Grounds for Rejecting L. A. Paul's Arguments." In *Permissible Progeny*, SARAH HANNAN, SAMANTHA BRENNAN, AND RICHARD VERNON (eds), 170–83. Oxford University Press, Oxford.

KUNG, PETER. 2010. "On Having No Reason: Dogmatism and Bayesian Confirmation." *Synthese* vol. 177 (1): 1–17.

KVANVIG, JONATHAN. 1986. *The Possibility of an All-Knowing God*. Macmillan Press, London.

———. 2005. "Truth Is Not the Primary Epistemic Goal." In *Contemporary Debates in Epistemology*, MATTHAIS STEUP AND ERNEST SOSA (eds), 285–96. Blackwell, Oxford.

KYBURG, H. 1961. *Probability and the Logic of Rational Belief*. Wesleyan University Press, Middletown.

LACKEY, JENNIFER. 2003. "A Minimal Expression of Non-Reductionism in the Epistemology of Testimony." *Noûs* vol. 37 (4): 706–23.

———. 2008. *Learning from Words: Testimony as a Source of Knowledge*. Oxford University Press, Oxford.

———. 2010. "A Justificationist View of Disagreement's Epistemic Significance." In HADDOCK ET AL. (2010), 298–325.

LAKOFF, ROBIN. 1975. *Language and Woman's Place*. Harper & Row, New York.

LANCE, MARK. 1995. "Subjective Probability and Acceptance." *Philosophical Studies* vol. 70 (1): 147–79.

LASERSOHN, PETER. 1999. "Pragmatic Halos." *Language* vol. 75 (3): 522–51.

———. 2005. "Context Dependence, Disagreement, and Predicates of Personal Taste." *Linguistics and Philosophy* vol. 28 (6): 643–86.

LASONEN-AARNIO, MARIA. 2010. "Unreasonable Knowledge." *Philosophical Perspectives* vol. 24 (1): 1–21.

LASSITER, DANIEL. 2011. *Measurement and Modality: The Scalar Basis of Modal Semantics*. Ph.D. thesis, New York University.

———. 2015. "Epistemic Comparison, Models of Uncertainty, and the Disjunction Puzzle." *Journal of Semantics* vol. 32 (4): 649–84.

LAUDAN, LARRY. 2003. "Is Reasonable Doubt Reasonable?" *Legal Theory* vol. 9 (4): 295–331.

———. 2006. *Truth, Error, and Criminal Law: An Essay in Legal Epistemology*. Cambridge University Press, New York.

LAUER, SVEN. 2012. "On the Pragmatics of Pragmatic Slack." *Proceedings of Sinn und Bedeutung 16* vol. 2: 389–401.

———. 2013. "Towards a Dynamic Pragmatics." Ph.D. thesis, Department of Linguistics, Stanford University.

LEAHY, BRIAN. 2011. "Presuppositions and Antipresuppositions in Indicative Conditionals." In *Proceedings of Semantics and Linguistic Theory (SALT) 21*, N. ASHTON, A. CHERECHES, AND D. LUTZ (eds), 257–74. CLC Publications, Ithaca.

LEUBSDORF, JOHN. 2015. "The Surprising History of the Preponderance Standard of Civil Proof." *Florida Law Review* vol. 67 (5): 1569–619.

LEVI, ISAAC. 1974. "On Indeterminate Probabilities." *Journal of Philosophy* vol. 71 (13): 391–418.

———. 1985. "Imprecision and Indeterminacy in Probability Judgment." *Philosophy of Science* vol. 52 (3): 390–409.

LEWIS, DAVID K. 1976. "Probabilities of Conditionals and Conditional Probabilities." In LEWIS (1986), 133–56. With postscript.

———. 1979a. "Attitudes *De Dicto* and *De Se*." *Philosophical Review* vol. 88 (4): 513–43.

———. 1979b. "Counterfactual Dependence and Time's Arrow." In LEWIS (1986), 32–51.

———. 1980a. "Index, Context, and Content." In *Philosophy and Grammar*, S. KANGER AND S. ÖHMAN (eds), 79–100. D. Reidel Publishing Company, Dordrecht.

———. 1980b. "A Subjectivist's Guide to Objective Chance." In LEWIS (1986), 83–132. With postscript.

———. 1986. *Philosophical Papers*, vol. 2. Oxford University Press, Oxford.

———. 1996. "Elusive Knowledge." In *Papers in Metaphysics and Epistemology*, 418–46. Cambridge University Press, Cambridge.

LIPPERT-RASMUSSEN, KASPER. 2011. "'We Are All Different': Statistical Discrimination and the Right to Be Treated as an Individual." *The Journal of Ethics* vol. 15 (1/2): 47–59.

LITTLEJOHN, CLAYTON. 2009. "Must We Act Only on What We Know?" *Journal of Philosophy* vol. 106 (8): 463–74.

LOAR, BRIAN. 1988. "Social Content and Psychological Content." In *Contents of Thought*, R. GRIMM AND D. MERRILL (eds), 99–110. University of Arizona Press, Tucson.

LOCKE, DUSTIN. 2013. "The Decision-Theoretic Lockean Thesis." *Inquiry* vol. 57 (1): 28–54.

LYCAN, WILLIAM. 2001. *Real Conditionals*. Oxford University Press, Oxford.

MACFARLANE, JOHN. 2011. "Epistemic Modals Are Assessment-Sensitive." In EGAN AND WEATHERSON (2011), 144–78.

———. 2014. *Assessment Sensitivity: Relative Truth and its Applications*. Oxford University Press, Oxford.

MAGIDOR, OFRA. 2015. "The Myth of the *De Se*." *Philosophical Perspectives* vol. 29 (1): 249–83.

MAGNUSSEN, SVEIN, DAG ERIK ELIERTSEN, KARL HALVOR TEIGEN, AND ELLEN WESSEL. 2014. "The Probability of Guilt in Criminal Cases: Are People Aware of Being 'Beyond Reasonable Doubt'?" *Applied Cognitive Psychology* vol. 28 (2): 196–203.

MAHER, PATRICK. 1993. *Betting on Theories*. Cambridge University Press, Cambridge.

MALCOLM, NORMAN. 1973. "Thoughtless Brutes." *Proceedings and Addresses of the American Philosophical Association* vol. 46: 5–20.

MALONEY, L. T. 2002. "Statistical Decision Theory and Biological Vision." In *Perception and the Physical World: Psychological and Philosophical Issues in Perception*, D. HEYER AND R. MAUSFELD (eds), 145–89. Wiley, New York.

MAMASSIAN, PASCAL, MICHAEL LANDY, AND LAURENCE T. MALONEY. 2002. "Bayesian Modelling of Visual Perception." In *Probabilistic Models of the Brain: Perception and Neural Function*, P. N. RAO, BRUNO A. OLSHAUSEN, AND MICHAEL S. LEWICKI (eds), 13–36. MIT Press, Cambridge.

MARCUS, RUTH BARCAN. 1990. "Some Revisionary Proposals about Belief and Believing." *Philosophy and Phenomenological Research* vol. 50 (Supp.): 133–53.

MATHIESEN, KAY. 2007. "Introduction to Special Issue of *Social Epistemology* on 'Collective Knowledge and Collective Knowers'." *Social Epistemology* vol. 21 (3): 209–16.

MCCAULIFF, C. M. A. 1982. "Burdens of Proof: Degrees of Belief, Quanta of Evidence, or Constitutional Guarantees?" *Vanderbilt Law Review* vol. 35 (6): 1293–336.

MCGEE, VANN. 1985. "A Counterexample to Modus Ponens." *Journal of Philosophy* vol. 82 (9): 462–71.

MCGRATH, MATTHEW. 2004. "Review of John Hawthorne, *Knowledge and Lotteries*." *Notre Dame Philosophical Reviews* vol. 8.

MCKINSEY, MICHAEL. 1991. "Anti-Individualism and Privileged Access." *Analysis* vol. 51 (1): 9–16.

MCMILLAN, JULIE R., A. KAY CLIFTON, AND DIANE MCGRATH. 1977. "Women's Language: Uncertainty or Interpersonal Sensitivity and Emotionality?" *Sex Roles* vol. 3 (6): 545–59.

MILLER, DAVID. 1999. *Principles of Social Justice*. Harvard University Press, Cambridge.

MONTAGUE, RICHARD. 1969. "On the Nature of Certain Philosophical Entities." *The Monist* vol. 53 (2): 159–94.

MOORE, G. E. 1939. "Proof of an External World." *Proceedings of the British Academy* vol. 25: 273–300.

MORRISON, JOHN. 2014. "Perceptual Confidence." *Analytic Philosophy* vol. 57 (1): 15–48.

MORTON, ADAM. 2004. "Against the Ramsey Test." *Analysis* vol. 64: 294–99.

MOSS, SARAH. 2011. "Scoring Rules and Epistemic Compromise." *Mind* vol. 120 (480): 1053–69.

———. 2012a. "On the Pragmatics of Counterfactuals." *Noûs* vol. 46 (3): 561–86.

———. 2012b. "The Role of Linguistics in the Philosophy of Language." In *The Routledge Companion to the Philosophy of Language*, GILLIAN RUSSELL AND DELIA GRAFF FARA (eds), 513–24. Routledge, New York.

———. 2012c. "Updating as Communication." *Philosophy and Phenomenological Research* vol. 85 (2): 225–48.

———. 2013. "Epistemology Formalized." *Philosophical Review* vol. 122 (1): 1–43.

———. 2014. "Credal Dilemmas." *Noûs* vol. 48 (3): 665–83.

———. 2015. "On the Semantics and Pragmatics of Epistemic Vocabulary." *Semantics and Pragmatics* vol. 8 (5): 1–81.

————. 2018. "Moral Encroachment." Forthcoming in *Proceedings of the Aristotelian Society*.

MUNTON, JESSIE. 2016. "Visual Confidences and Direct Perceptual Justification." *Philosophical Topics* vol. 44 (2): 301–26.

NAGEL, JENNIFER. 2011. "The Psychological Basis of the Harman-Vogel Paradox." *Philosophers' Imprint* vol. 11 (5): 1–28.

NESSON, CHARLES. 1979. "Reasonable Doubt and Permissive Inferences: The Value of Complexity." *Harvard Law Review* vol. 92 (6): 1187–225.

————. 1985. "The Evidence or the Event? On Judicial Proof and the Acceptability of Verdicts." *Harvard Law Review* vol. 98 (7): 1357–92.

NETA, RAM. 2009. "Treating Something as a Reason for Action." *Noûs* vol. 43 (4): 684–99.

NINAN, DILIP. 2012. "Counterfactual Attitudes and Multi-Centered Worlds." *Semantics and Pragmatics* vol. 5 (5): 1–57.

————. 2016. "What is the Problem of *De Se* Attitudes?" In *About Oneself: De Se Thought and Communication*, MANUEL GARCÍA-CARPINTERO AND STEPHAN TORRE (eds), 86–120. Oxford University Press, Oxford.

NISSAN-ROZEN, ITTAY. 2016. "Newcomb Meets Gettier." *Synthese*. Article published online first. DOI: 10.1007/s11229-016-1169-y.

NOZICK, ROBERT. 1981. *Philosophical Explanations*. Harvard University Press, Cambridge.

PARDO, MICHAEL. 2010. "The Gettier Problem and Legal Proof." *Legal Theory* vol. 16 (1): 37–57.

————. 2011. "More on the Gettier Problem and Legal Proof." *Legal Theory* vol. 17 (1): 75–80.

PARTEE, BARBARA AND MATS ROOTH. 1983. "Generalized Conjunction and Type-Ambiguity." In *Formal Semantics: The Essential Readings*, PAUL PORTNER AND BARBARA H. PARTEE (eds), 334–56. Blackwell, Oxford.

PAUL, L. A. 2014. *Transformative Experience*. Oxford University Press, Oxford.

PAUTZ, ADAM. 2016. "What Is My Evidence That Here Is a Cup?" *Philosophical Studies* vol. 173 (4): 915–27.

PERCUS, ORIN. 2006. "Antipresuppositions." In *Theoretical and Empirical Studies of Reference and Anaphora: Toward the Establishment of Generative Grammar as an Empirical Science*, A. UEYAMA (ed.), 52–73. Japan Society for the Promotion of Science. Report of the Grant-in-Aid for Scientific Research (B), Project No. 15320052.

PETTIGREW, RICHARD. 2015. "Transformative Experience and Decision Theory." *Philosophy and Phenomenological Research* vol. 91 (3): 766–74.

PHILLIPS, RICHARD. 1822. *New Voyages and Travels: Consisting of Originals, Translations, and Abridgements* vol. 5. Printed for Sir Richard Phillips, London.

PLANTINGA, ALVIN. 1993. *Warrant and Proper Function*. Oxford University Press, Oxford.

POLLOCK, JOHN. 2008. "Defeasible Reasoning." In *Reasoning: Studies of Human Inference and Its Foundations*, J. E. ADLER AND L. J. RIPS (eds), 451–70. Cambridge University Press, Cambridge.

PREYER, GERHARD AND GEORG PETER (eds), 2007. *Context-Sensitivity and Semantic Minimalism: New Essays on Semantics and Pragmatics*. Oxford University Press, Oxford.

PRITCHARD, DUNCAN. 2005. *Epistemic Luck*. Clarendon, Oxford.

————. 2006. "A Defence of Quasi-Reductionism in the Epistemology of Testimony." *Philosophica* vol. 78: 13–28.

_____. 2008. "Radical Scepticism, Epistemic Luck and Epistemic Value." *Proceedings of the Aristotelian Society* vol. 28 (1): 19–41.

_____. 2015. "Risk." *Metaphilosophy* vol. 46 (3): 436–61.

PRYOR, JAMES. 2000. "The Skeptic and the Dogmatist." *Noûs* vol. 34 (4): 517–49.

PUNDIK, AMIT. 2011. "The Epistemology of Statistical Evidence." *The International Journal of Evidence and Proof* vol. 15 (2): 117–43.

RAMSEY, F. P. 1927. "Facts and Propositions." In *Philosophical Papers*, D. H. MELLOR (ed.). Cambridge University Press, Cambridge.

_____. 1931. "General Propositions and Causality." In *The Foundations of Mathematics*. Routledge & Kegan Paul, London.

REDMAYNE, MIKE. 2008. "Exploring the Proof Paradoxes." *Legal Theory* vol. 14 (4): 281–309.

REICHENBACH, HANS. 1949. *The Theory of Probability*. University of California Press, Berkeley.

RICHARD, MARK. 1990. *Propositional Attitudes: An Essay on Thoughts and How We Ascribe Them*. Cambridge University Press, Cambridge.

RIGGS, WAYNE. 2002. "Beyond Truth and Falsehood: The *Real* Value of Knowing That *P*." *Philosophical Studies* vol. 107 (1): 87–108.

RINARD, SUSANNA. 2015. "A Decision Theory for Imprecise Credences." *Philosophers' Imprint* vol. 15 (7): 1–16.

ROBERTS, CRAIGE. 1996. "Information Structure in Discourse: Towards an Integrated Account of Formal Pragmatics." In *Papers in Semantics*, JAE-HAK YOON AND ANDREAS KATHOL (eds), 91–136. OSU Working Papers in Linguistics, vol. 49.

_____. 2016. "The Character of Epistemic Modality: Evidentiality, Indexicality, and What's at Issue." Ms., Department of Linguistics, Ohio State University.

ROSEN, GIDEON. 1998. "Blackburn's *Essays in Quasi-Realism*." *Noûs* vol. 32 (3): 386–405.

ROTH, ANDREA. 2010. "Safety in Numbers? Deciding When DNA Alone is Enough to Convict." *New York University Law Review* vol. 85 (4): 1130–85.

ROTHKOPF, CONSTANTIN, THOMAS WEISSWANGE, AND JOCHEN TRIESCH. 2010. "Computational Modeling of Multisensory Object Perception." In *Multisensory Object Perception in the Primate Brain*, MARCUS J. NAUMER AND JOCHEN KAISER (eds), 21–54. Springer, New York.

ROTHSCHILD, DANIEL. 2012. "Expressing Credences." *Proceedings of the Aristotelian Society* vol. 112 (1): 99–114.

_____. 2013. "Do Indicative Conditionals Express Propositions?" *Noûs* vol. 47 (1): 49–68.

ROTHSCHILD, DANIEL AND SETH YALCIN. 2016. "On the Dynamics of Conversation." Forthcoming in *Noûs*.

RUSSELL, BERTRAND. 1948. *Human Knowledge: Its Scope and Limits*. George Allen & Unwin, London.

RUSSELL, JEFFREY SANFORD AND JOHN HAWTHORNE. 2015. "General Dynamic Triviality Theorems." *Philosophical Review* vol. 125 (3): 307–39.

SALERNO, JOSEPH. 2016. "Epistemic Modals and *Modus Tollens*." *Philosophical Studies* vol. 173 (10): 2663–80.

SALMON, NATHAN. 1986. *Frege's Puzzle*. MIT Press, Cambridge.

SCHAUER, FREDERICK. 2003. *Profiles, Probabilities, and Stereotypes*. Harvard University Press, Cambridge.

SCHELLENBERG, SUSANNA. 2011. "Perceptual Content Defended." *Noûs* vol. 45 (4): 714–50.

SCHIFFER, STEPHEN R. 1978. "The Basis of Reference." *Erkenntnis* vol. 13 (1): 171–206.

———. 2007. "Interest-Relative Invariantism." *Philosophy and Phenomenological Research* vol. 75 (1): 188–95.

SCHOENFIELD, MIRIAM. 2014. "A Dilemma for Calibrationism." *Philosophy and Phenomenological Research* vol. 91 (2): 425–55.

SCHROEDER, MARK. 2008a. *Being For: Evaluating the Semantic Program of Expressivism*. Oxford University Press, Oxford.

———. 2008b. "What Is the Frege-Geach Problem?" *Philosophy Compass* vol. 3 (4): 703–20.

———. 2012. "Attitudes and Epistemics." In *Expressing Our Attitudes: Explanation and Expression in Ethics, Vol. 2*, 225–56. Oxford University Press, Oxford.

SCHROEDER, MARK AND JACOB ROSS. 2014. "Belief, Credence, and Pragmatic Encroachment." *Philosophy and Phenomenological Research* vol. 88 (2): 259–88.

SCHULZ, MORITZ. 2015. "Decisions and Higher-Order Knowledge." Forthcoming in *Noûs*.

SCHWARZ, NORMAN. 1998. "Accessible Content and Accessibility Experiences: The Interplay of Declarative and Experiential Information in Judgment." *Personality and Social Psychology Review* vol. 2 (2): 87–99.

SEARLE, JOHN. 1979. *Expression and Meaning*. Cambridge University Press, Cambridge.

SELLARS, WILFRID. 1962. "Philosophy and the Scientific Image of Man." In *Science, Perception, and Reality*, 1–40. Routledge & Kegan Paul, London.

SENNET, ADAM AND JONATHAN WEISBERG. 2012. "Embedding 'If and Only If.'" *Journal of Philosophical Logic* vol. 41 (2): 449–60.

SIDER, THEODORE. 2011. *Writing the Book of the World*. Oxford University Press, New York.

SIEGEL, SUSANNA. 2012. *The Contents of Visual Experience*. Oxford University Press, New York.

———. 2017. *The Rationality of Perception*. Oxford University Press, New York.

SILINS, NICHOLAS. 2007. "Basic Justification and the Moorean Response to the Skeptic." In GENDLER AND HAWTHORNE (2007), 108–42.

SINGER, PETER. 1978. "Is Racial Discrimination Arbitrary?" *Philosophia* vol. 8 (2): 185–203.

SKYRMS, BRYAN. 1980. *Causal Necessity*. Yale University Press, New Haven.

SLOTE, M. 1978. "Time in Counterfactuals." *Philosophical Review* vol. 87 (1): 3–27.

SOAMES, SCOTT. 1987. "Direct Reference, Propositional Attitudes, and Semantic Content." In *Propositions and Attitudes*, NATHAN SALMON AND SCOTT SOAMES (eds), 197–239. Oxford University Press, Oxford. Originally published in *Philosophical Topics* (15) 1987, pp. 47–87.

SORENSEN, ROY. 2009. "Meta-Agnosticism: Higher Order Epistemic Possibility." *Mind* vol. 118 (471): 777–84.

SOSA, ERNEST. 2007. *A Virtue Epistemology: Apt Belief and Reflective Knowledge*, vol. 1. Oxford University Press, New York.

———. 2010. "The Epistemology of Disagreement." In HADDOCK ET AL. (2010), 278–97.

DE SOUSA, RONALD. 1971. "How to Give a Piece of Your Mind: Or, the Logic of Belief and Assent." *Review of Metaphysics* vol. 25 (1): 52–79.

SPEAKS, JEFF. 2014. "What's Wrong with Semantic Theories Which Make No Use of Propositions?" In *New Thinking about Propositions*, JEFF KING, SCOTT SOAMES, AND JEFF SPEAKS (eds), 9–24. Oxford University Press, Oxford.

SPOHN, WOLFGANG. 2012. *The Laws of Belief: Ranking Theory and Its Philosophical Applications.* Oxford University Press, Oxford.

STAFFEL, JULIA. 2013. "Can There Be Reasoning with Degrees of Belief?" *Synthese* vol. 190 (16): 3535–51.

STALNAKER, ROBERT. 1970a. "Pragmatics." In STALNAKER (1999), 31–46.

———. 1970b. "Probability and Conditionals." *Philosophy of Science* vol. 37 (1): 64–80.

———. 1975. "Indicative Conditionals." In STALNAKER (1999), 63–77.

———. 1978. "Assertion." In STALNAKER (1999), 78–95.

———. 1984. *Inquiry.* MIT Press, Cambridge.

———. 1991. "Narrow Content." In STALNAKER (1999), 194–209.

———. 1999. *Context and Content.* Oxford University Press, Oxford.

———. 2002. "Common Ground." *Linguistics and Philosophy* vol. 25 (5–6): 701–21.

———. 2008. *Our Knowledge of the Internal World.* Oxford University Press, Oxford.

STANLEY, JASON. 2005. *Knowledge and Practical Interests.* Oxford University Press, Oxford.

———. 2007a. "Précis of *Knowledge and Practical Interests*." *Philosophy and Phenomenological Research* vol. 75 (1): 168–72.

———. 2007b. "Replies to Gilbert Harman, Ram Neta, and Stephen Schiffer." *Philosophy and Phenomenological Research* vol. 75 (1): 196–210.

STEPHENSON, TAMINA. 2007. "Judge Dependence, Epistemic Modals, and Predicates of Personal Taste." *Linguistics and Philosophy* vol. 30 (4): 487–525.

STRAWSON, P. F. 1952. *Introduction to Logical Theory.* Methuen, London.

SUTTON, JONATHAN. 2007. *Without Justification.* MIT Press, Cambridge.

SWANSON, ERIC. 2006. "Interactions with Context." Ph.D. thesis, Department of Linguistics and Philosophy, MIT.

———. 2008. "Modality in Language." *Philosophy Compass* vol. 3 (6): 1193–207.

———. 2010. "On Scope Relations between Quantifiers and Epistemic Modals." *Journal of Semantics* vol. 27 (4): 529–40.

———. 2011. "How Not to Theorize about the Language of Subjective Uncertainty." In *Epistemic Modality*, ANDY EGAN AND BRIAN WEATHERSON (eds), 249–69. Oxford University Press, Oxford.

———. 2016a. "The Application of Constraint Semantics to the Language of Subjective Uncertainty." *Journal of Philosophical Logic* vol. 45 (2): 121–46.

———. 2016b. "Probability in Philosophy of Language." In *The Oxford Handbook of Probability and Philosophy*, ALAN HÁJEK AND CHRIS HITCHCOCK (eds), 772–88. Oxford University Press, Oxford.

———. 2017. "Omissive Implicature." *Philosophical Topics* vol. 45 (2): 117–37.

TANG, WENG HONG. 2015. "Belief and Cognitive Limitations." *Philosophical Studies* vol. 172 (1): 249–60.

TARSKI, ALFRED. 1936. "*Der Wahrheitsbegriff in den Formalisierten Sprachen*." *Studia Philosophica* vol. 1: 261–405.

TAYLOR, DORCETA. 2014. *Toxic Communities: Environmental Racism, Industrial Pollution, and Residential Mobility*. New York University Press, New York.

THOMSON, JUDITH JARVIS. 1986. "Liability and Individualized Evidence." *Law and Contemporary Problems* vol. 49 (3): 199–219.

THORP, GARY. 2002. *Caught in Fading Light: Mountain Lions, Zen Masters, and Wild Nature*. Walker & Company, New York.

TRAVIS, CHARLES. 1985. "On What Is Strictly Speaking True." *Canadian Journal of Philosophy* vol. 15 (2): 187–229.

———. 2004. "The Silence of the Senses." *Mind* vol. 113 (449): 57–94.

TRIBE, LAURENCE H. 1971. "Trial by Mathematics: Precision and Ritual in the Legal Process." *Harvard Law Review* vol. 84 (6): 1329–93.

TYE, MICHAEL. 2003. *Consciousness and Persons: Unity and Identity*. MIT Press, Cambridge.

UNWIN, NICHOLAS. 1999. "Quasi-Realism, Negation and the Frege-Geach Problem." *The Philosophical Quarterly* vol. 49 (196): 337–52.

VAN FRAASSEN, BAS C. 1976. "Probabilities of Conditionals." In *Foundations of Probability Theory, Statistical Inference, and Statistical Theories of Science*, W. HARPER AND C. A. HOOKER, (eds), 261–308. D. Reidel, Dordrecht.

———. 1980a. "Rational Belief and Probability Kinematics." *Philosophy of Science* vol. 47 (2): 165–87.

———. 1980b. *The Scientific Image*. Oxford University Press, Oxford.

———. 1981. "A Problem for Relative Information Minimizers in Probability Kinematics." *British Journal for the Philosophy of Science* vol. 32 (4): 375–79.

———. 1990. "Figures in a Probability Landscape." In *Truth or Consequences: Essays in Honor of Nuel Belnap*, J. M. DUNN AND A. GUPTA, (eds), 345–56. Kluwer, Dordrecht.

VANBEVEREN, DANY. 2001. *The Influence of Binaries on Stellar Population Studies*. Kluwer, Dordrecht.

VELTMAN, FRANK. 1996. "Defaults in Update Semantics." *Journal of Philosophical Logic* vol. 25 (3): 221–61.

VENN, JOHN. 1866. *The Logic of Chance*. Macmillan, London.

VOGEL, JONATHAN. 1987. "Tracking, Closure, and Inductive Knowledge." In *The Possibility of Knowledge: Nozick and His Critics*, STEVEN LUPER-FOY (ed.), 197–215. Rowman & Littlefield, Totowa, NJ.

———. 1990. "Are There Counterexamples to the Closure Principle?" In *Doubting: Contemporary Perspectives on Skepticism*, MICHAEL D. ROTH AND GLENN ROSS (eds), 13–25. Kluwer, Dordrecht.

———. 1999. "The New Relevant Alternatives Theory." *Philosophical Perspectives* vol. 13 (s13): 155–80.

WACHTEL, TOM. 1980. "Pragmatic Approximations." *Journal of Pragmatics* vol. 4 (3): 201–11.

WASSERMAN, DAVID T. 1991. "The Morality of Statistical Proof and the Risk of Mistaken Liability." *Cardozo Law Review* vol. 13 (2–3): 935–76.

WEATHERSON, BRIAN. 2005. "Can We Do Without Pragmatic Encroachment?" *Philosophical Perspectives* vol. 19 (1): 417–43.

_____. 2008. "The Bayesian and the Dogmatist." *Proceedings of the Aristotelian Society* vol. 107 (1 pt 2): 169–85.

_____. 2011a. "Defending Interest-Relative Invariantism." *Logos and Episteme* vol. 2 (4): 591–609.

_____. 2011b. "No Royal Road to Relativism." *Analysis* vol. 71 (1): 133–43.

_____. 2012. "Knowledge, Bets, and Interests." In *Knowledge Ascriptions*, JESSICA BROWN AND MIKKEL GERKEN (eds), 75–103. Oxford University Press, Oxford.

_____. 2014. "Smith on Justification and Probability." Ms., Department of Philosophy, University of Michigan.

_____. 2016. "Games, Beliefs and Credences." *Philosophy and Phenomenological Research* vol. 92 (2): 209–36.

WEBB, JAMES, JANET GORE, EDWARD AMEND, AND ARLENE DEVRIES. 2007. *A Parent's Guide to Gifted Children*. Great Potential Press, Scottsdale, AZ.

WEDGWOOD, RALPH. 2002. "The Aim of Belief." *Philosophical Perspectives* vol. 16 (s16): 267–97.

_____. 2007. *The Nature of Normativity*. Oxford University Press, New York.

_____. 2012. "Outright Belief." *Dialectica* vol. 66 (3): 309–29.

WEISBERG, JONATHAN. 2013. "Knowledge in Action." *Philosophers' Imprint*, vol. 13 (22): 1–23.

WELLS, G. L. 1992. "Naked Statistical Evidence of Liability: Is Subjective Probability Enough?" *Journal of Personality and Social Psychology*, vol. 62 (5): 739–52.

WHITE, ROGER. 2006. "Problems for Dogmatism." *Philosophical Studies* vol. 131 (3): 525–57.

_____. 2010. "Evidential Symmetry and Mushy Credence." In GENDLER AND HAWTHORNE (2010), 161–86.

VAN WIETMARSCHEN, HAN. 2013. "Peer Disagreement, Evidence, and Well-Groundedness." *Philosophical Review* vol. 122 (3): 395–425.

WILLER, MALTE. 2013. "Dynamics of Epistemic Modality." *Philosophical Review* vol. 122 (1): 45–92.

WILLIAMS, BERNARD. 1978. *Descartes: The Project of Pure Enquiry*. Penguin Books, Harmondsworth.

WILLIAMS, J. ROBERT G. 2008. "Conversation and Conditionals." *Philosophical Studies* vol. 138 (2): 211–23.

WILLIAMSON, TIMOTHY. 2000. *Knowledge and its Limits*. Oxford University Press, Oxford.

_____. 2005a. "Contextualism, Subject-Sensitive Invariantism, and Knowledge of Knowledge." *Philosophical Quarterly* vol. 55 (219): 213–35.

_____. 2005b. "Précis of *Knowledge and its Limits*." *Philosophy and Phenomenological Research* vol. 70 (2): 431–35.

_____. 2007. "How Probable Is an Infinite Sequence of Heads?" *Analysis* vol. 67 (3): 173–80.

_____. 2015. "Justifications, Excuses, and Sceptical Scenarios." Ms., Department of Philosophy, Oxford University. Forthcoming in Julien Dutant and Daniel Dorsch (eds). *The New Evil Demon: New Essays on Knowledge, Rationality and Justification*, Oxford: Oxford University Press.

WINFREY, OPRAH. 2014. *What I Know for Sure*. Hearst Communications, New York.

WITTGENSTEIN, LUDWIG. 1916. *Notebooks 1914–16*. Blackwell, Oxford. Translated by G. E. M. Anscombe.

―――. 1953. *Philosophical Investigations*. Blackwell, Oxford. Translated by G. E. M. Anscombe.

YALCIN, SETH. 2007. "Epistemic Modals." *Mind* vol. 116 (464): 983–1026.

―――. 2010. "Probability Operators." *Philosophy Compass* vol. 5 (11): 916–37.

―――. 2011. "Nonfactualism about Epistemic Modality." In EGAN AND WEATHERSON (2011), 295–332.

―――. 2012a. "Bayesian Expressivism." *Proceedings of the Aristotelian Society* vol. 112 (2): 123–60.

―――. 2012b. "Context Probabilism." In *Logic, Language and Meaning*, MARIA ALONI (ed.), 12–21. Springer, Heidelberg.

―――. 2012c. "A Counterexample to Modus Tollens." *Journal of Philosophical Logic* vol. 41 (6): 1001–24.

―――. 2014a. "Comments on Sarah Moss." Presented at the 2014 Rutgers Semantics Workshop.

―――. 2014b. "Semantics and Metasemantics in the Context of Generative Grammar." In *Metasemantics*, ALEXIS BURGESS AND BRETT SHERMAN (eds), 17–54. Oxford University Press, Oxford.

―――. 2015. "Epistemic Modality *De Re*." *Ergo* vol. 2 (19): 475–527.

YALCIN, SETH AND JOSHUA KNOBE. 2014. "Epistemic Modals and Context: Experimental Data." *Semantics and Pragmatics* vol. 7 (10): 1–21.

ZUCKERMAN, ADRIAN A. S. 1986. "Law, Fact or Justice?" *Boston University Law Review* vol. 66 (4): 487–508.

Index